WESTMINSTER'S JEWEL
The Barbados Story

by
Olutoye Walrond

The author may be reached via email: oluwalrond@hotmail.com

ISBN: 978-976-8265-10-4

Cover Photo: © Ianpoole | Dreamstime.com - Big Ben And Boadicea Photo

The author acknowledges the work of the following persons whose own research, writings and memories have assisted greatly in the production of this book:

Warren Alleyne—The History of St. Patrick's Roman
Catholic Cathedral Barbados

Dr. Henderson Carter—Business in Bim:
A Business History of Barbados - 1900-2000

David Comissiong—The PEP Column

Wynter Crawford—I Speak for the People
(Edited by Prof. Woodville Marshall)

Glenford Howe and Don Marshall—"The Empowering Impulse
The Nationalist Tradition of Barbados"

Gary Lewis—White Rebel: The Life and Times of T.T.Lewis

Trevor Marshall—Essay on Lord Nelson

The Nation Publishing Company – Photographs of Christmas
in the Park and Kadooment

Bonham Richardson—Panama Money in Barbados 1900-1920

Marika Sherwood—Many Struggles
(West Indian Workers and Service Personnel in Britain 1939-1945)

Sir Garfield Sobers—Garry Sobers - My Autobiography

PREFACE

From the air it resembles a leg of pork, or – as some have said – the map of Africa upside-down. At 13 degrees north and 59 degrees west, Barbados is the most easterly of the Caribbean islands, one of a series of islands colonized by the British as far back as the 17th. century.

Unlike some of the other British-ruled islands, it wasn't blessed with a large land mass – it's merely 21 miles long and 14 miles wide. But size apart, Barbados' contribution to the economic power of the British Empire in the 17th. and 18th. centuries was so outstanding the island was regarded as one of the "jewels" of the imperial crown. The recently published book, **"Ten Cities that Made an Empire" by the British M.P,** Tristram Hunt, lists Bridgetown, Barbados among the ten. At the core of that reputation were thousands of African slaves whose unpaid labour on sugar plantations helped to fund the industrial revolution in Britain and enabled British sugar barons to live an opulent life.

The abolition of slavery in 1838 was a major blessing for the African population of the island – it liberated them from much of the brutality and grind of slavery, but it did little to advance their welfare otherwise. They continued to be ruled by a clique of British-descended planters and merchants who had everything but the interests of their black compatriots at heart. The period immediately following Emancipation was a period of struggle by radical middle-class figures against the oppression this clique visited on the mass of the people. But real progress would only come after the advent of universal adult suffrage and the introduction of black rule in the mid 20th. Century.

From a jewel in the imperial crown, Barbados, today, is a struggling economy, dependent on tourism and an ever-declining sugar industry. The jewel has lost its sparkle, even as the sun has set on the Empire. The ravages of slavery and colonialism are never far from the eye. But the history of slavery and colonialism has not only left an economic legacy, it has also left a major psychological legacy as well: a people with a woeful lack of self-confidence – who live in the shadows of those who once dominated their lives.

Westminster's Jewel seeks to tell that story – the story of Barbados from settlement by the British in 1627 up to the present.

WESTMINSTER'S JEWEL

Part 1 - Introduction

There's a statue of the British war hero Horatio Lord Nelson in the city centre. Elsewhere in the city and its environs you'll find place names like Prince William Henry Street, Prince Alfred Street, Victoria Street, Buckingham Road and Chelsea. The main health facility is the Queen Elizabeth Hospital, and you can enjoy the country air in the beautiful ambience of the King George V Memorial Park. If the first thought entering your mind is that you are somewhere in the British Isles, you are way out to sea – not even close. Go to your travel agency, book an airline ticket and fly in a south-westerly direction until you reach the most easterly of the Caribbean islands, Barbados or Little England as she's been nick-named.

More than three centuries of British colonialism has definitely left its mark on this 166-square-mile limestone rock. And that mark extends much further than place names. The Head of State of Barbados is not a Barbadian, but – the Queen of England. Barbadian men dress formally in European suits – heavy jackets and ties – in temperatures sometimes approaching 90 degrees Fahrenheit; the Anglican Church or Church of England is the dominant religious denomination and cricket is the national sport – this is the birth place of the West Indian cricket icon, Sir Garfield Sobers. Yes, we are a case study begging to be done. I will attempt to respond to this need in the course of this book.

Founded In Slavery

So, let's start at the beginning. And to do that we need to back-track to the late 15th. century when Christopher Columbus stumbled on the Caribbean, mistaking it for the East Indies. Columbus and his fellow travellers stepped ashore an island in the Bahamas on October 12th. 1492. They named the island San Salvador, planted in the ground the royal banner of Spain and claimed the island for the King and Queen of Spain. It did not matter to Columbus, his companions nor the Spanish sovereign that there were people already living on San Salvador. European arrogance of the day did not allow for the recognition of people of different races and cultures as equal beings with them. So from henceforth San Salvador was to be Spanish territory, and Columbus' arrival hailed as the 'discovery of the West Indies'. Up to the fourth quarter of the last century Caribbean students of history were still being taught that Columbus discovered the West Indies.

This accidental *'discovery'* was the launch-pad for the exter-mination of the indigenous Caribbean peoples – called Amerin-dians – and the control of the region by various European pow-ers. In the case of Barbados and the English-speaking Caribbean, that power was Britain, which managed to maintain control of the majority of islands. Some islands, like St. Lucia, Grenada and Dominica, fell into and out of French and British hands, but eventually ended up as British colonies. Barbados was singular in being the only island over which the British never lost control.

The first British ship landed at Barbados in 1625 under the command of Captain John Powell, who claimed the island on behalf of King James I. Two years later Powell's brother, Captain Henry Powell landed with a party of 80 settlers and ten slaves to occupy and settle the island. (Some historians say these were Irish and Scottish captives, used for indentured labour.) This expedition landed on the Barbadian west coast, at a place now known as Holetown, but which the pioneers named Jamestown. This settlement was funded by Sir William Courteen, a London merchant who owned the title to Barbados and several other unclaimed islands.

Bearded fig tree

The name *'Barbados'* is believed to be an adjectival derivative of the Portuguese word *'barba'*, which means 'beard'. It was given to the island by the Portuguese explorer Pedro a Campos, who passed by Barbados in 1536 on his way to Brazil. The name is believed to have been inspired by the presence on the island of large numbers of fig trees with aerial roots looking rather like beards. The early British settlers set about the task of developing the forested island into a productive, habitable place. Initially they cultivated cotton and tobacco for export, with the help of workers called indentured servants. These were young, unskilled labourers from Britain who were contracted to work for an employer for a fixed period of time in exchange for transportation, food, clothing, lodging and other necessities during the term of their indenture. Some of the indentured servants were free labourers; others were convicts or kidnap victims who were shipped to Barbados. Descendents of the indentured servants can still be found in small numbers in Barbados. They are known locally as *'Redlegs'* or *'Poor Whites'*.

African people, who now comprise the vast majority of Barbadians, were forced immigrants, who arrived in the mid 17th. Century as victims of the Atlantic slave trade. The trade in cotton and tobacco had become uneconomical and the British colonists found a replacement in sugar-cane, with the help of Dutch settlers in Brazil and Jews. But sugar demanded more strenuous labour than cotton and tobacco, and the colonists found this on the African continent. One estimate puts the number of Africans shipped to the British Caribbean over the period of the slave trade at nearly two million.

The unspeakable horrors of the trans-Atlantic slavery experience are still not within the consciousness of the mass of Caribbean people. People do have a notion that at some point in history there was slave labour in Barbados, but most remain blissfully ignorant of the extent and depth of the slavery experience. This lack of awareness is often manifested in glib comparisons with slavery in other parts of the world – e.g: slavery in biblical times or Arab slavery – the intention being to suggest that Caribbean slavery was nothing unprecedented. The truth is that trans-Atlantic slavery is unparalleled in the history of slavery, both in the extent of its brutality and in its attempt to de-humanize the enslaved persons.

The appalling torment of the experience is captured vividly by the Nigerian-born slave, Olaudah Equiano in his auto-biography. Born in 1745 Olaudah and his sister were kidnapped and sold to traders headed for the Caribbean. He ended up in the American state of Virginia and later England. This edited account from his narrative describes the trauma of his capture and the Atlantic crossing that followed:

Olaudah Equiano

Generally when the grown people in the neighbour-hood were gone far in the fields to labour, the children assembled together in some of the neighbours' premises to play, and commonly some of us used to get up a tree to look out for any assailant or kidnapper that might come upon us, for they sometimes took those opportunities of our parents' absence to attack and carry off as many as they could seize.

One day, as I was watching at the top of a tree in our yard, I saw one of those people come into the yard of our next neighbour but one to kidnap, there being many stout young people in it. Immediately on this I gave the alarm of the rogue and he was surrounded by the stoutest of them, who entangled him with cords so that he could not escape till some of the grown people came and secured him. But alas! ere long it was my fate to be thus attacked and to be carried off when none of the grown people were nigh.

One day, when all our people were gone out to their works as usual and only I and my dear sister were left to mind the house, two men and a woman got over our walls, and in a moment seized us both, and without giving us time to cry out or make resistance they stopped our mouths and ran off with us into the nearest wood. Here they tied our hands and continued to carry us as far as they could till night came on, when we reached a small house where the robbers halted for refreshment and spent the night. We were then unbound but were unable to take any food, and being quite overpowered by fatigue and grief, our only relief was some sleep, which allayed our misfortune for a short time.

The next morning we left the house and continued travelling all the day. For a long time we had kept to the woods, but at last we came into a road which I believed I knew. I had now some hopes of being delivered, for we had advanced but a little way before I discovered some people at a distance, on which I began to cry out for their assistance; but my cries had no other effect than to make them tie me faster and stop my mouth, and then they put me into a large sack.

They also stopped my sister's mouth and tied her hands and in this manner we proceeded till we were out of the sight of these people. When we went to rest the following night they offered us some victuals, but we refused it, and the only comfort we had was in being in one another's arms all that night and bathing each other with our tears. But alas! we were soon deprived of even the small comfort of weeping together. The next day proved a day of greater sorrow than I had yet experienced, for my sister and I were then separated while we lay clasped in each other's arms. It was in vain that we besought them not to part us; she was torn from me and immediately carried away, while I was left in a state of distraction not to be described. I cried and grieved continually, and for several days I did not eat anything but what they forced into my mouth.

I now saw myself deprived of all chance of returning to my native country or even the least glimpse of hope of gaining the shore, which I now considered as friendly; and I even wished for my former slavery in preference to my present situation, which was filled with horrors of every kind, still heightened by my ignorance of what I was to undergo. The first object which saluted my eyes when I arrived on the coast was the sea, and a slave ship, which was then riding at anchor, and waiting for its cargo. These filled me with astonishment, which was soon converted into terror when I was carried on board...I was soon put down under the decks, and there I received such a salutation in my nostrils as I had never experienced in my life – so that with the loathsomeness of the stench and crying together, I became so sick and low that I was not able to eat, nor had I the least desire to taste anything.

I now wished for the last friend, death, to relieve me; but soon, to my grief, two of the white men offered me eatables, and on my refusing to eat, one of them held me fast by the hands and lay me across I think the windlass, and tied my feet while the other flogged me severely. I had never experienced anything of this kind before, and although, not being used to the water – I naturally feared that element the first time I saw it – yet nevertheless could I have got over the nettings I would have jumped over the side, but I could not; and besides, the crew used to watch us very closely who were not chained down to the decks, lest we should leap into the water…The white people looked and acted, as I thought, in so savage a manner; for I had never seen among my people such instances of brutal cruelty, and this, not only shown towards us blacks, but also to some of the whites themselves.

One white man in particular I saw, when we were permitted to be on deck, flogged so unmercifully with a large rope near the foremast that he died in consequence of it; and they tossed him over the side as they would have done a brute. This made me fear these people the more, and I expected nothing less than to be treated in the same manner. . . .

The stench of the hold while we were on the coast was so intolerably loathsome that it was dangerous to remain there for any time, and some of us had been permitted to stay on the deck for the fresh air; but now that the whole ship's cargo were confined together it became absolutely pestilential. The closeness of the place and the heat of the climate, added to the number in the ship, which was so crowded that each had scarcely room to turn himself, almost suffocated us. This produced copious perspirations, so that the air soon became unfit for respiration from a variety of loathsome smells, and brought on a sickness among the slaves, of which many died….The shrieks of the women and the groans of the dying rendered the whole a scene of horror almost inconceivable. Happily, perhaps, for myself I was soon reduced so low here that it was thought necessary to keep me almost always on deck, and from my extreme youth I was not put in fetters. In this situation I expected every hour to share the fate of my companions, *some of whom were almost daily brought upon deck at the point of death, which I began to hope would soon put an end to my miseries.*

Often did I think many of the inhabitants of the deep much more happy than myself. I envied them the freedom they enjoyed, and as often wished I could change my condition for theirs. Every circumstance I met with served only to render my state more painful, and heighten my apprehensions and my opinion of the cruelty of the whites.

One day they had taken a number of fishes, and when they had killed and satisfied themselves with as many as they thought fit, to our astonishment who were on the deck, rather than give any of them to us to eat as we expected, they tossed the remaining fish into the sea again, although we begged and prayed for some as well as we could, but in vain; and some of my countrymen, being pressed by hunger, took an opportunity when they thought no one saw them of trying to get a little privately, but they were discovered, and the attempt procured them some very severe floggings.

One day, when we had a smooth sea and moderate wind, two of my wearied countrymen who were chained together, preferring death to such a life of misery, somehow made it through the nettings and jumped into the sea. Immediately another quite dejected fellow, who on account of his illness was suffered to be out of irons, also followed their example; and I believe many more would very soon have done the same if they had not been prevented by the ship's crew, who were instantly alarmed.

Equiano was no less horrified about the treatment of the African captives after arrival in the Caribbean than he was about the experience of the Atlantic crossing. He writes:

It was very common in several of the islands, particularly in St Kitts, for the slaves to be branded with the initial letters of their master's name, and a load of heavy, iron hooks hung about their necks. Indeed on the most trifling occasions they were loaded with chains, and often instruments of torture were added. The iron muzzle, thumbscrews...are so well known as not to need a description, and were sometimes applied for the slightest faults.

I have seen a negro beaten 'til some of his bones were broken for even letting a pot boil over...The wretched field-slaves, after toiling all the day for an unfeeling owner who gives them but little victuals, steal sometimes a few moments from rest or refreshment to gather some small portion of grass, according as their time will admit. This they commonly tie up in a parcel...and bring it to town or to the market to sell. Nothing is more common than for the white people on this occasion to take the grass from them without paying for it; and not only so, but too often also to my knowledge our clerks and many others at the same time have committed acts of violence on the poor, wretched, and helpless females....

Is not this one common and crying sin enough to bring down God's judgement on the islands? He tells us the oppressor and the oppressed are both in his hands; and if these are not the poor, the broken-hearted, the blind, the captive, the bruised, which our Saviour speaks of, who are they? One of these depredators once in St Eustatius came on board our vessel and bought some fowls and pigs of me, and a whole day after his departure with the things he returned again and wanted his money back: I refused to give it and not seeing my captain on board, he began the common pranks with me, and swore he would even break open my chest and take my money.

I therefore expected, as my captain was absent, that he would be as good as his word, and he was just proceeding to strike me, when fortunately a British seaman on board, whose heart had not been debauched by a West India climate, interposed and prevented him. But had the cruel man struck me I certainly should have defended myself at the hazard of my life, for what is life to a man *thus oppressed? He went away, however, swearing, and threatened that whenever he caught me on shore he would shoot me, and pay for me afterwards.*

But if you find Equiano's graphic account of the Atlantic crossing shocking, then the Zong Massacre will surely electrocute you. In 1781 Captain Luke Collingwood's ship, the Zong, was taking much longer to make the Atlantic crossing and was running short on water. Well, Collingwood's solution was simple: get rid of some cargo. He had his crew throw more than 130 Africans over-board, fully aware that the ship's owners, a syndicate of slave traders in Liverpool, had taken out insurance on its "cargo".

When the insurers rejected the claim the ship's owners took the matter to court and initially won judgment. The trial by jury, at the Guildhall in London on 6 March 1783, was presided over by the Lord Chief Justice, the Earl of Mansfield. But the insurers appealed and the case went before Mansfield and two other Judges of the King's Bench. In his summary of the Jury's rationale for siding with the plaintiffs, Mansfield delivered himself of what would now be some quite revolting remarks. He said the Jury *"had no doubt – though it shocks one very much – that the case of slaves was the same as if horses had been thrown over board... The question was whether there was not an absolute necessity for throwing them over board to save the rest....the Jury were of the opinion there was."*

Equiano, who had migrated to England by this time, drew the case to the attention of the abolitionist campaigner, Granville Sharp, who tried to enter a case for murder. The Solicitor General, Justice John Lee, would have none of it. As far as he was concerned: *"What is this claim that human people have been thrown overboard? This is a case of chattels or goods. Blacks are goods and property; it is madness to accuse these well-serving honourable men of murder. They acted out of necessity and in the most appropriate manner for the cause. The late Captain Collingwood acted in the interest of his ship to protect the safety of his crew. To question the judgement of an experienced well-travelled captain held in the highest regard is one of folly, especially when talking of slaves.* **The case is the same as if wood had been thrown overboard."**

The ordeal of the Atlantic crossing was but the beginning of travail for the kidnapped Africans. Their first stop was Barbados, then the clearing house for the trade in African labour in the Caribbean and the Americas. From here, many – like Equiano – were bought in auction houses and trans-shipped to other Caribbean islands and North America to begin new lives as unpaid labourers in harsh and brutal conditions. In this new dispensation they would be stripped of their humanity and treated more like property.

CRUELTIES OF SLAVERY.

Whipping of Slaves

With a legislature in place in Barbados since 1639, it was to be expected that the law would become a buttress for the system of slavery, and that is exactly what happened. The earliest of a series of slave laws was passed in 1661. The Barbados Slave Code, as it was called, created the legal basis for the practice of slavery. It was in this code that the enslaved Africans were first defined as chattel or property. In its introduction the Code said its purpose was to *"protect them (the enslaved) as we do men's other goods and Chattel."* The Code was a particularly inhuman piece of legislation that permitted the enslaving planters almost free reign to brutalise their slaves. It was a time in human society distinguished by a general propensity for brutality; but historical accounts of the treatment of enslaved African people in the Caribbean are especially gruesome, far more so than the treatment of slaves in previous dispensations. Quite apart from the merciless beatings, a slave could have his nostril slit, his limb or ear severed or even be burnt alive!

It was the grave misfortune of Scotsman, James Ramsay, working on sugar plantations in the island of St Kitts, to witness this savage assault on enslaved people. Ramsay quit his job as Ship's Surgeon with the British Navy in September 1762 to take up holy orders. Following his ordination he elected to work with the enslaved people of St. Kitts. So moved he was by the cruelty meted out to the enslaved that he recounted it in a book called *"Essay on the Treatment and Conversion of African Slaves in the British Sugar Colonies" (1784)*:

> *"The ordinary punishments of slaves, for the common crimes of neglect, absence from work, eating the sugar cane, theft, are cart whipping, beating with a stick – sometimes to the breaking of bones; the chain; an iron crook about the neck; a ring about the ankle, and confinement in the dungeon. There have been instances of slitting of ears, breaking of limbs, so as to make amputation necessary, beating out of eyes and castration..."*

The Barbados code would turn out to be a model for similar legislation in Antigua, Jamaica and the American colony of Carolina. The 1661 law was replaced in 1688 by a new code. It was the view of the governing elite that stronger measures were required to deal with what was described as the *"barbarous, wild and savage nature"* of the enslaved Africans. Clearly, European arrogance of the day didn't allow for any description of 'savage' to be applied to the inhuman treatment of the enslaved. The 1688 slave code criminalized a whole set of activities in which free people engage. It took away the right to own property, marry, attend dances and funerals without permission – it even banned the possession and beating of drums and other loud instruments.

These instruments were identified as the means by which the enslaved gave *"signal and notice to one another of their wicked plans and purposes."*

One activity of the enslaved which proved to be the bane of the planters was itinerant vending. Contrary to the view of many, the enslaved were not un-enterprising labourers whose lives were limited to plantation work; from the latter part of the 17th. Century some of them were engaged in a robust trade in food crops, fruits and domestic animals. The ruling elite was concerned about this from two perspectives: they suspected that the commodities being traded were being stolen from the plantations and there were complaints from white, small-scale commodity retailers about competition from the enslaved hucksters.

And so throughout the course of the 17th. and 18th. Century the authorities found themselves resorting to repressive regulations to curtail the commercial enterprise of the black population. One piece of legislation passed in 1708 not only sought to curtail trading by the enslaved, but the involvement of planters and other whites in the trade. It recognised that some whites *"do daily send their negroes and other slaves to the several towns in this island to sell and dispose of all sorts of quick stock, corn, fruit and pulse and other things...."*

Another major piece of legislation was passed in 1733 stating emphatically:

> *"It shall not be lawful for any Negro or other slave to plant to his use or any use other than that of his master, any cotton or ginger whatsoever, and...if any Negro shall be found with any such or exposing the same for sale, such cotton and ginger shall be deemed as stolen goods."*

In 1779 yet another Act of Parliament prohibited *"goods, wares and merchandises and other things from being carried from house to house or about the roads and streets in this island, to be sold or bartered or disposed of...."* But five years later in 1784 the Barbados Mercury newspaper was reporting that the number of Vendors in Bridgetown was continuing to rise. And in apparent concession that the '*problem*' of trading by the enslaved had become overwhelming, the Judiciary advised the government to drop its opposition to the trade and focus instead on organization.

The government accepted the Court's advice. It legalized public vending by slaves but restricted it to the Shambles – what we now know as Cheapside. Clearly, the enslaved people of Barbados were not merely hewers of wood and drawers of water; they had the capacity for industry and commerce, which, in spite of their best efforts, the authorities could not eradicate. It is impossible to resist drawing parallels between the attitude of the authorities to huckstering by the black population in pre-Emancipation Barbados and that of the current political and law enforcement authorities to street vending today. The similarities are striking. In each instance, the political elite had a negative view of the commercial enterprise of an under-class and tried repeatedly – without success – to control, if not eradicate it. The one difference – in all its irony - is the racial make-up of the political directorate then and now.

It is nothing short of miraculous that the African Barbadian has survived the experience of plantation slavery. The blissful ignorance of many modern-day Barbadians about that experience is often reflected in suggestions that without it "*we would not be here*". This outrageously insensitive view is known to fall from the lips of persons who've had the benefit of higher education. If only they knew what it took for them to be here – if only they knew….

Parliamentary Roots

It didn't take long for the British settlers to plant political roots on the island.

By 1639 they had created the first parliament, making it the third oldest in the Americas and the Commonwealth. Known as the House of Burgesses, it comprised 16 land-owners. (The House of Burgesses was the first elected assembly of English settlers in North America. The inaugural meeting took place in 1619 in Virginia. "*Burgess*" means an official of a municipality, or the representative of a borough in the English parliament).

The first sitting was held in premises known as the Sessions House, located somewhere in the vicinity of Marhill Street and Spry Street. The site now bears a monument erected in 1989 by the government of the day. It became somewhat of an itinerant parliament over the next hundred and thirty years, moving from place to place: from taverns to the homes of landlords and merchants. Indeed, Governor, Jonathan Atkins was moved to remark in 1674:

> "*I must confess I am a little astonished to see so honourable an assembly…meet in a place so considerable as the island is, and have no house to receive us but a public tavern.*"

A step towards the creation of a house of parliament was made in 1724, when the assembly approved a plan to erect a building on Coleridge Street to house the legislative council (fore-runner of the Senate) the assembly, the law courts and the jail. This building would later house the High Court and Court of Appeal. But even with this building available, the assembly apparently continued its itinerant ways, with meetings in private homes and taverns.

Parliament Buildings

The existing home of parliament, originally called the Public Buildings, but re-named the Parliament Buildings, was built in the early 1870's and is the final resting place of the Barbados parliament. It comprises two wings adjacent to each other, separated by a courtyard. Parliament – i.e the House of Assembly and the Senate - meets in one wing while the other houses a parliamentary museum.

The long parliamentary tradition of the island is often confused with its history of democracy. In 1989 when the island celebrated the 350th. anniversary of parliament, it was not uncommon to hear references to 350 years of democracy. In fact, real democracy has only been in existence for a small fraction of the life of parliament. What democracy existed previous to full adult suffrage in 1950 was limited to the sugar planters, free coloureds (persons of mixed race) and others with the required income and property qualifications. The Franchise Act of 1721 limited voting rights to free men who were white, Christian, British, 21 years or older, and who possessed ten or more acres of land. It specifically declared that no person *"whose original extraction shall be proved to have been from a Negro"* was to be considered a freeholder or permitted to vote or give evidence in court, except in the trial of *"negroes"* or slaves.

These conditions were modified over the years, and eventually abolished by the passage of The Representation of the People Act of 1950 which gave the absolute right to vote to everyone over the age of 21. The first election held under this new dispensation occurred in 1951; but black control of the House of Assembly actually took place five years previously with a coalition government, after the 1946 general election.

The Charter of Oistins

From very early on the planter-merchant government enjoyed a fair degree of autonomy from London. The local authorities were allowed a certain latitude in law-making, appointments to public office and in trade. This limited independence appeared to be under threat when civil war erupted in England. Between 1642 and 1651 a power struggle between the Crown and Parliament resulted in a series of conflicts and political manoeuvrings, and the execution of the King, Charles the First. The war ended in victory for Parliament at the Battle of Worcester and the replacement of the English monarchy, first with the Commonwealth of England and then with a Protectorate under the rulership of Oliver Cromwell.

Naturally, the political upheaval in England had implications for the colonies. After the execution of Charles the First, his son, Charles the Second emerged in exile as heir to the throne, and approved an earlier appointment of Francis Lord Willoughby as Governor of Barbados. The Barbadian planters were divided between those who supported the new King and Governor, and those backing the republicans. The former faction was concerned about the loss of the latitude they enjoyed in domestic affairs and trade with the Dutch. The two factions, backed by their own supporters from within the militia, threatened to bring a miniature version of the English civil war to Barbados; but it was the royalists who had the upper hand.

In fact, the island became a refuge for royalists from England, as the German-born Explorer/Historian, Robert Schomburgk tells us:

"The history of Barbados is by no means barren of events which have materially affected the British Empire... It was here and in St. Christopher's that England founded its first colonies in the southern part of America; it was here that the first sugar-cane was planted upon the soil of the British dominions ; it was here that many of those attached to the royal cause, during England's civil wars and the interregnum which ensued, sought and found an asylum, until the chivalric opposition of that small spot to the mandates of Cromwell roused his ire and vengeance."

Westminster responded to the events in Barbados by taking steps to bring the island in line. They introduced laws halting trade between Barbados and England, and mandating that only English ships were to be used by the colonies for trading purposes. They followed this up with more drastic action: sending a military fleet to force the Barbadians royalists into subjection. Fleet Commander Sir George Ayscue's mandate was to blockade the island until surrender. In Barbados the royalists were defiant. The parliament endorsed Charles the Second as King and steps were taken to punish those who resisted the authority of Governor, Francis Lord Willoughby. In a brazen display of irony the royalists invoked the threat of slavery to galvanize support against any military attack by the authorities in Westminster, calling on Barbadians to defend themselves against *"the slavery that is intended to be imposed on them."*

And in a national declaration, the Governor, Legislative Council (forerunner of the Senate) and the House of Assembly sought to impress on Barbadians that they would be *"brought into contempt and slavery"* if the island were to be invaded by the English. The declaration also made it clear to the English authorities that the planters were prepared to fight to defend their freedoms and privileges. The royalists did put up some resistance, but it was Cromwell's men who got the upper hand. Articles of surrender were drawn up and signed by either side as The Charter of Barbados on 11th. January 1652. The signing, which was followed by ratification by parliament later the same month, took place at what was known then as The Mermaid Tavern in Oistins.

But even though they capitulated, the planter royalists did manage to secure some significant concessions from the other side. Two of the principal provisions of the Charter were that there would be no taxation on the island without its consent and that local authorities would have a greater measure of independence in the administration of the island's affairs. Sticking out like a sore thumb in all of this is the absence of the enslaved Barbadians. It is clear that this episode in Barbadian history was all about Englishmen and how they would prosper on the backs of African people. Theirs (the enslaved) was not a threat of some metaphorical slavery from Westminster; theirs was literal slavery of the worst possible kind.

Indeed one of the provisions of the Charter was that the Barbadian planters would regain control of any property they had lost, including human 'property'. Article 12 of the charter puts it this way:

> "That all persons on both sides be discharged and set free with the full benefit of enjoying these articles, and that all horses, cattle, servants, **negroes and other goods** whatsoever, be returned to their right owners...."

So – there was nothing at all in this for the suffering lot of enslaved African Barbadians.

If they were enslaved before, they would continue to be enslaved. All of this would appear to be lost on those descendants of the enslaved Africans and others, who now seek to adorn this episode in local history and place it on a grand, social pedestal.

Against The Odds

The all-embracing strictures and brutality of slavery notwithstanding, some enslaved persons managed to achieve a measure of economic advancement and personal status that was worthy of note. This can be attributed to a combination of fate and personal acumen. The most famous of these slave success stories is that of Olaudah Equiano. Equiano made the torturous trans-Atlantic crossing in 1756 from his native Nigeria. He escapes the Auctioneer's hammer in Barbados but is sent on to the American state of Virginia, where he is bought by British Navy Lieutenant, Michael Pascal. Pascal re-names him Gustavus Vassa, and takes him on naval trips for the next eight years.

He eventually ends up in England with Pascal's sister, where he is baptised and learns to read and write. As fate would have it, he returns to the Caribbean – this time to Montserrat – after Pascal sells him to a Captain Doran, who sells him to an American Quaker called Robert King. Under King Equiano is able to further his education in reading and writing and engage in some trading; but more importantly he's permitted to purchase his freedom. Eventually he returns to England where he throws himself into the movement against the slave trade.

Initially, Equiano was a prominent member of an abolitionist group called 'Sons of Africa', but later on he threw in his lot with the Society for the Abolition of the Slave Trade, working with the likes of Granville Sharpe and Thomas Clarkson to end the trade. In 1789 Equiano wrote and published his life story: **"The Interesting Narrative of the Life of Olaudah Equiano, or Gustavus Vassa, The African"**. The book traces his journey from the Nigerian village where he was born to his arrival in Barbados and subsequent trans-shipment to America and England.

Notwithstanding its cumbersome title, the book became a best-seller, earning for the author considerable wealth, and helping to advance the cause of abolition.

The name Rachel Pringle is one that introduces us to another example of enslaved Barbadians who were able to break free from the economic and social confines of slavery. Influenced by the numerous sketches in historical and other publications, Barbadians have an impression of her as a woman of enormous proportions with a chubby face, topped by an elevated head-tie. This caricature almost completely minimizes the success story that Pringle represents. Rachel was born a slave in the early 1750's, the off-spring of an African woman and her white, English enslaver, William Lauder.

The turn in her fortunes came – ironically – from an unfortunate episode in her early life. Her father found the voluptuous Rachel irresistible and tried to exploit her sexually. When she fought off his advances he became furious and ordered that she be punished by the public whipper. By good fortune she was rescued by the Captain of a ship in port, called Thomas Pringle who claimed her and placed her in a new home in the city. She subsequently abandoned the name Lauder and adopted the surname Pringle. Well, they didn't live happily ever after. Pringle abandoned Rachel; but her charms would capture the imagination of another Englishman called Polygreen whose name she took also.

No doubt attributable to her relationships with wealthy Englishmen, Rachel ended up a property owner, her assets including a mansion believed to be Barbados' first hotel. The hotel became a popular place to stay among British seamen, one of whom was no less a person than King William the 4th. Prince William Henry, as he was then, visited Barbados in the late 1780's in his capacity as a Leeward Islands naval Captain.

The story goes that the youthful Prince and his companions were in such high spirits that they engaged in an orgy of destruction, culminating it by heaving Rachel and her chair head over heels, to the great amusement of all present. It is said that Rachel displayed no emotion through it all, but at the end simply made an inventory of the damage and presented the Prince with a bill for 700 pounds before his departure, which he paid in full.

Rachel used the money to refurbish the property and re-named it the Royal Naval Hotel. Besides her hotel, she owned some ten properties on Canary Street, now George Street, St. Michael. Her death in 1791 at the age of 38 was the final chapter in the story of a Barbadian slave woman whose personal attributes enabled her to escape from the coop of slavery.

Enter London Bourne, a slave born in 1793 to William Bourne, a successful Cooper and political activist. The elder Bourne was a man of means who owned properties on Bay Street and Roebuck Street. London Bourne's wife, a free, black woman, owned property in her own right which she brought to the marriage. Bourne's assets included a property in Bridgetown; Grazettes, Friendship and Dear's estates and a business in London. The building – now demolished – which was known as Exchange Building, on land now occupied by London Bourne Towers, was one of the Bourne properties.

His oldest son, Joseph, whom he educated in Scotland, joined his father in what became known as London Bourne & Son. Unfortunately, the business eventually foundered and Bourne's assets fell into new hands. Additional to his involvement in business, Bourne also had an active interest in Pan Africanist activity. He was a member of groups devoted to education about Africa and repatriation to the continent. In this regard he was following in the footsteps of his father, who was a party to the founding of the Colonial Charity School – later called St. Mary's – believed to be the first primary school for black children in Barbados. London Bourne continued his father's work with the school, sitting on the board as Treasurer. Given the circumstances into which fate so unmercifully threw them, the stories of Equiano, Pringle and Bourne are tales of extra-ordinary success, and a demonstration that even from the depths of the bottom-less pit it is sometimes possible to rise to the top of the mountain.

Resistance

There's a presumption some have that the enslaved Africans in the Caribbean were a docile lot who simply put their tails between their legs and accepted their plight. Nothing could be further from the truth. The evidence suggests that in spite of the harshness of their existence they beat drums, danced, engaged in trading and – yes – resisted their enslavement. Some did so by running away. In Barbados, a small island with no mountains or forests, this option was not very attractive; but in much larger countries like Jamaica and Suriname with mountainous terrain and vast forestland runaway Africans were able to establish communities known as Maroons.

And then there were those bold souls who dared to take the fight to the European enslavers. The poster boy of slave revolts in the Americas, of course, is the Haitian revolution of the early 1790's, which drove the French from Haiti and established the first black republic in the western world. No such luck for the enslaved Barbadians who took up arms in 1816. The rebellion was led by an African-born slave called Bussoe – later spelt 'Bussa' - now listed in the pantheon of ten national heroes of Barbados. He was a Ranger – somewhat of an Overseer – at Bayley's Plantation in St. Philip. The plantation house is now the home of the Guyanese Singer and record producer, Eddie Grant.

In addition to Bussa, the ring-leaders of the rebellion were Washington Franklin, a free, coloured man; King Wiltshire, a Carpenter at Bayley's; Nanny Grigg, a Domestic Servant at Simmons plantation and Jackie, a Driver (Supervisor) at Simmons. It was a complete surprise for the authorities; there had been relative peace among the enslaved people for the preceding 100 years. Indeed, one plantation owner and member of the assembly called Robert Haynes expressed his utter surprise in these terms:

"The night of the insurrection I would and did sleep with my chamber door open, and if I had possessed ten thousand pounds in my house I should not have had any more precaution, so well convinced I was of their attachment ..." The revolt was planned for April 17th., but erupted three days earlier on the 14th. The action started in the evening in the parish of St. Philip and spread to the neighbouring parishes of Christ Church, St. George and St. John. This extract from a letter to the then Governor, James Leith, from the Commander of the imperial troops, Colonel Edward Codd, gives an insight into how things unfolded:

"...on arriving in the Parish of St. Philip, I found that the system of plunder and devastation, which had been pursued by the insurgents, had been very alarming in its extent and ruinous in its consequences. Canes, plantations, provision grounds, a few dwelling houses and rocks on some of the estates in that and the neighbouring Parish of Christ Church having been involved in a general flame, whilst household furniture of every description – rum, sugar, wine, corn, and every species of food which had been stored were promiscuously scattered in the roads and fields near to the dwelling houses, with a rapidity and destruction that evinced the fury of the insurgents."

But it was a tall order for Bussa and his men. They were outmatched by the local militia and the imperial troops. At the end of it all Bussa and hundreds of his fighters were killed; others were tried and executed or deported. Colonel Codd was effusive in his letter to Governor Leith as he described the performance of the black soldiers in the Imperial troops: *"The insurgents did not think our men would fight against black men, but thank God they were deceived. I assure you the conduct of our Bourbon Blacks, particularly the Light Company under Captain Firth...has been the admiration of everybody, and deservedly."*

One week after the revolt Governor Leith made a public speech calling for a return to normalcy among the enslaved population. He blamed the insurrection on what he called *"the misrepresentation and instigation of ill-disposed persons"*, who, he said, had been spreading the claim that the slaves had been granted freedom, but were being denied it.

He then went on to indulge in some specious rationalisations of slavery in terms not very different from those employed today: *"slavery is not the institution of any particular colour, age or country. It has ever existed and does still exist among white as well as black men. That the blacks of Africa have countenanced slavery, and with the whites have been its joint authors in the West Indies is a fact personally known to all of you who have come from Africa under the compulsive transfer of your persons by your own countrymen by whom you were held in bondage in your native land..."*

Governor Leith took the opportunity to express his gratitude to those slaves who supported their 'masters' during the revolt:- *"I cannot omit to express my satisfaction at the good sense and feeling of so large a proportion of you who rallied round your masters and their families when your deluded brethren so shamefully forgot the ties of duty and gratitude where benefits have been conferred on them."* He then appealed for a speedy return to *"general confidence and industry, and of that comfort and cheerfulness which so large a proportion of you seem to enjoy."* This Governor should have been given a medal for his audacity. He thinks nothing of congratulating those enslaved persons who, instead of supporting the effort to end slavery, felt constrained to rally around the very people who were exploiting and brutalizing them; and then appeals to them to return to their status as cheerful slaves.

For his heroic efforts against the iniquitous system of slavery the government of Barbados named Bussoe among the pantheon of national heroes in the late 1990's. Additionally, it erected a statue in tribute to the struggle against slavery. It's officially called the Emancipation Statue but, for whatever reason, is referred to by Barbadians as the Bussa Statue. The statue is the work of the deceased Guyanese-born Sculptor, Karl Broodhagen. It depicts an enslaved man breaking the chains of slavery.

The Emancipation Statue

The Bussa revolt was the first of three major uprisings among the enslaved of the British Caribbean. In 1823 Guyana erupted, and then in 1831 there was a major outbreak in Jamaica. It was perhaps inevitable that these attempts by the enslaved Africans would fail but Historians believe that their heroic efforts contributed to the momentum which eventual led to the abolition of slavery in the British Caribbean.

Apprenticeship and Freedom

August 1st. 1834 must have been a day of glorious redemption for the mass of enslaved Africans in Barbados. That was the day on which the Act abolishing slavery in the British Empire became effective. There should have been dancing and merriment across the island – but that was not yet to be. For the Abolition Act contained a provision called Apprenticeship, which tied the enslaved to the plantation for periods of four and six years – depending on whether they were field or house slaves. There's general agreement among Historians that apprenticeship represented very little departure from slavery, and hence they recognise August 1st. 1838 – the end of apprenticeship – as the real Emancipation Day.

The apprentices were subject to almost as many restrictions on their activities as existed under slavery. Enslavement was replaced by mandatory labour contracts that bound them to the plantations for which they worked previously. This contract provided for a minimum of forty-five hours of free labour before they got paid. There was no option to seek employment elsewhere even if terms were better. And at less than a shilling a day, the wages paid by the Barbadian planters were among the lowest in the Caribbean. Unlike their counterparts in the larger islands like Jamaica, Dominica and Trinidad who had access to vast areas of uncultivated land, the Barbadians were virtual prisoners of the plantation and therefore could not develop a peasantry. They could count on no help from the planters who did their best to keep them tied to the plantation.

The British government and the Barbadian planter-elite were not at all nonchalant about the change from slavery to freedom. To ensure that the terms of the apprenticeship were observed on both sides, Britain sent down special Magistrates as mediators between the apprentices and their former enslavers. The Magistrates were mandated to submit periodic reports to Westminster on such things as the conduct of the slaves in their new status, criminal and civil offences and the relationship between the apprentices and the planters. As it turned out Apprenticeship was abandoned in 1838 and full freedom granted to all.

"*Lick and Lock-up Dun Wid*" (beating and locking up over), a Barbadian folk song, has become the anthem of Emancipation. Sung with much gusto by folk groups and enhanced with the irresistible rhythms of the national beat, Tuk (a syncopated serving of bass drum, kettle drum, cow-bell and flute), there is no stronger invocation to the dance. And dance they did – according to legend – on the morning of August 1st. 1838 when the system of Apprenticeship ended. Historical accounts of this first Emancipation Day say the newly freed Barbadians danced in the streets as they sang "*Lick and lock up done wid (with), hurrah for Jin Jin* (Queen Victoria) *Lick and lock up done wid, hurrah for Jin Jin. The Queen send from England to set we free, so Lick and lock up done wid, hurrah for Jin Jin.*" Well, it must have been an unspeakable joy, indeed, on that first morning of freedom from the beatings, confinements and other afflictions of slavery.

There were no illusions among the planters that after Apprenticeship the legal control they enjoyed over the African labour force would come to an end, with all the implications they feared that held for their businesses and security, and they were not about to fold their arms and wait for it to happen. Leading up to, and immediately after August 1st. 1838, a series of legal mechanisms were put in place to control the activities of the black populace and keep them tied to the plantation. For instance, in 1835 we had the creation of a temporary police force, a move which, no doubt, anticipated a large body of African people with free mobility and decision-making. Another control mechanism adopted by the plantocracy was the Masters and Servants Act of 1840, which limited the options of the former enslaved to hire themselves out. Under this law they were mandated to give five days of labour to the plantation in exchange for specified wages, and were required to pay rent for their accommodation.

These measures were springing up like overnight mushrooms: An Act for the Better Ordering of the Poor of this Island, and the Prevention of Bastardy; An Act to Punish and Suppress Vagrancy and to Determine who are Vagrants, Rogues and Vagabonds; An Act to Regulate the Hiring of Servants and for the More Expeditious Recovery of Wages; an Act for the Prevention of Tumults and Riotous Assembly, an Act to Authorise the Appointment of Rural Constables. To its credit, the Colonial Office challenged, and in some instances disallowed these proposed legislative measures. The plantocracy was so preoccupied with establishing control mechanisms over the newly freed blacks that it invested the majority of its budget on security between 1838 and 1850. During this period, spending on law and order accounted for up to 60% of all government expenditure, while education, health and welfare got less than ten percent. This, at a time of considerable hardships for the working people.

But the limitations imposed by law could not out-weigh the benefits which freedom brought. One of these was an upliftment in family life. With the rigours of slave labour gone and a bit more time at their disposal the African labouring class invested more of themselves in family life. One cleric made the following observation: "*The married people on the estate conduct themselves more soberly and chastely, and more rare indeed is the instance of a couple going to live with each other without being lawfully married.*"

Another observer from the white community commented thus: "*Family relations are becoming more sacred; mothers are more fond of their children; and it is believed that the number of births is greater, and the number of deaths among children considerably less than it was during slavery.*" Education was also one of the things on their new agenda. They wrote a letter to the then Governor, Sir Evan Macgregor, asking for help with the education of themselves and their children. Those who were once deemed to be savage and uncivilised, and unworthy of human status were now poised to stand shoulder to shoulder as equals with their oppressors.

These developments represent the genesis of a major re-definition in the lives of these early African Barbadians. They led ultimately to black control of the commanding heights of political, if not economic power in Barbados.

Blood Money – Those Who Profited

But if life for the enslaved Barbadians was a bed for thorns, the opposite is true for those who kept them in bondage and exploited their labour. By all accounts, slavery in Barbados redounded to the benefit of resident English planters, absentee landlords and British society as a whole. The planters lived like Lords in spacious mansions, with free labour at their beck and call; the absentee plantation owners in England reaped the rewards from the sale of sugar and the British treasury was enriched by taxes on the industry.

Plantation great houses like Sunbury in the parish of St. Philip and Nicholas Abbey in St. Peter are now treasured by conservationists and visited by tourists as heritage sites, but were once residences of opulence for those whose whips extracted blood from the backs of enslaved Barbadians.

But the pleasures of the slave plantation were not limited to sugar. In his book, "**The Sugar Barons**", Historian, Matthew Parker, gives an account of one 18th. century plantation Manager in Jamaica, named Thomas Thistlewood who engaged in routine sexual exploitation of enslaved women. According to Parker, Thistlewood admitted to having sexual encounters with black women more than three thousand eight hundred times. It is not unreasonable to assume that a similar thing happened in Barbados.

Back in Britain the wealth from plantation slavery in the Caribbean was also making a big impact. Among the wealthiest Britons were those engaged in business ventures related to the slave trade and plantation slavery. They used their massive profits to build huge mansions and establish new industrial and commercial enterprises, including the Bank of England and Barclays Bank.

At the national level, the British economy was the biggest winner. By the late 1780's about 70% of the national income was derived from taxes on the products of slave labour. Indeed, according to one estimate, by the close of the 18th. century British Caribbean plantations were contributing four million pounds to the British economy, four times the figure from the rest of the world. At the nucleus of this hideous enterprise sat the British Crown as charterers of the slave-trading Royal African Company and as beneficiaries of the proceeds from the company's dealings in slave trading.

The sugar colonies in the Caribbean had become the hub of the British Empire, Britain's most valuable overseas possessions. It is therefore a claim with some credibility that the industrial revolution in Britain was partly funded by Caribbean slave labour. Indeed, Matthew Parker asserts that modern Britain was built on sugar. But the contribution of Barbados has been singled out. By the close of the 17th. century the island was being called *"the brightest jewel in the English crown"*, and by the late 1700's *'the richest spote of ground in the worlde'*.

The Caribbean contribution to a developed Britain was something not lost on the British Prime Minister, Winston Churchill. Addressing a banquet of West Indies sugar planters in London in 1939, Churchill declared: *'Our possession of the West Indies, like that of India... gave us the strength, the capital, the wealth, at a time when no other European nation possessed such a reserve. It enabled us to come through the Napoleonic wars, the keen competition of the 18th and 19th centuries and enabled us to lay the foundation of that commercial and financial leadership which gave us a great position in the world.'*

The Atlantic slave trade itself was a major contributor to the enrichment of Britain in the 18th. century. To quote one James Houston, an employee of a firm of 18th-century slave merchants: *"What a glorious and advantageous trade this is...It is the hinge on which all the trade of this globe moves."* But while the beneficiaries of Caribbean plantation slavery revelled in the glories of their blood-stained wealth, they were, unwittingly, laying the foundation for the physical under-development that is now so characteristic of the region.

The abolition of slavery in the late 1830's was the golden opportunity for the British to begin the process of redressing the injustice of slavery. For inherent in the act of abolition must have been some notion about the wrongness of enslavement. But in a most bizarre affront to natural justice the British government considered the enslaving planters worthy of compensation for the loss of their slave 'property' and voted the sum of twenty million pounds for reparations to them. Half of the amount went to slave holders in the Caribbean and the remainder to British-based slave holders. The figure was equivalent to 40 percent of the government's annual expenditure, and in today's terms would be worth more than 16 billion pounds.

It was a massive pay day, the glorious legacy of which is still being savoured by the descendents of those who engaged in this despicable enterprise. Well, documents recently made public in Britain have been shedding some light on who those people are. Nick Draper, of the University College of London who had a look at the papers estimates that as many as 20% of wealthy Britons of the period got their wealth from the trade. They include ancestors of British Prime Minister, David Cameron, and author George Orwell.

To date, the British government has not apologized for its role in the slave trade and slavery – presumably because it thinks that to do so would be an admission of liability for reparations. Well, to its credit, the Church of England voted unanimously in 2006 to acknowledge its involvement in the trade and apologize. Addressing the General Synod before the vote, the Bishop of Southwart, Thomas Butler, said the profits from the slave trade were part of the bedrock of Britain's industrial development.

The Synod heard of the role played in slavery in Barbados by the Church's Society for the Propagation of the Gospel in Foreign Parts, through ownership of the Codrington estates in the rural parish of St. John. In an emotional meeting of the Church's governing body, a senior member of the clergy, Rev Simon

Bessant, told his colleagues the organisation owned the Codring-ton Plantation in Barbados, where slaves had the word "*Society*" branded on their backs with a red-hot iron. The physical pain of slavery and its legacy of impoverishment notwithstanding, the demand for apologies and reparations continues to fall on the deaf ears of those who built their mansions and filled their barns with the blood, sweat and tears of African people dripping from their hands.

Reparations

The monumental miscarriage of justice in the British compensation package for the slave owners remained unchallenged for nearly all of the 180 years following the coming into effect of the Abolition Act in 1834. It must surely raise an eyebrow somewhere that none of the governments of the post 1950's period (Adult suffrage being enacted in that year) considered it necessary to raised the matter of reparations with Britain until we come to the first decade of the 21st. century.

Oh, what a striking contrast to the story of Jewish reparations from Germany. About the middle of the 20th. century Jewish organisations, with the backing of their government, initiated negotiations with Germany and managed to secure an agreement to compensate the Jewish state for the slave labour and persecution of Jews during the Holocaust and to compensate for Jewish property stolen by the Nazis. The Agreement was signed on September 10, 1952, and came into effect on March 27, 1953. Subsequent to that agreement Germany, in partnership with German industry, established a separate fund to compensate Jews and non-Jews for slave and unpaid labour during the war. The Jewish people clearly have a sense of identity which causes them to place a value on their lives and property.

At a governmental level, the first serious broaching of the reparations issue on behalf of the Caribbean was done by former Barbados Prime Minister, Owen Arthur, in a speech marking the bicentenary of the abolition of the trans-Atlantic slave trade, at Holy Trinity Church, in the city of Hull, England in 2007. The former Barbadian leader praised the efforts of the British abolitionist, William Wilberforce, but said there was some unfinished business to be dealt with. He then went on to make the case for reparations:

Owen Arthur

"*It is to be noted that when slavery was abolished in 1833 over 20 million pounds was paid by the British government of the time to the Caribbean slave-holders as reparations for the loss of their property. Not a penny was paid to the former slaves. Now I know that reparation, at least for the victims of the transatlantic slave trade and their descendants, has been a controversial issue. I suggest it need not be. It is a matter, not of retribution, but of morality. We need to bring equity to the emancipation process, and closure to the criminal activity that was racial, chattel slavery. I submit also that the cause being fought for reparation is not a mission of mendicancy.*

And it is not unknown as a practice over time. During the 19th century, Europeans accepted and enforced multiple forms of reparations. By ordinance of 17th April, 1825, the French Government recognized the Independence of Haiti on the condition that it agreed, inter alia, to pay reparations of 150 million gold francs. For the 97 years between 1825 and 1922 Haiti struggled to pay reparations, a drain of its resources that can help explain its present distressing circumstances. The effects of 500 years of chattel slavery are still shaping the realities of black people the world over.

The principle of Reparations should be upheld, advocated and promoted through the establishment of a fund to facilitate material compensation to countries which were victimized, and by the pursuit of national and international policies to confront and eradicate the legacies of slavery. For I conceive of reparations as a national and international responsibility. Indeed the Government of Barbados, from the inception of universal adult suffrage in 1950, and especially since independence in 1966, has accepted its duty of making national reparations through a wide variety of successive policies and programmes such as the provision of free education from primary to tertiary level, and the effective redistribution of land by the Tenantries Freehold Purchase Act of 1980.

It is now time that in the specific case of Britain and the Caribbean this historical injustice should be redressed. But it should be done, not in anger, but in a spirit of reconciliation, healing and social justice. Moreover, it should be done in a way that strengthens the lasting bonds of friendship between Britain and the Caribbean."

Since the firing of that first salvo over the bow by Arthur, Barbados has taken concrete steps to put the reparations issue firmly on the national and international agenda. In 2012, it established a 12-member Reparations Task Force, to be responsible for sustaining the local, regional and international momentum for reparations. The Barbadian initiative has now been superseded by a regional one involving the member states of the Caribbean Community, CARICOM. At a meeting in St. Vincent in 2014 the group established a reparations commission and agreed to a 10-point list of demands to put to European governments. Among the demands: a full formal apology for slavery; a repatriation programme for those wanting to return to Africa; a development plan for the indigenous, Amerindian people; transfer of scientific and technological know-how and cancellation of debt.

The CARICOM commission has asserted that victims of crimes against humanity and their descendants have a legal right to justice and that those who have been enriched by the profits of the slave trade have a case to answer. In a presentation to the United Nations, Prime Minister Ralph Gonzales of St. Vincent described trans-Atlantic slavery as a historical wrong that has to be righted:

Ralph Gonzales

"*The awful legacy of these crimes against humanity,* he said, "*ought to be repaired for the developmental benefit of our Caribbean societies and all our peoples.*"

The CARICOM states have hired a British law firm to handle their case. A spokesman for the firm described the CARICOM package as "*a very comprehensive and fair set of demands on governments whose countries grew rich at the expense of those regions whose human wealth was stolen from them.*" The Caribbean states are hoping to open a dialogue with Europe on the issue, but say they are prepared to take the case all the way to the International Court of Justice. So far Britain has remained cool on the idea of reparations. Former British Prime Minister Tony Blair would go only so far as to express "*deep sorrow*" about the slave trade, saying it was one of the most "*inhuman enterprises in history*". Mr. Blair admitted that Britain's ascension to imperial dominance "*...was partially dependent on a system of colonial slave labour....*"

The concept of reparations is one that is well recognised in law. The law of Tort is founded on the principle that one who suffers at the hands of another is entitled to redress. Perhaps it was this principle – albeit wrongly applied – that persuaded the British government of the day to compensate slave holders consequent upon the abolition of slavery. The German pay-out to the Jews is not the only instance of reparations for past injustice. The government of New Zealand also fulfilled its duty to right the wrongs done to the indigenous Maori peoples by the invading British forces more than 150 years ago. Then there's the case of Japanese Americans who were rounded up and forcefully relocated to special camps during the Second World War, after Japan's attack on Pearl Harbour.

The U.S government formally acknowledged that its action was motivated by "*race prejudice, war hysteria, and a failure of political leadership*", and paid out $1.6 billion in reparations. Japan had its own reparations obligation – to thousands of Korean women living in Japan who were forced into sex slavery for Japanese soldiers during World War 2. In 1993 Japan acknowledged the existence of the wartime brothels and made a monetary award and an apology to the victims. But no such good fortune for the descendants of trans-Atlantic slavery. The reaction across the board to calls for redress has been consistently negative; even the demand for an apology from national governments has so far failed.

The history of the modern movement for slavery reparations can be traced back to the Pan African Congress on reparations which took place in Nigeria in 1993. The case for reparations at the conference was put by none other than British Queen's Counsel, Lord Anthony Gifford. He based it on three main planks:

Lord Anthony Gifford

1. That slavery was a crime against humanity;
2. That international law demands that those who commit such crimes must make reparation and
3. That there is no legal, barrier to prevent those who still suffer the consequences of crimes against humanity from claiming reparations, even though the crimes were committed against their ancestors.

Lord Gifford told the conference he believed the cause of reparations is rooted in fundamental justice: "... *a justice which over-arches every struggle and campaign which African people have waged to assert their human dignity.*" He deemed the mass kidnap and enslavement of Africans as the most wicked enterprise in recorded history, noting that no compensation was ever paid by any of the perpetrators to any of the victims, and that the consequences of the crime continue to be massive, both in relation to the enrichment of the descendents of the perpetrators, and in relation to the impoverishment of the descendents of the victims.

So, as we have established, the concept of reparations for past injustices is widely accepted. The question which begs to be answered, then, is: what is special about reparations for slavery. The late Jamaican Pan Africanist, Dudley Thompson, thought the answer is to be found, not so much in the merits of the case, but in the identity of the beneficiaries. Lord Gifford struck a similar note in his presentation to the 1993 Pan African conference. According to him, the case for reparations would be misconceived if (it) "...*were merely an appeal to the conscience of the white world... For while there have been many committed individuals and movements of solidarity in the white world, its political and economic power centres have evidenced a ruthless lack of conscience when it comes to black and African peoples.*"

If Lord Gifford and others are right, then the real opposition to reparations might very well be rooted in the same, old racist toxin that undergirded slavery itself and has poisoned relations between African people and Europeans ever since.

Confederation, Resistance and Riots

The merchant-planter elite running the affairs of Barbados since the institution of Parliament in 1639 found itself facing another challenge to its power in 1876. The colonial government in London was proposing a federation of Barbados with the Windward Islands of Grenada, St. Lucia, St. Vincent and Tobago, having made two previous attempts to federate the Leewards. The three Windward islands were already in some kind of partial federation: in 1833 they shared a common Governor in Barbados, though retaining parliamentary independence; and had a common Court of Appeal headed by the Chief Justice of Barbados.

The plan called for a unified administration of the four islands with a single parliament comprising 12 members appointed by the Governor. This would be a far cry from the traditional Barbadian two-chamber Parliament comprising the appointed Legislative Council and the House of Assembly, administering the affairs of the island as they deem fit. Indeed, Barbados was one of very few Caribbean colonial outposts to retain this kind of local, political authority.

It was to Irishman, Pope John Hennessy, appointed Governor of Barbados, that fell the unenviable task of persuading the power brokers in Barbados to accept the confederation proposal, and consequently the elimination of their political power. In 1876, the year after he arrived, Hennessy presented the proposal to the legislature. He tried to impress on the House the benefits of confederation: employment opportunities in the Windwards and freedom of movement among them. As expected, the political elite rejected the proposal. They met and formed what they called the Barbados Defence Association, with the aim of preserving their constitution and protecting their interests. The association denounced the confederation plan as damnation, saying it would lead to further taxation and oppression.

In a series of meetings and press advertisements it sought to rally the support of Clerks, Bridgetown Porters and Planters, but failed to attract support from the working people, the majority of whom appeared to back Governor Hennessy. In fact, Hennessy, himself, tried to garner the support of the under-classes when he realized that the merchant-planter alliance was against him. It would not at all be implausible to conclude that the black and coloured under classes were of the view that if the ruling elite didn't want it, then it must have been something good.

Well, apparently the populace was so galvanized over the issue that violence and rioting erupted, beginning on April 18 at a plantation in St. George, where workers raided potato fields. Looting and arson were the order of the day – or should we say 'night', when most of it occurred – as the riots continued for the next four days, spreading to other parishes. In the city, frightened merchants and their families took refuge in ships anchored in Carlisle Bay. Military troops succeeded in restoring the country to normalcy, but only after eight people were killed, several injured and hundreds arrested. Britain withdrew the confederation plan and John Pope Hennessy was later transferred to Hong Kong.

Once again, then, the fiercely nationalistic spirit of the Barbadian elite class had been able to defend their interests against the will of the imperial government. There can no better representation of that spirit than the following verse published in a Barbadian newspaper at the height of the confederation issue:

Let every patriot in his heart
Resolve to do a manly part
To stem the current of the hour
Though lobbied by imperial power

Let every man but firmly stand
Upon the charter of the land
Nor Britain's might shall dare to wrest
The charter from a free man's breast.

Migration

Mention the word 'migration' in Barbados and we think immediately of the outward movement around the middle of the 20th. century to Britain, Canada and the United States. But, in fact, migration from Barbados is as old as the hills, dating as far back as the 17th. Century, the very start of the settlement of the region. When sugar replaced cotton and tobacco as Barbados' main cash crop it spelt bad news for the small farmer. For unlike the previous crops, sugar did not lend itself to small-scale cultivation, and before long the small farmers were all gobbled up by the larger estates. With their livelihoods gone, these farmers saw dim prospects for a good future in an over-crowded island lacking in natural resources, and sought to pitch their tents elsewhere.

One of the places to which they turned in search of fresh fortunes was the American south – the origin of the famous Barbados-Carolinas connection. But we need to backtrack a bit, because the Carolinas enterprise did not originate with the Barbadian planters. In 1663, a consortium of eight Lords Proprietors as they were called, each of whom had received grants of land in North America from King Charles 2nd., agreed to establish settlements in Carolina. But before doing so they despatched agents to Barbados to have a look at the workings of the sugar industry, and subsequently sent an exploratory group of Barbadian planters to Carolina.

The Barbadians were impressed with what they found and bought a portion of land from the indigenous Indians. They named the new colony Clarendon and appointed a Governor. In 1665 the Governor and a group of explorers arrived from Barbados and founded a town which they called Charles Towne. For environmental and other reasons this settlement was a failure; but this was no deterrence and by 1670 another group of settlers was on its way to Carolina. Comprising planters and enslaved labourers, the group sailed from Speightstown to Carolina. On arrival, they established a town on behalf of the King of England, which they also called Charles Towne. Within a matter of a few years more than half of the new settlers of the colony had come from Barbados. These pioneering Barbadian-Carolinians soon recognized the vast potential for wealth creation in the new colony and immediately set about to exploit this potential. So they literally rolled their sleeves up and started to build their new home into a thriving colony. The Barbadian adventurers took with them a successful model that would shape the social and economic future of South Carolina for centuries to come. Strong trading links developed between Barbados and Carolina providing much of the money that helped to build the colony.

Not surprisingly, there was more than a hint of Barbados in the newly developing colony. Its early architecture was highly suggestive of the Barbadian chattel house, and some have detected a strong hint of Barbadian dialect in the speech of the Gullah people, as the African Carolinians are known. The most notable Barbadian import was the plantation system, which made the colony economically sustainable, to the point where it became the wealthiest of England's American colonies.

This early migratory movement was by no means limited to planters. The brutality of slavery may have been over with Emancipation, but life for the former slaves was anything but a bed of roses. In the first place the reparations which rightfully should have gone to them were awarded to the planters. They were literally thrown to the mercy of freedom, with the rags on their backs.

Add to this an increasing population, rising unemployment, mal-nutrition and starvation, and perhaps the lowest wages in the region and you have a very powerful push factor for migration. And migrate they did. Many left to seek opportunities in Brazil, Suriname (Dutch Guiana then), Guyana, then called British Guiana, Costa Rica and Trinidad. An 1891 census for Trinidad recorded that in a population of 208 thousand there were 33 thousand immigrants from the British West Indies, nearly 14 thousand of whom were from Barbados.

But Guyana was a particularly attractive destination for Barbadians. It was a large country with lots of land space and employment opportunities. Its sugar industry was an expanding one in the period after Emancipation, and generally speaking wages there were better than those in the Caribbean. Employment could also be found in the Guyanese mining and forestry industries.

Between 1835 and 1863 more than 20 thousand Barbadians emigrated to Guyana; but another 25 thousand went between 1864 and 1885 under a bounty system offered by the Guyanese planters – such was the demand in Guyana for Barbadian workers at the time. This migratory trek continued up to the 1920's, but a less significant movement to Guyana continued up to as late as the 1960's. This was mostly skilled and professional labour going for jobs in the civil service, teaching and Police service. The Barbados-Guyana connection has produced many Guyanese of Barbadian ancestry, including such high-profile people as Presidents Forbes Burnham and Desmond Hoyte.

In later years, the United States and Britain became major destinations for migrant Barbadians. The first big trek to America from the Caribbean started at about the close of the 19th. Century and lasted until the early 1920's. Most of these early migrants were unskilled labourers driven in search of a better life, at a time of great hardship in the Caribbean. The regional sugar industry was buckling under the pressure of tough competition from cane-producers like Cuba and Brazil, and from European beet sugar. In Jamaica, for instance, the number of plantations plummeted from more than 600 in 1836 to 74 by the end of the 1910. Unemployment was high. But by the second decade of the 20th. century the Americans were tightening the screws on immigration to everyone except the peoples of northern and western Europe.

U.S immigration laws in the early 1920's imposed a quota system that was clearly biased against people of African descent.

Under the new system the number of Barbadians and other Caribbean people entering the United States plunged from more than ten thousand in 1924 to just over three hundred in 1925. But by the 1960's this position would be reversed with another significant movement of Barbadians and other Caribbean people to the U.S.A. To a lesser extent Barbadians were also seeking new opportunities in Canada.

The Canadians, too, eventually put entry restrictions in place, but in 1955 they introduced a programme to attract domestic workers from Barbados and Jamaica. Single women of basic education were offered immigrant status in exchange for their service under the programme.

But the greatest migratory trek of them all was the Panama exodus, the mass movement of Barbadians and other Caribbean people for work on the construction of the Panama Canal. This monumental capital project appeared to have an insatiable appetite for Caribbean workers.

Barbadians leaving for Panama

The first attempt to construct the canal began in 1880 under French leadership, but was abandoned after nearly 22 000 workers died, largely from disease and landslides. But in 1904 the United States picked up the challenge, and in the process created employment for thousands of Caribbean people, many of them

Barbadians. The Isthmian Canal Commission, the American body appointed to oversee the canal project, sent a recruitment agent to Barbados with the very attractive offer of free deck passage to and from Panama and what at the time was a very good daily wage of ten cents an hour. In the dire economic straits of their lives at the time, Barbadians were enchanted by the Panamanian opportunity, and by 1911 about 40,000 of them were already in the Canal Zone. Altogether an estimated 45 thousand to 60 thousand left these shores for Panama. And so, once again, Barbadians in their numbers were turning their backs on a post-slavery society with very little to offer them except the legal freedom that came with Abolition.

Panama was no bed of roses for the Caribbean migrants. Let's start by recognising the topography of the area: this was fifty miles (spanning from east coast to west coast) of jungle territory, inhabited by dangerous snakes and other life-threatening creatures. As if the arduous task of digging the canal trench was not enough, the migrants faced hardships in other facets of their existence. They lived in slums and jungle camps; many were victims of explosive accidents and vector-borne disease; and on top of all this they suffered racial discrimination from their American employers.

A system of virtual apartheid operated in the Canal zone. The Americans were classified as skilled workers and paid in gold coins, whereas the black, mostly Barbadian and other Caribbean workers were classified as unskilled and paid in silver at half the earnings of white workers. The discrimination also extended to fringe benefits, whites getting better accommodation than the slums in which their black counterparts lived, and enjoying paid vacation and sick leave.

These differentials may have been considered inconsequential by the Caribbean migrants, more focussed on the opportunity to make a *'decent'* living for the first time in their lives than on the injustice of discrimination. And in fact, *'Panama money'* did become an uplifting factor in the lives of many of the Barbadian migrants on their return home. Between the start of canal construction and the end of the second decade of the

20th. Century, there was a significant increase in the number of Friendly Societies in Barbados, the fore-runner to the credit union.

These societies offered loans to their members for such needs as sickness and death expenses. Panama returnees also invested their new-found wealth in shops and plots of land. Estimates vary about the total value of Panama money in Barbados, but one authoritative source suggests it could exceed one million pounds Sterling, at today's dollar value, the equivalent of about 37 million pounds or 61 million U.S dollars.

A happy ending for some but, sadly, many Barbadian migrants never got the opportunity to return and enjoy the fruits of their labour. They would have been among the thousands who succumbed to the malaria mosquito and the other life-threatening hazards of the canal zone – an estimated fifty-eight hundred men. There were some others who did not return at the completion of the canal project. They chose instead to re-migrate to neighbouring countries like Honduras and Costa Rica for work on the banana plantations, while others moved on to Cuba and the Dominican Republic. Inevitably, some chose to settle, planting seeds in the Canal Zone that have germinated and blossomed into pockets of Barbadian/Caribbean communities in Panama.

The Panama Canal project was undoubtedly a monumental engineering and construction undertaking. As a link for the Atlantic and Pacific Oceans, it effectively cuts by more than half the journey via the South American Cape Horn. Barbadian and other Caribbean workers whose labour made it possible have secured their place in the annals of world history. They could want no greater encomium than that given by Colonel George Goethals, the Supervisor of the project: "*In the construction work, the West Indian workers had a high turnout and a lot of credit ... it can truthfully be said that by providing a wide supply of labour, the work is made easier to achieve than would have been possible without them.*"

The migratory tradition established in the pre and immediate post Emancipation period culminated in another significant wave, but this time the destination of choice was the proverbial '*mother country*'. Caribbean people have been migrating to Britain since the 17th. and early 18th. century, when some enslaved people made the trans-Atlantic crossing. The next major influx occurred during the first world war, when fifteen thousand Caribbeans left to serve in the British army.

But it was the so-called Windrush migration of the mid 20th. century that symbolised the big trek from the Caribbean to Britain. The second world war had left Britain with a labour shortage and citizens of countries in the British empire were encouraged to fill the void. The Caribbean, particularly Barbados and Jamaica, became hunting grounds for workers to take up vacancies in social services like London Transport, the health care sector and British Rail.

The Empire Windrush

The symbolic origin of mass migration from the Caribbean to Britain occurred in 1948, when the motor vessel, **Empire Windrush**, docked at the British port of Tilbury with 492 Jamaican immigrants. The **Windrush** passed through Jamaica on its way home from Australia to Britain, and many Jamaicans responded to an advertisement offering low-cost transportation for the onward journey to Britain. The year 1948 is significant since it was also the year the British passed a nationality Act, granting British citizenship to people from Commonwealth countries, with the right to enter and live in Britain.

Barbadians and other Caribbean people jumped at the opportunity to explore the prospects of a better life in what they regarded as the '*Mother Country*". The government of Barbados, itself, recognised the employment opportunity and sought to exploit it on behalf of its work-hungry citizens. In 1955 it set up a Sponsored Works Programme with a Liaison Officer in London to find jobs for Barbadians; and just over ten years later 27 thousand Barbadians had found employment in England.

But the treatment of these black British citizens in the so-called 'Mother Country' would be anything but motherly. For while they had been indoctrinated with the view that they and their British counterparts were all part of one big, happy family, there was no such notion on the part of the British, many of whom regarded them as black intruders into their space. The inevitable racist treatment met them at almost every turn: employment, housing, education, entertainment, even church. The racism was quite open in some instances. For example, a notice for rental might read "*No blacks, no dogs, no Irish*".

Racial intolerance combined with Police antagonism and economic adversity to create a volcano in the Caribbean community, which would erupt in a series of riots in the 1950's in various parts of the country. Following the riots the government bowed to overwhelming public pressure and introduced legislation aimed at curbing the flow of Caribbean and other non-white immigrants to Britain. The Commonwealth Immigrants Act of 1962 removed the automatic right of entry and citizenship available to citizens from member states of that organisation. Henceforth *Commonwealth citizens would require employment vouchers for entry, unless they were students, members of the armed forces or persons who could support themselves without working.* A subsequent law imposed the more stringent requirement that immigrants have ancestral roots in the United Kingdom, the clearest indication yet of the intention to restrict non-white immigration. Some of those already in the country were affected by other regulations requiring them to produce a work permit for a specific job, and to register with the police. After one year they would have to re-apply for permission to stay. The government was also offering free passage to those who wished to return to their countries of origin.

Another eruption occurred in the 1980's, with a major flash point in Brixton, London. After the Brixton riots the government commissioned an inquiry by British Jurist, Lord Scarman, which blamed racial discrimination, disadvantage and disproportionate targeting of Caribbean people in Police stop-and-search operations, and called for urgent remedial action.

Thirty years later and there is yet another eruption of violent protest among the Caribbean community in Britain. August 2011 and several districts in the city of London, and towns across England are inflamed, with looting, arson and other acts of violence. The trigger was the alleged Police mistreatment of a girl taking part in a demonstration over the shooting by Police of a black man. At the end of the melee five people were dead, more than three thousand arrested, and an estimated £200 million worth of damage done to property. The journey to the 'motherland' for the Caribbean migrants was turning out to be far more eventful than they had anticipated. They were discovering, many for the first time, that things they took for granted back in the Caribbean, like the colour of their skin and texture of their hair, could impact negatively on the quality of their lives.

But a far more insidious threat came in the form of gangs of young men motivated by racial intolerance, who went around attacking non-white people. Among the many victims of these violent gangs was Stephen Lawrence, the 18 year-old son of Jamaican immigrants, who was rushed by a group of white youths as he waited for a bus and fatally stabbed in 1993. The murder, which went unsolved for nearly two decades, sparked a major national affair in Britain, with strong overtones of racism and corruption within the Metropolitan Police Service.

The government ordered an inquiry into the case which found – among other things – that there was institutional racism within the Police Service. The Macpherson Report as it is known

Stephen Lawrence

accused the Metropolitan Police of *"pernicious and institutionalised racism"*. It found that the Police had failed to make a swift arrest of the five suspects, lost evidence, ignored witnesses and misplaced or destroyed documents. In January 2012, eighteen years after the murder, two of the killers were convicted and sentenced to jail terms on the basis of new forensic evidence.

Five years after the death of Stephen Lawrence, and another African Caribbean man dies in questionable circumstances at a state institution in Britain. David Bennett, in his late thirties died at a psychiatric hospital after he attacked a Nurse and was subdued by hospital staff. In an apparent scuffle with the staff he was restrained and held face down to the ground for almost half an hour.

The death once again raised the spectre of institutional racism in Britain, specifically the treatment of black people in mental hospitals. A Coroner's inquest found that his death was due to prolonged restraint and long-term anti-psychotic drug therapy. It recorded a verdict of accidental death aggravated by neglect. But the Bennett family was not happy with these findings and launched a campaign for a more rigorous inquiry, prompting the government to set up a commission of inquiry.

The commission's report expressed the view that there was institutional racism throughout the health service, and suggested that greater effort was needed to combat it. It continued: *"Until that problem is addressed, people from black and minority ethnic communities will not be treated fairly. Black and minority ethnic communities have a fear of the NHS* (National Health Service) *– that if they engage with the mental health services they will be locked up for a very long time, if not for life, and treated with medication which may eventually kill them. The cultural, social and spiritual needs of patients must be taken into account."* The report recommended that the government take steps to wipe out institutional racism in mental health services and appoint a national director for mental health and ethnicity to oversee the improvement of services to black and ethnic minority patients.

The Bennett case was a national wake-up call about the not-so-nice experience of Caribbean people and other minorities with the mental health-care system. National surveys have shown that black and other ethnic minorities in Britain comprise a significantly disproportionate percentage of persons admitted to British psychiatric hospitals. The surveys show that they are more likely than white Britons to be referred to these hospitals by the Police and the Courts and that once admitted, are more likely to be subjected to restraint or confinement.

But the rigours of living in Britain notwithstanding, many Barbadian and Caribbean people were able to make a success of their lives. They donned their coats and took on the English weather; they challenged racism, and got anti-discrimination legislation; they offered themselves and served as councillors and Parliamentarians, and in spite of all, they befriended the British people, the majority of whom received them with open arms. These friendships have enabled many British people to enjoy – perhaps otherwise unaffordable holidays in the Caribbean. What a glorious alternative to xenophobia and racial intolerance.

The Windrush migration is now a closing chapter in Caribbean and British history. Those migrants still alive are now retirees. Many have chosen to re-settle in the Caribbean where the fruits of their labour are visible in the high quality of life they now enjoy. Certainly, in Barbados, many have built nice homes and drive their own vehicles.

As retirees, they enjoy the privilege of spending their days as full-time holiday-makers - sea-bathing, sight-seeing and socialising with friends. Having weathered the turbulence of the windrush they are now savouring the calming breezes of the Trade Winds and basking in the warm and golden rays of the tropical sun.

Education

From the earliest times education was established as one of the bedrocks of the Barbadian society. This is probably the reason why the island has been able to boast for some time now of a near 100 % literacy rate. Yes, you heard that right: an underdeveloped former colony of mostly slave-descended people with a long history of high literacy.

The roots of structured education in Barbados go all the way back to the 17th. century – 1686 to be exact, when two planters from the parish of St. George donated the land and money for a charity school. But this effort by John Elliot and Rowland Bulkeley was intended for the benefit of poor, white children only; the education of enslaved children was not on the agenda at this time. There were other private initiatives on behalf of the education of poor, white children, including one by Colonel Henry Drax of Drax Hall plantation in St. George parish, who made the following provision in his will:

> "Herein I give and devise for the erecting and enduring a free school or college in Bridgetown in the island of Barbados, to endure and continue forever to be paid by my executors in England, three years after my decease, two thousand pounds to the extent and purpose aforesaid."

Colonel Drax died in 1683, but it would be another twelve years (1695) before the school opened its doors. At first, its student intake was limited to poor, white children from the St. Michael parish, but by the first two decades of the 19th. century the catchment was expanded to poor-whites from the other parishes. After slavery was abolished, black children were admitted.

The school was first located at what is now Constitution Road, on the site of the old Queen's College school. At various times it was known as Drax Parish School, the Parochial Charity School, the Colonial Charity School, the Free School and the Boys' Central School. Like its name, its location has changed over time. It moved from Constitution Road to Weymouth and from Weymouth, in 1958, to its present location, where we all know it as Combermere School, the oldest school in the island.

The name *'Combermere'* comes from the title *'Lord Combermere'* borne by Sir Stapleton Cotton, a Governor of Barbados who was instrumental in raising the money to erect a building and reorganize the old Free School into the Boy's Central School.

The record also indicates that a Girls' Central School was also established in Bridgetown. Like Combermere, this school owed its creation to the bequest of Henry Drax; in fact the evidence suggests that the two schools functioned as a bicameral institution. This would later evolve into what we now know as Queen's College, originally a girls' school, but now a coeducational institution.

Queen's College as an independent school came into existence in 1883 when an Education Commission recommended a first grade school for girls. The idea the commissioners had in mind was an institution offering an education to girls comparable with that of the top schools in England at the time. The name Queen's College was given to it in 1883, but, like its sibling, Combermere, it bore various names previously: Girls' Central School, Drax's School, The Parish School of St. Michael, The Free School and the Parochial Charity School. Queen's College shared a site at Constitution Road with Combermere, until 1943 when Combermere moved to Weymouth.

With the means at their disposal, the planters would send their children back to England to be educated. One example of this practice is Christopher Codrington, the benefactor of Codrington College. Codrington was born in Barbados but joined his father – then Governor of the Leeward Islands – in Antigua, from where he was sent to Oxford University.

Codrington, himself, figures prominently in the history of education in Barbados. The establishment of Codrington (*theological*) College in the rural parish of St. John is a direct result of instructions in his Will. When he died in 1710 Codrington (a slave owner) left his sugar estates in St. John to the British missionary organization known as the Society for the Propagation of the Gospel in Foreign Parts with instructions that: "*...three hundred Negroes at least (be) always kept thereon and a convenient number of Professors and Scholars maintained there, all of them to be under the vows of poverty, chastity and obedience, who shall be obliged to study and practise physic (medicine) and chirurgery (surgery) as well as divinity.*"

Codrington College

Construction of the college started in 1714 and finished in 1743. Two years later Christopher Codrington smiled in his grave when the doors of Codrington College swung open, not yet as a theological institution, but as the Codrington Foundation School (*one of several names by which it was known*). Its primary purpose was to educate boys who would subsequently matriculate at Codrington College for the study programme envisaged by Christopher Codrington.

This school would later evolve into the Lodge School, taking its name from the Chaplain's lodge which alternated with the college as its home in those early years. Its curriculum included reading, writing, Latin, and accountancy. The college opened in 1745, thirty-five years after Codrington's death, but it took another 85 years before it began functioning exclusively as an institution for theological studies. Today it is the principal institution for the training of Anglican Priests in the Caribbean, and for education in theological studies. None of those who go there is trained to treat man's physical being, as Codrington wished, but they may be able to respond to his spiritual needs.

The year 1733 is another significant one in the history of education in Barbados. It's the inaugural year of what is regarded as Barbados' leading secondary school, Harrison College. The benefactor was Thomas Harrison, a merchant, who wanted it to be *"a Public and Free School for the poor and indigent boys of the parish"*. Some have described it as the Eton of Barbados (*Eton being the most elite of Britain's secondary schools*) because of its long tradition of academic excellence and elegant ethos. Up to the present time it's the first choice of parents for children making the transition from primary to secondary education, in spite of a general standardization in the education system. Among those who've walked through its portals in the course of time are five Barbadian Prime Ministers and the so-called "Grand Old Man" of English cricket, the England Captain and Wisden Cricketer, Pelham Warner (1873–1963).

One of the earliest educational institutions in the northern part of the island opened its doors in 1785. The benefactor was Baronet, Sir John Gay Alleyne, a descendant of the first British settlers, who owned Bawden's and River Plantations in St. Andrew. In 1770 Alleyne, a Member of Parliament and Speaker of the House of Assembly, provided the financial means for the founding of a seminary for poor white boys. The seminary was later transformed into a secondary school, which we now know as the Alleyne School.

The children of poor whites in the parish of Christ Church were not to be left out of this wave of philanthropy which appeared to be moving among wealthy, white land owners. What we now know as the Foundation School began as a charity school, the result of a donation of one hundred acres of land from one Francis Williams. The donation was made in 1709 and exactly a hundred years later the first stone in the construction of the school was laid.

The year 1818 marks another milestone in education in Barbados: the first public school for coloured boys opened its doors in Bridgetown. It was built with money donated by the public and a religious organization called the Church Missionary Society. As the education net continued to widen, another school opened for black and coloured children; and a decade later girls came into the picture, when the first public school for coloured girls opened.

By the early years of the 1820's the thrust in education was no longer being limited to poor whites. Attention was then being paid to mass instruction of the enslaved, though this had more to do with exposure to religious doctrine and customs than academic education. The religious teaching was part of a package of measures prescribed by the British authorities for improvement in the lives of enslaved people in the British dominions in the lead up to the passage of the Emancipation Act. It was essentially an indoctrination exercise to "*Christianize*" and "*civilize*" the black population, designed more to make them better servants than improve their intellectual status.

Indeed, the first Anglican Bishop of Barbados, Bishop William Coleridge, who was a driving force behind it, said as much when he suggested that an instructed slave would be more "*obedient, honest and industrious*" and consequently – we may add – more valuable.

Coleridge is to be credited with an expansion in educational op-

Bishop William Coleridge

59

portunity. From ten in 1825, one year after he took up his post as Bishop, the number of schools administered by the Anglican Church stood at more than 150 in 1834. Altogether there were more than 200 schools – including private ones – in Barbados by the end of Coleridge's tenure in 1842. Teaching was done by Anglican Priests, but Wesleyan and Moravian Missionaries were also involved in this drive, though to a lesser degree. But even previous to these efforts, in 1797, Parliament approved religious instruction to the enslaved by Anglican Priests; but the plantocracy sought to ensure that any teaching of the enslaved did not include reading and writing and, in fact, enacted legislation rendering it illegal to teach an enslaved person to read and write.

The planters' concerns had everything to do with the subservient relationship between them and the enslaved. They feared that an educated slave might be empowered to the point where he is less obedient and ultimately less productive. Even the philanthropic Bishop William Coleridge was not disabused of this snobbish patronage towards the black, labouring class. He was of the view that once the novelty of emancipation wore off, the former slaves would settle down and accept their status as providers of labour. As he put it: *"they may not yet fully understand their position in the social scale…They may think that a state of freedom admits of more liberties than are consistent…with the various continual demands of West Indian agriculture."*

This desire to keep the enslaved illiterate was not limited to the Barbadian planters; it seemed to have been a regional strategy. For example a Guyanese newspaper of the day called the **Colonist** quoted one planter thus: *"While we have no desire to treat our Africans with undue rigour, we cannot be ignorant… that our power over them can exist only so long as we are more highly educated and enlightened."*

The education net widened significantly in the years immediately following the passage of the Emancipation Act in 1833. This was consistent with the British government's policy of investing in the education of the soon-to-be-free African population. The money was channelled into a fund called the Negro Education

Grant (1835). With the passage of the Abolition Act by the local Parliament in 1834 a number of schools were established on sugar plantations. The intentions of this latest blitz in education were no different from those of the earlier ones: to give the liberated African just enough knowledge to make him a better servant. This citation from the planter newspaper, The Agricultural Reporter of 1905 shows this in clear terms:

> *"It is admitted that the negro, if properly handled, is an excellent labourer. The question then is one of proper handling. Handle the negro properly and there would be no lack of workers. Such handling would involve, amongst other things, the giving of a sound practical education. Some book learning is, of course, essential, but the mistake of conveying to the child the idea that such education as he acquires at school is calculated to make him eligible for the highest honours in life must be avoided."*

Two more schools for white and coloured boys were established in the period spanning 1825 and 1852. These were the Coleridge School, named in honour of Bishop Coleridge, and the Parry School, named after the second Bishop of Barbados, Thomas Parry. These schools were established by the Anglican Church, and were inaccessible to non-Anglicans and the children of unmarried parents. A school for girls was the final one to be established in the north of the island in this pre-20th. century period. Located in coastal Speightstown, it opened in 1894 with the name Alexandra – after the then Princess of Wales, and wife of Edward, Prince of Wales, later King Edward VII. Like most other secondary schools in the island it's now co-educational.

The last of the so-called older secondary schools is what we now know as The St. Michael School. It was established by the St. Michael vestry in 1928 as St. Michael's Girls School. In 1979 the first boys were admitted to the School. In those early years these schools were truly elite, drawing their student body almost exclusively from the white and privileged coloured groups. They charged school fees which were above the means of the vast majority of black Barbadians. The only other avenue for entry to these schools was a parochial Vestry scholarship; but even here black and other underprivileged Barbadians had the odds stacked against them, as these scholarships almost invariably went to the children of upper-class folks, irrespective of intellectual ability. The practice of class snobbery was so blatant in those times that an applicant for a scholarship might be asked what work his mother does, and if he said she was a Maid, that answer might prevent him from receiving the award. The following extract from a letter published by the Barbados Advocate newspaper in 1911 underscores the race and class prejudice of the day. Under the caption, H.C REJECTS COLOURED SCHOLAR the writer castigated the management of Harrison College for turning down the application of a Mr. Sealy on grounds of colour:

"Since the rejection of Mr. E. M Sealy, Barbados scholar at Oxford, who was appointed to the vacancy in the mathematical department at Harrison College, Dr. Dalton, the Head Master, and his advisers have cut a very sorry figure and appeared most contemptible to the people of this community. The rejection of Mr. Sealy, an educated and deserving son of the soil, merely because he is a coloured man, is in my humble opinion the most unjust and nefarious attempt to ride roughshod over the rights and liberties and privileges of a free people that can be imagined...."

This iniquitous practice of colour and class-based admission to school was effectively blocked by the introduction of the Common entrance Examination in 1959 and the abolition of fees across the board in 1962. Prior to that, in the early 1950's a number of secondary schools were established by the government led by Grantley Adams to meet the educational needs of children whose parents could not afford the fees of the older schools. These schools were called Secondary Modern Schools – later Comprehensive Schools. The first of these was St. Leonard's (boys and girls schools) which opened at Richmond in St. Michael in 1952. In subsequent years several more of these schools were opened. They became known as *"newer secondary schools"* distinguishing them from the *"older secondary schools"*. This description must not be taken lightly, for as we shall see momentarily, the distinction between these two sets of schools in the minds of Barbadians is akin to that between a turbo prop and a supersonic jet.

The expansion in public educational opportunities was accompanied by a vibrant enterprise in private education. Among the earliest of these schools were the Ursuline Convent (1894), a creation of the Roman Catholic Church; St. Winifred's, Girls School (1901) and Codrington High School (1917 – no connection with the Codrington Estate). These schools drew their student body almost exclusively from the white community. Then in the mid 1900's a series of private secondary *"high"* schools as they were called, patronized by the children of black Barbadians sprang up. The Modern High School, Lynch's Secondary, The Federal High, The Community High, The Washington High, The Seventh Day Adventist School, the Wakefield High and the Barbados Academy among them.

These commercial educational institutions offered working-class Barbadians an opportunity to educate their children, other than through the public school system.

In the realm of tertiary education there was the creation of the Cave Hill campus of the University of the West Indies, Erdiston Teacher Training College, the Barbados, Community College, offering advanced level tuition and associate degrees, and the Samuel Jackman Prescod Polytechnic.

The legacy of this vast expansion in educational opportunity is that today, access to free primary, secondary and – until recently – tertiary education is readily available to every Barbadian child. In fact, for some time now we have been at a point where every child can be guaranteed a primary and secondary education. How, then, do we account for the Barbadian obsession with the transfer of children from primary to secondary school? The examination by which this transfer is made, called the Common

Entrance and sometimes the Eleven Plus Exam, is easily the biggest national neurosis.

The obvious question to ask when in the company of parents with children around the examination age is: when would they be sitting the eleven-plus, or some other question related to the taking of this test. Children around the ages of ten and eleven are never perceived as having an identity that is separate and distinct from the Eleven Plus Examination. The actual day of the test is a veritable red-letter day. The Press publishes photographs of children and adults praying, and news reports will speak of *"the most important day in the lives"* of the little ones. Let's bear in mind that these are 11-year-olds transferring from primary to secondary school, and that whether they do the test or not there are enough places in those schools for them.

Children praying before taking the 11+

Well, you can imagine what happens when the results are announced. The newspapers are a-washed with pictures: the hugs and kisses, the top boy and top girl and the top schools they will be going to. There is no doubt that this examination occupies a large space in the minds of Barbadians. It is impossible for anyone not familiar with this system to understand the paranoia which this test generates in the Barbadian mind. And the question you may be asking is: since the examination apparently serves no real purpose, why not abolish it and let children transfer to the nearest secondary school?

Celebrating after the 11+

The answer lies with those two sets of schools I referred to earlier as older and newer secondary schools. These schools generally follow the same curriculum, have the same Teachers who were educated and trained at the same institutions, and are administered by the same department of government, the Ministry of Education. To the best of my knowledge they share equally in the resources of the state. As centres of education there is virtually no difference in their software. There is, however, a huge difference in their reputations with Barbadians. The order of school preference for parents each year before the writing of the Common Entrance Exam is almost instinctively Harrison College, Queen's College, Combermere and the remainder of the older schools, followed by the newer ones.

This preference for the older schools is rooted in their history as institutions for the poor whites and later, schools for the upper classes. This elite reputation has remained with them ever since. That reputation is boosted by the performance of students. Since everyone wants to go to the older schools, these schools always attract the intellectual cream of the primary schools. They therefore have a higher academic profile as reflected in their performance in examinations. It does not matter in the least that many students who have attended newer schools have performed equally well.

But there is one genuine distinction between the older and newer schools. For reasons related to their student intake the older schools tend to have a better ethos than the newer ones, as exemplified in the deportment of the students. I suspect this is a significant factor in the appeal which these schools have for parents, who always want to know their children are in a safe and disciplined environment.

The prejudices and misconceptions notwithstanding, Barbadians continue to emerge from secondary education, whether older or newer school, and go on to high academic achievement. Perhaps the most dramatic repudiation of the myth of unequal education in the secondary school system is the fact that today there are older secondary schools with Principals who went to newer schools. In recent times the two "*top*" schools, Harrison College and Queen's College, have both had Principals who were educated at newer secondary schools. All indications are that it is the student who makes the school and not the school that makes the student.

The confusion and paranoia can all be laid at the doorstep of the people who administer education in this country – i.e: the Ministry of Education. This institution – headed by a Minister of government – has failed miserably to provide visionary leadership to education in this country. To a man, its policy makers have simply come to office and carried on from where their predecessors left off. Innovation and change are not things that fascinate them. Where is the leadership in this eleven-plus affair? Here's an examination that serves no purpose other than to give parents a choice of which school their children will attend. I make this claim because there's no attempt to use the results of the test to provide help for students who show signs of weakness in the two subjects tested, nor to advance those who have mastered the subjects and are ready to go forward – which should be the whole purpose of the test. Those student who do well should be allocated to schools where they can progress at their pace without being held back by those needing remedial help; those who score below par should be graded according to their needs and allocated to institutions that will cater to those needs.

Far from showing leadership, Ministers of Education buy into the Eleven-Plus mania by hosting Media conferences after the results are made known. It makes absolutely no sense – and in fact looks quite stupid – for a Minister of Education to convene a press conference to announce the top boy and top girl in a school test, and what schools they are from. I thought Ministers of Education would have been more concerned about policy directions, than about what some eleven-year-old did in a graduation test for secondary school. The energy spent on this test far out-weighs its importance to the nation's well-fare.

But sadly, those entrusted with the duty of providing leader-ship in this issue are themselves so caught up in the mindless-ness of it all that they are unable to offer anything but the most mundane, unimaginative ideas. The window-dressing exercise of having a periodic investigation by a commission that always arrives at the status quo is not enough; there is need for a major rationalization. Tell us why we have this test: what are its objec-tives and how these are being achieved.

This and numerous other issues in education cry out for attention from the army of occupation in the Ministry. One other such issue is the low level of certification at the secondary level. It's estimated that roughly 60% of students leave second-ary school without certification in any subject. Quite apart from that, many leave with little more than basic literacy. A perusal of the various internet blogs might leave you appalled at the low level of language ability of many of our people. Following is a sample I collected over a period of time:

Thanks lord you have **gaven** me a **next** year to **cheer** (share?) joy and happiness on this very special day.

I am **applaud** (appalled?) at the bad ratings Barbados is receiving.

That is good, cause it seem the ppl at the… FTO is **laing** (lying?) in bed with the…so we have to put **prusuure** on them.

You ppl don't have a heart posting **does** (those?) sort of comments.

I hope justice is served soon so that the family can have a **piece** of mind.

He should be **May** to apologise

I am so disappointed in him, he should b **band** for d rest of d yr.

The students did not realise how good **there** had it. Now the well run dry.

Most tourist just love our island an its people; if we don't see that then we **or** too blind to see.

Barbados is one of **does** Caribbean islands with the less crime….

It's showing the kids if **their** work hard what **their** can accomplish in life.

Our Country **have** been classified, as having a **depth** (debt?) problem.

Weather the guy is a criminal or not I don't know.

*Errol Barrow, not only made a political speech, but he **profocide**, (prophesied?) that one day we would wake up an find Barbados is not our own, but he didn't **relized** that his own party would have sold out to the highest bidder.*

*By just looking one **wid** never know this is a funeral.*

*I dont think students should pay those high fees. What govt should **of** dun is let students that fail courses pay to resit them.*

*Why was **their** no one supervising these kids?*

*So sorry hope the government give her some help if she **wasant** insured.*

*It **dose** not matter what your hair looks like.*

*Why not get your car clean today for as **littel** as $35.00.*

*That **song** fishy to me....*

*I like your comment and I am so proud of you may god **continental** (continue?) to bless you*

*My prayers **goes** up to your family, leave it all up to prayer.*

*Ninety per cent of men think it is ok to leave women holding their children in their early years and then **excerpt** (expect?) to return later in their lives.....*

*Don't know **were** you live but here in Barbados more and more men are stepping up to **they** responsibilities as fathers...*

*Do you know anyone that can make it as fast and as cheap **than** China.*

Baving (bathing?) in the East Coast is like play lotto...you take a chance

*Didn't the police **told** him not to engage?*

*Keep up the good work my brother, you're doing a **oneder-ful** job.*

*We must understand that we **or** our brother's keepers.*

*This is one sad government-run **intertie** (entity?).*

When we consider the amount of time wasted in schools perhaps we ought not to be surprised at the paucity of language skills exhibited above. I live near a primary school and I continue to be amazed at the amount of noise to be heard coming from that school way after assembly at 8:45 in the morning. I mean – well past 9:30 when you would imagine that a teaching and learning ambience would have taken over, a cacophony of children's voices disturbs the morning peace.

The wastage of time actually begins with something called morning assembly, a relic of the era of ecclesiastical control of education. I am hearing children singing religious songs at a time when they should be settling into class. There is this prevailing notion among many of our people that religion is the solution to all our problems and is especially good for our children. The now, more enlightened notion that religious persuasion is a personal matter to be left to the individual is yet to take firm root in these parts. This is especially so given the diversity in religious doctrine and practices and the disunity even within the Christian church.

In a secular society like Barbados, for instance, on what basis are we to decide what prayers should be said in school or what songs sung. What Christian songs will a Muslim student sing? It comes down eventually to personal bias, and no one should have the right to impose their biases on anyone else – not even children.

Religious minorities may be just that, but they are no less citizens of Barbados with all of the rights and responsibilities that come with that. Of course, this is not to say that certain values common to all of us cannot be inculcated in our children at school. Values education: yes; religion: no. But has anyone in the Ministry of Education ever thought about this matter? I doubt it very much.

Notwithstanding the poverty in language skills mentioned, the investment made in education through the ages has done Barbados well. Our long-standing reputation as a country with 98% literacy attests to that. But from the above it is clear that way too many of our people have not moved very far beyond basic literacy. The ability to express themselves in internationally-recognised English remains a struggle for a significant number, many of them with secondary education. Our high literacy rate may remain a proud boast, but an education system that can only deliver basic literacy is woefully inadequate in a modern world.

Perhaps if those who administer it would emerge from their hundred years of slumber we would be on our way to addressing the myriad maladies in the system.

Our War Heroes

Every year around the end of the first two weeks of November there's a military ceremony in what used to be called Trafalgar Square – now called Heroes Square – in honour of those who served in the two European wars, widely known as World War One and World War Two. Known in Barbados and elsewhere in the Commonwealth as the Remembrance Day ceremony, it is essentially a hangover from British colonial rule. The event is attended by officials of state, representatives of the diplomatic corps, contingents from the military and other uniformed groups and, of course, the few surviving men who served with the British army in the wars.

War Veterans at Remembrance Day Parade

They are referred to honourably as '*our war heroes*' – strange that is, since Barbados never fought a war with anyone. Indeed the only military conflicts involving the Caribbean countries were those among the Europeans themselves and those which led to the extermination of the Amerindian people. It's another of the numerous examples of a people living vicariously in the skins of their colonizers. More on that score later.

The first of the two world wars erupted in July 1914. Its cause was a complex set of factors in which territorial disputes, militarism, alliances, imperialism, and nationalism all had their part to play. The trigger was pulled when the heir to the Austro-Hungarian throne, Franz Ferdinand, and his wife, were assassinated by a Serbian. This led to a declaration of war on Serbia by Austria-Hungary. Thereafter a series of military alliances became activated.

Russia, allied with Serbia, entered the fray; Germany, allied to Austria-Hungary, declared war on Russia; France, in alliance with Russia, was automatically at war with Germany and Austria-Hungary; Britain, committed to defending Belgium, was implicated when the Germans invaded Belgium in pursuit of its aggression against France; Japan, honouring a military agreement with Britain, declared war on Germany; Austria-Hungary responded by declaring war on Japan.

The United States and Italy, at first neutral, eventually joined the war on the side battling Germany and Austria-Hungary. So what does all of this have to do with Barbados and other Anglophone Caribbean countries? We had no alliances with anyone. I daresay the vast majority of those Barbadians alive at the time had no idea what the fighting was all about and probably did not even know some of the warring countries existed. We went into this war as colonies of Britain. The prevailing understanding was that Britain was the '*Mother Country*' and we were duty bound to support our '*mother*' in a time of war. This was demonstrated in very clear terms when, in the face of the considerable economic stress faced by the mass of people in the region at the time, colonial authorities in the islands donated gifts of cotton, logwood, rum, oil, sugar, aeroplanes and ambulances to Britain, equivalent in value to several million pounds, today's currency.

This support was also reflected in the street. Quite unsolicited by the British, Barbadians and other Anglo-Caribbeans were virtually lining up to fight for the '*Mother Country*'. When the war started some of them simply packed up and went to Britain to volunteer for service – although, in the depressed conditions of the times some may also have volunteered for economic reasons. The problem for these loyal sons and daughters, of which they were, as yet, blissfully unaware, was the colour of their skin. Britain simply did not want black people fighting their war, and tried – sometimes not so subtly – to make this known. The British War Office attempted to stem the tide, and even threatened to repatriate new arrivals.

Among those making the trip were nine Barbadian men who stowed away on a ship passing through Barbados from Trinidad, on its way to London. The report of their arraignment in a local, British newspaper called the Stratford Express (*19ᵗʰ. May 1915*) makes for some interesting reading:

> "*Nine black men,* **natives** *of Barbadoes, West Indies, were charged with being stowaways on the S.S. Danube. Mr J.W. Richards, who prosecuted for the Royal Mail Steam Packet Company, said that the S.S. Danube made a voyage from Trinidad to England, and the day after leaving Trinidad the ship called at Barbadoes. It was presumed that the men came aboard there for the day. Afterwards they were found on the vessel.*
>
> **Mr Gillespie (Magistrate)** *In a dark corner, I suppose?* **(Laughter)**.
>
> *Mr Richards continued that the men were put to work, and they did not cause any trouble. He was told that the men were desirous of enlisting in the Army.*

Mr Gillespie: What, do they want – to enlist in the Black Guards? (Laughter).

Det. Sgt Holby said he had made enquiries at the local recruiting office and they told him they could not enlist because of their colour, but if application was made to the War Office no doubt they could enlist in some regiment of black men.

Remanded for a week."

But the '*natives*' of Barbados and the Anglophone Caribbean were in far less light-hearted spirits about what they considered their duty to King and country. So great was the agitation in the region to be involved that the British Governors in the various islands felt constrained to make representation to London. The intensity of the lobby, coupled with heavy losses suffered by Britain and her allies, eventually persuaded London to consider the enlistment of the Caribbean volunteers. Consultations between the Colonial Office, the War Office and the reigning monarch, King George V, culminated in approval for the formation of a British West Indies Regiment (BWIR) in May 1915.

BWIR Soldiers

About ten thousand of the nearly 16 thousand volunteers in the BWIR came from Jamaica; others came from Barbados and the rest of the English-speaking Caribbean. Another recruitment exercise was taking place almost simultaneously with that for the BWIR, but this time among white Caribbean men in Barbados and Trinidad. The Barbados Citizens' Contingent and the Trinidad Merchants' and Planters' Contingent, comprising white and near-white men, petitioned the British government and got permission to be integrated in British regiments. Yet, still, not everyone in the Caribbean was bitten by the patriotic bug. Some adopted the view that it was a white man's war in which black people had no business. Indeed, when some black Canadians expressed a wish to enlist they were told it was a *"white man's war"*. Eventually, the British army bowed to the pressure and created an all-black battalion in 1916, called the Number 2 Construction Battalion.

I don't think it would have taken long for the eager Caribbean soldiers in the BWIR to realize that they did not fit neatly into the British army. Some, on arrival in Europe, were housed in cold, sub-standard accommodation, unlike their British counterparts. One account suggested that even German prisoners of war were treated to heated rooms and blankets. Because of the severity of the cold, many of the men were affected by frostbite and other ailments. A similar fate befell one contingent en route to England via Canada. Dressed in light, tropical clothing, the men were no match for the Canadian frost. The wintry weather afflicted hundreds of the men with frostbite, resulting in amputations and some deaths. As it turned out, the Caribbean men had been denied the heavier, wintry garb with which the British soldiers were outfitted.

But if the Caribbean volunteers had any romantic notions about going valiantly into battle, they would be sorely disappointed, for the British had no intention of employing them as combat units. They were posted away from the European warfront to places like Egypt, Palestine and Africa, and engaged as labour battalions for such menial task as digging trenches and ferrying ammunition. Eventually some of the men were allowed to engage in combat with the British against Turkish soldiers in the Palestine war zone. What the Caribbeans didn't know was that as a matter of policy the British War Office avoided putting black soldiers to fight against Europeans. Apparently they didn't consider the Turks to be fully European.

Accommodation and other services were also strictly delineated along racial lines, with the Caribbean men treated to inferior conditions compared with their white counterparts.

In hospitals, the BWIR's were isolated from white soldiers and placed with continental Africans and Asians; in recreational sport a cricket game would pit black soldiers against white. Even in religious assemblies there was discrimination. Black soldiers were barred from attending religious convocations at the YMCA. They were turned away by no less a person than the Chaplain, who told them they could sit and listen from outside.

(Yes – the 'C' in YMCA stands for 'Christian', a philosophy that says we are all brothers and sisters in Christ. Amen). As far as promotions were concerned, the black soldiers were not allowed to rise higher than the level of Sergeant.

The racial discrimination was not restricted to the Caribbean soldiers; an order by the British Commander of a South African labour battalion read: *"Care should be taken to prevent all familiarity between Europeans and natives as it is subversive of discipline and impairs their efficiency."* But perhaps one of the most insulting of racial incidents occurred as Caribbean men were arriving in Egypt for duty in 1916. Imbued with their own sense of British nationalism, a contingent from what was then British Honduras – now Belize - approached a YMCA building, the strains of *"Rule Britannia"* echoing from their mouths, only to be rebuffed by British troops inside: *"Who gave you niggers authority to sing that song. Clear out of this building; only British troops admitted here."*

Inferior treatment notwithstanding, the Caribbean men contributed to a decisive victory against the Turks in Palestine, winning for themselves 16 medals. But it would not be enough to earn them the respect and esteem of the army high command. They would be treated to what would be the ultimate act of humiliation in the final year of the war. A pay increase given to other troops was denied them. The British War Office said the denial was due to the fact that they were *"natives"*. Clearly, the British didn't consider white Bermudans to be *"natives"* since the all-white Bermuda Volunteer Rifle Corps got the increase. In a letter of protest sent to the Governor of Barbados, some of the men said the action was *"not only an insult to us who have volunteered to fight for Empire, but also an insult to the whole of the West Indies."*

The second-class treatment of the Caribbean soldiers culminated in a violent revolt at the Italian naval port of Taranto, where the men of the West Indies Regiment were assembling at the end of the war. As was their lot throughout the war, they were saddled with the menial tasks, but this time were subjected to the additional indignity of being instructed to clean the toilets of the white soldiers. Disgruntlement was rife in the Caribbean camps over this, the withholding of the pay increase given to the other troops, and the denial of promotion above the rank of Sergeant, and on December 6th. 1918 trouble erupted at Taranto. In one battalion soldiers attacked their officers and assaulted the unit Commander. Over the next few days there was one bombing, a fatal shooting and a strike. Order was restored after a company of British soldiers armed with machine guns, supported by troops from the Worcestershire Regiment, arrived at Taranto. The revolting battalion was disbanded, and several of the Caribbean soldiers later tried and sentenced to jail for mutiny.

Interceding on behalf of the Caribbean men on the pay issue, the British Colonial Office argued that to deny the Caribbean soldiers the pay rise would affect the loyalty of the *'negro'* to the Empire and *"...incur...a weakening of our hold on the West Indian islands."* This representation succeeded in securing the increase, retroactively, for the men of the British West Indian Regiment.

But the return of normalcy to Taranto was merely external; the mental scars which the experience inflicted on the Caribbean men was more lasting. It generated in men, previously indoctrinated with the notion that they were mere subjects of the British Crown, a new vision of themselves as persons, and of the Caribbean as a nation in its own right. In the immediate after-math of the mutiny, a group of Sergeants from the disbanded battalion convened a meeting to discuss their grievances. They formed an organization, which they named *"The Caribbean League"* to represent their interests and to promote closer ties and self-determination in the Caribbean.

A subsequent meeting of the League provided a more vivid indication of the mental revolution generated by Taranto. One Sergeant put the question of Caribbean independence on the table, in words more compatible with the black radical movement of the 1960's than with the pre-independence era in the Caribbean. To loud applause from those present, he said the black man should have freedom and govern himself in the Caribbean, and that if necessary force and even bloodshed should be used towards this end.

One of the leading members of the League was Barbadian Clennell Wickham, who in later years would become Editor of the radical Herald newspaper. But the life of the League was cut short after British military authorities found out about it and broke it up. As part of their punishment, the Caribbean men were denied participation in the victory ceremonies and sent back home under armed guard, to be greeted, not with the banners and bugles of victory, but with the mistrust of the colonial authorities, who feared their new-found political spunk might cause trouble. The British had taken the precaution of despatching three war ships to Barbados, Jamaica and Trinidad ahead of their arrival.

On May 26, 1919, the steam ship Ajax, docked in Port of Spain after a journey from Europe with 450 men from the BWIR. They paraded before the Mayor of Port of Spain before marching for two miles to the Savannah where they received a token welcome by the Governor and were disbanded. On return to civilian life many met difficulty finding employment. In stark contrast, the white contingent returned some time thereafter to a champagne reception at the Governor's residence. Jobs awaited them as they reintegrated into civilian life.

The lament of Barbadian volunteer, George Blackman, would suggest that the black Barbadian servicemen fared no better. *"When the war finish, there was nothing. I had to come and look for work. The only thing that we had is the clothes and the uniform that we got on – the pants, the jacket and the shirt and the boots".*

It was a sad and bitter end of an emotional journey that began on the high road of loyalty to King and country – a defining moment for the Caribbean men who clamoured to fight on behalf of their *"Mother Country"*. Perhaps, for the first time, these loyal sons of the British Empire had come to understand that they and the British were not one and the same after all; that their love and allegiance to the so-called Mother Country was woefully misplaced. It was a realization partially echoed in a secret memo emanating from an official in the Colonial Office, calling for recognition that things had changed in the relationship between Britain and her black Caribbean subjects: *"Nothing we can do will alter the fact that the black man has begun to think and feel himself **as good as the white**."*

Lt. Walter Tull

But there was one exception to the otherwise shabby treatment of the black service-men and women. His name is Walter Tull, and he was the son of a Barbadian-English couple. The story begins in a suburban neighbourhood in Barbados called My Lord's Hill where a Carpenter, called Daniel Tull grew up. Daniel was one of the many Barbadians who migrated in search of a better life in the difficult years after Emancipation. He went to St. Lucia, first, but move on to England in 1876 where he settled in the south eastern county of Kent and married an English girl named Alice Palmer, in 1880. The marriage produced three children, the first of which – a girl – died weeks after her birth. But the Tulls went on to have two boys, named William and Walter.

Tragedy struck the two boys early in life; they lost both their parents to chronic diseases and ended up in an orphanage. In his early, adult life, Walter became a professional footballer, playing for Tottenham Hotspur and Northampton Town, at the time one of the few non-white football professionals in Britain.

With the eruption of World War One, Walter joined the army, serving in the Footballers' Battalions of the Middlesex Regiment up to the rank of Sergeant, the highest level for a non-white soldier. Unlike many of the other black soldiers, he experienced active duty in France, Belgium and Italy, and was commended by his superior Officer for gallantry and coolness. He was even recommended for a medal of bravery, but did not receive it. So impressed were his military superiors with his performance that he was returned to England to be trained as a Lieutenant, a rank which, up to then, the Army did not give to non-white soldiers. In 1917, one year before the end of the war, he was commissioned as Second Lieutenant Walter Tull. But the glory of his promotion would be shot-lived; he was killed in combat one year later in France, at the age of 30.

Tull was recommended for the Military Cross honour for his heroism, but it was never granted, some believe, because of army rules against black men leading white soldiers. There's been a campaign in Britain for the honour to be awarded posthumously, but it appears the rules do not permit retroactive awards.

Portrait of 2nd. Lt. Walter Tull on Five Pound Coin

But the Barbadian-descended British hero has not gone un-recognised. In 2014 the Royal Mint chose his portrait for one of a limited-edition set of five-pound coins commemorating the centenary of the outbreak of World War One.

His sterling qualities amazed them all –
Cool, brave and disciplined;
And on sober reflection were they forced to admit
That the worth of a man is not measured by his skin.

The Second World War erupted in September 1939 when Germany invaded Poland, prompting Britain and France to declare war on Germany. As with the previous war, various al-liances came into play, expanding the conflict to much of the rest of the world. The Caribbean response to World War Two bears many similarities to that of the first war. Once again, the islands barred no holes in their generosity to their 'mother coun-try'. Donations of money and materials flowed from the region to London. One estimate puts the financial contribution from the region at more than two million U.S dollars. Material gifts came in the form of things like mobile canteens and recreational booths and even fighter planes.

The colonial governments of the Caribbean had once again demonstrated – if there was any doubt – that loyalty to kith and kin ranked far higher in their scheme of things than the welfare of the mass of under-privileged people they governed. But the people, themselves, also seemed to have had some misplaced loyalties. For, as if they had learnt nothing from the shabby treatment meted out to them by the British on the first occasion, Caribbean people were again begging for an opportunity to enlist in the British army. *"We were British,"* declared Jamaican, Connie Mark, who volunteered and served with a branch of the army called the Auxiliary Territorial Service, ATS. *"England was our mother country. We were brought up to respect the Royal Family. I used to collect pictures of Margaret and Elizabeth...I adored them. It was the British influence. We didn't grow up with any Jamaican **thing**; we grew up as British."* Her view would have been typical of the prevailing mind-set among Caribbean people of the day: a denial of self and identification with the imperial power.

A note from the Colonial Office to the British cabinet reported an *"intense wave of loyalty sweeping through the...West Indies".* But the authorities in London advised the island governments to discourage the movement for enlistment. The argument was put that the Caribbeans would be of more help staying at home and maintaining local production of goods and services. What was not known – at least to the mass of people – was that enlistment in the British Army, Navy and Air force was limited to men of **pure European descent** – i.e: white men. This rule, adopted in 1938, automatically ruled out more than 90% of the inhabitants of Britain's Caribbean colonies. One of them was Jamaican Dentist, Leo March, who tried to enlist in the British Air Force in 1939. March complained to the Colonial Office that he had been turned down because he was not of pure European descent. Some black Britons who also tried to enlist were rejected on the same grounds.

As was the case in the first war, the racial bar also existed in the American and Canadian armies, as Barbadian, Owen Rowe, discovered when he joined the Canadian army in 1942. Rowe was assigned to service in the Pacific with Canadian forces who were under the direction of the Americans. The assignment was cancelled on the verge of his departure; his superior officer told him the U.S Army was segregated and they didn't want to expose him to segregation. He later transferred to the Canadian Air Force.

Besieged by the Colonial Office on the question of the racial bar, the military authorities in London finally agreed (at least in words) to a relaxation of the bar in October 1939. The announcement, made in both houses of Parliament, declared a lifting of the colour bar on non-Europeans from the colonies, for the duration of the war. As it would turn out, this exercise was purely cosmetic, for merely one month later the British Foreign Affairs Office sent out a memo to diplomatic offices to the effect that *"only offers of service from white British subjects should be considered."* And the Colonial Office followed this up with a secret memo to the Governors of the colonies indicating that *"it is not desirable that non-European British subjects should come here for enlistment. How you handle this we leave to your discretion."* In a subsequent memo later in the war, the Office instructed the foreign missions *"We must keep up the fiction of there being no colour bar while only those with specific qualifications are likely to be accepted."*

So that when a Barbadian medical student in Scotland – a Mr. K. Ward – attempted to join the Royal Air Force he was turned down: only men of pure European descent. But as agitation among the Caribbeans for enlistment mounted, the colonial Governors were forced to continue their lobby for the acceptance of non-white volunteers. The Colonial Office, in response, recommended to the Army administrators the revival of the West India Regiment, a regional militia established in 1795 and disbanded in 1927. The regiment had been pressed into use during the First World War, serving in Africa and the Middle East. What the Office had in mind, though, was labour, rather than battle-front units.

The proposal was rejected; the Army chiefs didn't even want black, Caribbean labour in their war. Well, the Governor of Trinidad apparently decided that *'if you can't beat them, join them'*. He wrote the Colonial Office in May 1940 to report that Trinidadian merchants wanted to outfit and send a group of white men, as they had done during the First World War. The Governor's note continued: *"It is necessary to find an outlet for the strong local desire to render loyal service."* Undeterred by the lack of response from

London, the Trinidadian war enthusiasts held a public rally in Port of Spain two months later and adopted a resolution, which they sent to London, suggesting a Caribbean corps of 250 thousand, including 25 thousand Trinidadian men.

The case made in the resolution for the use of Caribbean volunteers reflected a pitiful delusion in the minds of Caribbean people at the time, of a mutual affinity between them and the British: "...*it would be most unfair to our **Mother Country** should we not, like our English **brothers**, also taste the horrors of actual warfare and the unspeakable sacrifices attendant there to.*"

One branch of the British Army that was more receptive to the Caribbean volunteers was the Royal Air Force. Owing to a labour shortage very early in the war, authorities in London approved the enlistment of Caribbeans for ground duty with the Air Force, including service with support agencies like the Women's Auxiliary Air Force. Altogether, about seven thousand Caribbean volunteers signed up with the RAF, including about 400 Pilots and other air men.

But up to 1943, four years after the start of the war, the authorities in London were maintaining their objection to the recruitment of non-white volunteers in the regular army. The colour bar also applied to women volunteers who were being assigned to a female ancillary unit called the Auxiliary Territorial Service or ATS. In 1943 the Governor of Barbados protested to London that the head of the Service had indicated that only girls of "*pure European descent*" could be recruited.

Caribbean women in the A.T.S.

The reply from the War Office confirmed this: "*We are prepared to accept any European girl...but we cannot agree to accept coloured women for service in this country.*" In fact, there were some black women in the ATS in Britain, believed to have been resident at the time of their recruitment. The colour bar was eventually removed and a contingent of ATS recruits, black and white, was accepted for service.

A break-through was also happening for the cherished dream of a Caribbean corps in the Army. Influenced partly by the heavy loss of men on the ground, the British cabinet agreed in January 1944 to the formation of a Caribbean Regiment – ten thousand men signed up. But even this late acceptance would not end the trail of rejection following the Caribbean men. The military authorities in London met with repeated refusal from the Commander-in-Chief in India to accept the Regiment. A similar response came for a proposal to send them to Italy: not wanted. The regiment was finally sent to Italy, where it was used for non-combat duties behind the front line, and then posted to Egypt where its duties included clearing mines around the Suez Canal area.

But if there is one bright spark in the whole Caribbean war experience, then it must be the contribution of the men who joined the Air Force. Although largely ignored by historians and war-movie makers, the Caribbean airmen rendered distinguished service to the WW 2 air operations. Barbados' first Prime Minister, now national hero, the late Errol Barrow, was among the company of Caribbean RAF airmen. Barrow flew more than forty bombing missions during the war, eventually rising to become a Flying Officer and personal navigator to the Commander of the British Zone of occupied Germany.

Other Caribbean airmen who crisscrossed the European war skies with Barrow include Trinidadian, Ulric Cross, a decorated Squadron Leader; Dudley Thompson, who later became a cabinet minister in Jamaica, Lawyer and Pan Africanist; Michael Manley, Prime Minister of Jamaica from 1972 – 1980 who joined the Canadian Air Force; Julian Marryshow, son of the Grenadian newspaper Editor and Publisher, Theophilus Marryshow and

Guyanese scholar and author of the book, "To Sir With Love", Edward Brathwaite.

Ulric Cross

The Caribbean air men distinguished themselves in the R.A.F, earning 103 medals. The most distinguished of them was Squadron Leader, Ulric Cross, who was awarded the Distinguished Flying Cross and Distinguished Service Order.

Historians are of no doubt that these brave Caribbean men and their colleagues on the ground contributed immensely to the defeat of Hitler's agenda in Europe. They may have lacked the required purity in their racial composition, but they were able to prove that their metal was greater than their melanin.

In The Name of God

As wine to the French, so is religion to Barbados. The fewer than 300 thousand Barbadians must certainly be the most religious in the world – you can find a church virtually at every corner. The island's religious roots go all the way back to the arrival of the British in the late 1620's. Within a year of their arrival they had built a church not far from their landing site, now known as the St. James Parish Church. It must be the mother of all paradoxes that those who would spend the next 300 years inflicting the most inhumane treatment on fellow humans felt the need to commune with the God of love and justice.

The denomination of choice for the British settlers was the Church of England, known in these parts as the Anglican Church. In those early years the local church was under the direction of the Bishop of London. It would not be before 1824 that the first Bishop is appointed for Barbados. The 35-year-old William Hart Coleridge was appointed to the diocese of Barbados, the Leeward Islands, Trinidad & Tobago and Guyana.

The Church functioned as an extension of the state, joining the executive, Parliament and the Judiciary, which, along with the plantation, constituted the system of power and control. Indeed, one month after his arrival, in January 1825, Bishop Coleridge was appointed to the Legislative Council, the precursor to what is now the Senate, a non-elected parliamentary assembly. As a state church, its Priests were paid from the Treasury and possessed pensionable rights. And when the system of local government known as the Vestry System was introduced, its Chairmen were invariably Anglican Priests. It might therefore not be surprising that, unlike the Methodists, who were to come later, the Anglican

Church proved to be no strident crusader against the injustices of slavery, choosing, instead, to sit on the fence.

Bishop Coleridge's tenure is largely identified with a significant boom in church building and in educational opportunities for the lower classes. The Church was also instrumental in education at a higher level, pioneering teacher education in the Anglophone Caribbean. The progenitor of this was the Rev. Richard Rawle, a Principal of Codrington College, who organized lectures for Caribbean Teachers in the period 1847 – 1864. This work was resumed in 1912 with the creation of the Rawle Institute – also at Codrington College. The institute was replaced by Erdiston Teacher Training College in 1948.

Since 1969 the Anglican Church has ceased to be the state church of Barbados. By an Act of Parliament, passed in April 1969, the government of then Prime Minister Errol Barrow dis-established the Church. As a result of this Act the Church ceased to receive financial support from the state and is now fully responsible for its own sustenance.

St. John's Anglican Church

Dis-establishment also effectively abolished the post of Bishop of Barbados, though the title is still used by the office holder – I suspect for reasons of prestige.

It is almost impossible to over-state the ascendancy of the Anglican Church and the aura of respectability with which it was cloaked in Barbados. In the pre-disestablishment era it literally ruled the roost in all matters ecclesiastical, and figured prominently in other things social. Not only did its Bishop have constitutional status as the Bishop of Barbados, he was also appointed to the local Privy Council. Anglican clergymen enjoyed primacy in the choice of persons for national religious duty – Chaplain of the House of Assembly and Senate, or chairmen of boards. Religious invocations at national events were almost invariably done by Anglican Priests. It was the church of choice for a majority of Barbadians, not only for Sunday worship, but for special events like weddings, baptisms and funerals.

Its involvement in the education system persisted even well after the state assumed control of the public schools once controlled by the Church. As children attending school in the rural parish of St. John, our weekly routine would include a religious assembly at St. John's Parish Church whether we were Adventists, Catholics, atheists or agnostics. Those were not days when respect for religious freedom was rife. Church attendance also took place on special days like Ash Wednesday. There has been some diminution in the Church's influence over the years, but by and large it still possesses some of its original clout. The Chaplains in the houses of parliament are still both Anglican and national religious events more often than not involve Priests of the Anglican Church. And while school church attendance has been all but abandoned, it is still known to occur on special religious occasions.

The Church has also lost the patronage of a significant portion of its membership over the years. A national census in 1980 recorded that 40% of Barbadians were Anglicans, but by the year 2010 that figure had fallen to 24%. Some of that decline is, no doubt, attributable to a general cooling of religious fervour among Barbadians, but many of those leaving the Church became affiliated with other denominations. Some have attributed this loss to the Church's failure to make itself more culturally compatible with Caribbean society. They point, for instance, to its rigid adherence to a worship format inherited from the English that is at variance with the vibrancy and rhythm of Caribbean culture.

The propensity to follow the Church of England prototype even manifests itself in the speech patterns of the clergy, many of whom deliver their sermons with Anglicized accents, characterized by unnatural drawls on their vowels. Change is not something that comes easily in the conservative society that is Barbados, and in the Anglican Church that change has been long and slow in coming. Nevertheless, the Church has made some modest steps towards reforming its worship format. But I suspect the reforms which some might think necessary would change the character of Anglicanism as we have come to know it.

The religious order took a different turn in the second half of the 17th. century with the arrival of the Quakers, the Methodists and the Moravians. In contrast to the pro-establishment Anglican Church the Quakers and Methodists would ruffle quite a few feathers among the planter-merchant community. The Quakers emerged in England in 1652 as a reformist off-shoot of the Church of England, under the leadership of George Fox. They called themselves the Religious Society of Friends. Doctrinally, they held to many of the beliefs and practices of mainstream Christianity.

George Fox

With a mandate to go into the world and convert people, they sent missionaries to Barbados, Jamaica and other Caribbean countries – Barbados, then being a major transit point for trade between Britain and the American colonies. Quakers journeying to America would stop at Barbados before moving on to their destination, and would use the intransit time to evangelize. Fox, himself, visited Barbados in 1670 for three months.

The local Quaker community was said to be the largest in all the British colonies – at one point numbering over a thousand – and could boast of having among its ranks sugar planters, Doctors and other business people. They tended to eschew officialdom: they kept their own registers of births, marriages and deaths; had their own burial grounds and refused to take official oaths, serve in the military or pay dues to the Anglican Church.

Their doctrine also put them at variance with the established Anglican Church and they published pamphlets attacking the church and its Priests. In other respects a sect given to peace and non-violence, they displayed uncharacteristic stridency in their opposition to the Anglican Church, sometimes intruding on, and disrupting services.

As a result of this virulent campaign, a group of Anglican clergymen presented the authorities with a petition demanding the suppression of the sect. The petitioners complained of the frequent interruption of services and the vilification of the Church. It accused the Quakers of *"poisoning...many of our flock, who being infatuated and inveighed with these pernicious tenets, desert the established Church and withdrawn into private and unlawful conventicles."*

Though they eventually took a stand against slavery, members of the faith were, themselves, involved in the use of slave labour in the early years of the movement. But in the early 1670's founder George Fox led a chorus of anti-slavery declarations, calling on Barbadian slave holders to treat their slaves kindly and ultimately free them. This platform reached its zenith in 1688 with the first public statement by Quakers in the American state of Pennsylvania against enslavement. There-after they gradually eradicated slavery from among their ranks and were among the first campaigners to call for the abolition of slavery. Local Quakers also broke new ground by inviting enslaved persons to their meetings, causing embarrassment to the Anglican Clergy and concern among the political authorities of the day.

It was inevitable that their activities and dogmas would run them into trouble with the Barbadian planter-merchant ruling class, and in 1676 the authorities passed *"An Act to Prevent the People called Quakers from bringing Negroes to their Meeting"*. The Governor followed this up with an order in 1680 calling for the closure of the Quakers meeting room in the city, though this was later revoked. Some were arrested for refusing to submit to military service, failure to pay taxes and opening their businesses on religious holidays; and Quaker meetings were sometimes broken up. Local authorities were forced eventually to liberalise religious expression by the Toleration Act, passed in the British Parliament in 1689, which granted freedom of worship to non-conformists.

By the late 18th. century there had been a mass exodus of Quakers to Pennsylvania. Today in Barbados the Society of Friends is no more. With the exception of a few burial grounds and the street called Quakers Road, in Carrington's Village, there is no physical legacy of the bold, religious crusaders from England who dared to stand up to the power brokers of pre-emancipation Barbadian society.

The Quakers were followed by Moravian missionaries. This faith originated in the provinces of Bohemia and Moravia in Czechoslovakia as a reformist movement within the Roman Catholic Church in the late 14th. Century. In the early 1730's the church undertook an international missionizing campaign which brought them to Barbados in 1765. They became known, not only for their evangelical work, but for their efforts to educate the enslaved population. Like the Quakers, they encouraged slaves to attend their meetings; but unlike their predecessors, they opted not to rock the boat by challenging the injustices of slavery. The Moravian Church still exists in Barbados, though with a modest membership.

But the presence of none of the religious crusaders would prove to be more eventful than that of the Methodists, who elicited an unprecedented level of anti-religious sentiment among the white population. It all began with the visit of Methodist missionary, Thomas Coke, and three companions in 1788. But the man who would be the spark that lit the fuse of the anti-Methodist bomb was The Rev. William Shrewsbury, who arrived in 1820. The vitriol against Shrewsbury might have had more to do with the events that unfolded before and after his arrival than with Methodism itself. The 1816 Bussa revolt in Barbados and the Demerara revolt of 1823 had created some nervousness among the white community. They thought abolitionists and (Methodist) missionaries were to blame for spreading the idea of human equality among the enslaved.

It probably did not help that Shrewsbury himself was an opponent of slavery and befriended the enslaved. By his own account, Shrewsbury's sermons were hot talking points among the whites. He was accused of jeopardizing the peace of the colony and of having secret meetings with slaves to pass on news from the Anti-Slavery Society in Britain. He was the target of verbal attacks and his services were often disrupted by violent mobs hurling missiles and discharging firearms.

In a letter to a friend, Shrewsbury described in clear terms the kind of odium to which he was subjected in his public appearances:

"If I passed in the streets, indignant eyes met in every direction. Gentlemen in stores would come to the door and stand gaping at me as at a monster until I was out of sight. And sometimes they would utter such sayings as these: 'that fellow ought to have a rope tied around his neck'; 'hang him'; or more elegantly '...the damn rascal of a Methodist Parson; he ought to be kicked into hell'.

This hostility even extended to Parliament. In a message to the Governor on April 5, 1825 the House of Assembly sought to draw his attention to a legal provision requiring all people to be subject to the authority of the Church of England. The assembly informed the Governor that they considered the Church of England and its ministers sufficient enough to care for the needs of the people of Barbados and that no other hostile groups or sects should be allowed to subvert the principles of the established Church.

The anti-Methodist zealots first served notice of their violent tendencies on October 5th. 1823. A group of young men rode past the Methodist chapel while a service was in progress and threw bottles of a foul smelling liquid into the church. Things took a turn for the worst when the anti-Methodists crusade resolved to demolish the Methodist chapel.

A secret group circulated pamphlets calling for the destruction of the chapel, and on the evening of Sunday, October 19th. 1823 a large group of white men assembled at the chapel with hammers, crowbars, hatchets and other implements. They broke into the chapel and proceeded to carry out the demolition, labouring well into the night. Unable to complete the task in one night, the party returned the following morning.

Like the prophetic destruction of the Jewish temple, not one stone of the chapel was left standing on another when the job was completed. Meanwhile, Shrewsbury and his pregnant wife had retreated to the home of his brother for safety. They passed the night peacefully, and the next day were put on a boat for St. Vincent.

The destruction of the chapel and Shrewsbury's departure were not the death knell of Methodism in Barbados, owing largely to the dauntless work of a free, coloured (mixed race) woman called Ann Gill and her sister in law, Christina Gill (Ann Gill is now a national hero of Barbados). Ann sought to keep the faith alive by holding meetings in her home. This was in contravention of an order from the Court; the Magistrates had banned Methodist meetings using an outdated piece of legislation called the Conventicles Act as justification, and had put surveillance on members' homes. The act, passed during the reign of Charles 2nd. to control non-conformist religious gatherings, outlawed meetings of more than five persons if such meetings were in conflict with the established church.

In fact, this law had been superseded by the Toleration Act of 1689 which gave conditional freedom of religion. Mrs. Gill found herself a target of the Police and the Court, which warned her to cease her religious activities. To that order she replied: "*We ought to obey God rather than men.*" It was the kind of defiance that called for exceptional courage, given the mood of fanaticism demonstrated in the destruction of the Methodist chapel. Indeed, Mrs. Gill home was the target of a plan for arson to mark the first anniversary of the chapel's destruction. The plan was made known by a group called the Committee of Public Safety in a proclamation leading up to the anniversary:

"*...it is hereby made known to all whom it may concern that for the avowed purpose of rooting eternally from their shores the damned doctrine and public exhibition of methodistical hypocrisy, now again rearing its baneful head and spreading its beasted and pestilential principles among us, we have decreed that from and after the said memorable, the blessed 21st. of October...that we will, with fire and sword, root out and destroy all and every abettors of Methodism and Methodists. So help us God.*" In response to an appeal from Mrs. Gill, the Governor ordered troops to guard her home on the anniversary night, which passed without incident.

The terrorist activities of the Barbadian whites against the Methodists did not escape the notice of the British Parliament nor that of the Anti-Slavery Society. In a motion tabled in the House of Commons in June 1825, co-founder of the Society and leader of its parliamentary group, Thomas Buxton, expressed "*amazement and detestation*" at the "*scandalous and daring violation of law*" which had occurred in Barbados, and demanded that the authorities in Barbados re-build the chapel at their own expense. Back in Barbados, there were signs of a thaw in the anti-Methodist hysteria. The Courts dropped all charges against Mrs. Gill; and a successor to Shrewsbury, a Moses Raynar who had previously served in Barbados, returned to take over the leadership of the Church. Raynar was able to conduct meetings without interference either from mobs or the authorities.

The last census put the Methodist membership at roughly five percent, a relatively small number of the religious community in Barbados, who now practise their faith with none of the turmoil and terrorism in which it was founded.

Though not persecuted as badly as the Methodists, the early Roman Catholics in Barbados also met some resistance from the authorities. Roman Catholics have been present in Barbados almost from the beginning of British settlement. Certainly by the early 1630's there were English and Irish Catholics here, though the faith had no organization at that time. By the early 1650's a visiting Priest from Suriname, Antoine Biet, was able to report the presence of Catholics *"not small in numbers"*, the majority of whom would have been Irish people, banned into servitude by the Cromwell administration in Ireland.

Those days were previous to the advent of religious tolerance, and as such no Catholic Priests were admitted or allowed to remain in the island, even among those under sentence of penal servitude. The minutes of a Legislative Council meeting of May 21st. 1656, relative to the presence of four Catholic Priests in Barbados, give a clear indication of the attitude in governmental circles to the promotion of Roman Catholicism in Barbados:-

"It is ordered that Richard Shelton, James Tuite, Robert Eagan and Redman More, Irish Priests, do within three daies (days) *bring into the Secretary's Office ye* (your) *place o … abode, and that they have 15 daies libertie to seeke passage for their departure from this island to anie* (any) *place without the dominions of ye Commonwealth of England."*

The year 1829 was a significant one for the faith. That's the year in which the Roman Catholic Emancipation Act was passed in Britain, doing away with many of the restrictions on Catholics. Authorities in London sent a copy of the Act to Barbados with a recommendation that it be adopted by the local legislature. It would take three decades before this happened. Meanwhile back in 1839 a committee of local Catholics petitioned the Bishop for a resident Priest. The petition was successful and a Rev. William Rogers was contracted from British Guiana. Rev. Rogers lost no time setting plans in train for the erection of a church. In addition to local efforts, he undertook a fund-raising tour of the islands. The corner-stone was laid in 1840, but work on the erection of the church would not begin until 1847 the same year Rev. Rogers demitted office. It was completed the following year and consecrated on March 10th. 1850 as St. Patrick's Catholic Church, now St. Patrick's Cathedral.

Catholic membership in Barbados has been hovering around 4% in the last few decades. A significant segment of it comprises Barbadians and residents with ancestral roots in those Caribbean and Latin American countries where Roman Catholicism is dominant – St. Lucia, Dominica, Trinidad, Venezuela.

The most recent of the Christian entrants to the Barbadian religious arena are the Evangelicals. This definition can be misleading, because although they have some doctrinal and other things in common, they are, by no mean, a homogenous group. Evangelicals encompass a diverse body of Christians ranging from Pentecostals, to Adventists, to Jehovah's Witnesses. The evangelical presence can be traced back to the latter part of the 19th. century, and the activities of American missionaries. This activity, which stretched well into the 20th. century, led to the establishment of such churches as the Christian Mission, the Nazarene, the Pilgrim (Wesleyan) Holiness, New Testament Church of God and the Brethren.

These churches are characterized by the highly spirited and boisterous nature of their meetings, and the oftimes "*fire and brimstone*" preaching from their pulpits. They profess to practise true Christianity, as exemplified by the application of the principles of the bible, and avoidance of smoking, alcoholic consumption and what they regard as "*worldly*" pleasures – attendance at dances and carnivals and other social entertainment events.

In more recent times a new brand of the Pentecostal subset, heavily influenced by American evangelical culture and theology, has been making its presence felt. These new Pentecostals are characterized by their more youthful membership and their departure from traditional Evangelical traditions – the women are far less modest in their attire: the wearing of jewellery and trousers, once spurned as being "*worldly*", is now commonplace. Another noticeable change is reflected among the clergy. When

I was growing up Pentecostal Pastors were never addressed by the title "*Reverend*" and did not wear cassocks or other religious accoutrements like collars. I think this had something to do with Jesus' denunciation of the Pharisees for seeking to set themselves apart by their titles and dress. Well – today we have Pentecostal and Evangelical "*Reverends*", Bishops and Apostles who can be seen decked in clerical collars and sometimes robes. The American influence is evident in their worship – they've replaced traditional Evangelical hymns with North American-type songs and choruses accompanied by drums and other percussion instruments – and in their relationship with the right-wing evangelical movement in the United States. They've pitched their tents with the likes of Benny Hinn, Creflo Dollar, Jimmy Swaggart and other American televangelists of that ilk.

The American influence may sometimes also extend to the speech patterns of some preachers – it is not unusual to hear a preacher, born and bred in Barbados, pouring forth in a quasi-American accent. This latter practice speaks to a post-slavery/colonialism syndrome to which I will make reference later.

Outside of Christianity, there are small pockets of religious activity – mostly of the Hindu and Islamic faiths. Those involved are mostly immigrants from India or Indians from other parts of the Caribbean who came into Barbados between the late 19th. and early 20th. centuries. They practise their faith openly, in a country that recognizes the freedom of all in matters of conscience and faith – no threats of arson; no destruction of mosques nor temples. Time is a great change agent.

The Radicals

Throughout the course of human existence the fields of oppression have always been fertile ground for the seeds of justice and liberation. Whether they come in the form of Mandela, Fidel Castro, Wilberforce, Harriet Tubman or Clement Payne, bold agents of change have always emerged to resist or reform the existing order, if not destroy it altogether. In the near four centuries of its history as a British colony, Barbados has had its fair share of those who challenged injustice, sometimes at its very root. We've already mentioned the heroism of Bussa and his cohorts of the pre-Emancipation period; but leading up to 1838 and thereafter, those daring to stand up to the wrongs of the plantocracy continued to make their presence felt.

Samuel Jackman Prescod (1806 –1871)

One of the most prominent of them was a man called Samuel Jackman Prescod, the son of a free coloured woman and a white, land-owning father. He made his mark as a Journalist, newspaper Publisher, political activist, labour leader and Member of Parliament, dedicated to the cause of the free coloured and enslaved people. In the years immediately preceding and following Emancipation, he would prove to be a champion of the oppressed coloured and black people, and the scourge of the powerful planter elite.

The platform for his passionate campaign could be said to have been launched on Emancipation Day, in a declaration he made to the free coloureds and blacks from the pages of his Liberal newspaper: *"Fellow men and friends, I have lived to see you declared free men, and I hope to live to see you made free."*

It was in his role as a Journalist that Prescod conducted much of his militant activity, first as Editor of a newspaper for the Free Coloureds (people of mixed race) called the New Times, and then as Editor and Publisher of his own paper, the Liberal. His work, both as Editor/Publisher of the Liberal and later as a Member of Parliament, may be categorized under three general heads: expansion of the right to vote, then limited to people with ownership of real estate; a campaign against the oppressive, post-Emancipation laws and political party organization.

His campaign to expand the franchise was partially successful when, in 1831, free coloured and free black people (who met the required property qualifications) were given the vote. Another change to the Franchise legislation was made in 1840. But Prescod was still dissatisfied even after these two changes, which left the vote largely within the same narrow clique. Writing in "The Liberal", he criticised the 1840 bill as inadequate, saying there was never any intention to extend the franchise. And Governor, Evan McGregor, who gave his assent to the bill didn't escape Prescod's ire either: *"The credit of the character of this colony would be considerably improved if Sir Evan McGregor was not so much of a planter Governor...If those who have no voice... were to occupy a little more of his attention...he would never have given his assent to the Franchise Bill."*

The slew of repressive anti-worker legislation that came with the abolition of slavery consumed much of Prescod's intellectual and physical energies – laws such as the Hiring of Servants Act (also known as the Contracts Act) which virtually tied workers to the plantation; the Offences Against the Person and Property Act; the Trespass Act and the Emigration Act. Prescod saw these laws as nothing but an attempt by the plantocracy to maintain control over a free people. As he put it, they would *"...leave the emancipated classes but the semblance of freedom without its substantial privileges and immunities."* On the Contracts Act, he advised the workers not to sign onto any contract that could lead to the curtailment of their rights. Many followed this advice and there were strikes in the sugar industry.

He was strongest in his objection to the Emigration Act, which sought to prevent workers from leaving the country for job opportunities, and criminalized the actions of anyone who helped them to do so. *"I tell you that this law would make us all slaves, all except the planters and those who have...an interest in keeping the labour market full and wages low. It takes from every other person in the island...the right of freely advising and assisting on any occasion a fellow subject to do that which may be for his benefit, and which the law says he has the right to do. It takes from every labourer and tradesman the right of...hiring himself to any person, or to go out of this island to any other colony or place...."*

The Emigration law had been introduced to stem the tide of workers seeking jobs overseas in the hard times after Emancipation. As part of his campaign against it Prescod held a meeting of supporters at St. Mary's School, adopting resolutions to petition the British houses of Parliament and Queen Victoria. Governor, Evan McGregor, also got another lashing; the meeting expressed deep regret that he would grant his assent to a law *"so unconstitutional in its principles (and) so iniquitous in its tendency..."* Not satisfied to confine his agitation within the island's borders, Prescod took his protest to the Secretary of State for the Colonies in London via memo. In one such memo, he sought to draw to the Secretary's attention that while the colonies had abolished slavery and apprenticeship, they had sought to curtail the freedoms of the former slaves with unjust and illegal restrictions.

"Legislative despotism" is how Prescod described these measures, which he said were designed to give the planters a monopoly of labour and keep workers in a condition of praedial servitude. In furtherance of his campaign he joined forces with the British-founded Central Negro Emancipation Committee on

102

whose behalf he drafted and despatched the following memo to the Colonial Secretary in 1838:

"That the majority of the colonies have abolished the apprenticeship system and thus destroyed the last vestige of legalized slavery is a matter for unfeigned thankfulness; that they have clogged the infant liberties of the negroes with unjust and illegal restrictions and thus destroyed the grace of this act is a matter for deep regret...."

In another missive to the Secretary, Prescod outlined some of his own expectations of Emancipation as follows:

"...the apprenticeship of the emancipated slaves was to be immediately succeeded by personal freedom in that full and unlimited sense in which it is enjoyed by all other British subjects; the Governors of the colonies were to be precluded...from giving their sanction to any ordinance perpetuating or continuing after the termination of the apprenticeship, any distinctions or exclusions arising out of a previous servile condition; all laws, ordinances or orders in council that contravene the imperial statute or were repugnant to any part thereof were to be null and void and of no effect; the British legislature and Her Majesty's government were to...carry into full and complete effect the great measure for the entire abolition of slavery throughout the colonies, and to secure to the enfranchised bondsmen all the rights and all the privileges of freedom."

In 1840 he became a hero who suffered for his cause. A successful libel suit against him landed him in jail for eight days. He was released after a pardon from the Governor, undeterred from his task of attacking the injustices of the government. Three years after he would create local history by becoming the first Barbadian of African descent to be elected to the House of Assembly. For Prescod this was nothing more than a higher platform from which to advance the cause of the under-classes. It was from parliament that he organized the Liberal Party, comprising supporters within the House as well as other small land owners, coloured Clerks and businessmen. For more than two decades afterwards, the party functioned as the parliamentary opposition on the platform established by its founder.

In 1860, at the early age of 54, Prescod retired from political activity, but later functioned as an Appeals Court Judge. His death, in 1871, at the age of 65 was the final page of an important chapter in the struggle for equality and justice for the oppressed masses of Barbados. Today, he is numbered among a pantheon of ten national heroes; a technical college, The Samuel Jackman Prescod Polytechnic, is named in his honour, and his face is on the 20-dollar note (Barbados currency).

Despised as a rebel, a radical, and a rogue by the wealthy elite of his time, today his name is celebrated by both the descendents of those against whom he battled, and those for whose upliftment he wielded his pen and his voice so valiantly.

Charles Duncan O'Neal (1879–1936)

Prescod's death may have ended a chapter in the struggle for justice in 19th. century Barbadian society, but a mere eight years after his passing, the grounds of oppression in Barbados would throw up another Moses in Charles Duncan O'Neal, the son of black, well-to-do parents. After graduating from the Parry School (what is now the Coleridge & Parry School) O'Neal went to Scotland to study medicine, graduating with distinction. It was in Scotland that his interest in politics first manifested itself.

He contested local government elections and won a seat on the Sunderland County Council. But, perhaps, his real interest was in the politics of Barbados, and in 1910 he returned home. Not happy with the conditions he found, he set sail again, this time for Trinidad and Dominica. On his return, he thrust himself into the local politics taking up the plight of the under-classes with the radical Journalist, Clennell Wickham, of whom we shall hear next.

Like Prescod, O'Neal used the Press as a vehicle to project his message to the wider society, but he also employed the strategy of grassroots organization, forming the Democratic League, a quasi-political party, the Working-men's Association, which functioned as the business and industrial arm of the League, and the Loan and Friendly Society. The association was an investment organisation with a share-owning membership drawn from various parts of the island. Its office was located at the corner of Reed Street and Baxters Road in the City.

But it was the Democratic League, a grouping of coloured and black middle class people, that gave him his greatest political leverage. The League's programme, as articulated by O'Neal, included such (at the time) revolutionary proposals as free education and free dental care for children; the abolition of child labour; the introduction of Universal Adult Suffrage and improved conditions for women in the workplace. He tried his best to impress on the political directorate the need to alleviate the abject poverty afflicting the underclass, manifested in poor nutrition and housing and high infant mortality.

Two months after its creation in 1924 the League achieved success at the polls, when its candidate, Chrissy Brathwaite, was elected as a representative for St. Michael in the House of Assembly. O'Neal, himself, would have to wait for another eight years before he could ascend the steps of Parliament. In the Assembly, he made good use of the parliamentary question to get his ideas across. In one such question related to the use of child labour – which he opposed – he asked: "*whether the government will introduce such legislation as is deemed adequate to prohibit the carrying and using of whips by drivers of 'third gangs'* (child labour units) *when on duty"*, and *"whether the government will fix the number of working hours during which a child under 14 years of age may be employed for agricultural purposes on estates during vacation."*

The government spokesman who answered the question said there was no need for such legislation or regulation. One planter MP said the young people in the 'third gang' were *"learning their vocation"*. He went on to describe the gang as *"...the most useful vocational school in this island."* In his follow up comments, O'Neal told the House: *"we have passed those barbarous days when it was found necessary to use the whip to get work out of people...its use on third gang labourers is barbarism, and we in this country should rather be more highly advanced than to permit such instruments to be used in our names...These children are driven by necessity to work, and knowing that, the driver uses all his power to get the last ounce of blood out of them."*

Child labour was an issue about which O'Neal had strong feelings. He once led a delegation, including Wickham and others, to appeal to the Governor to use his authority to have it banned. The appeal was not successful. His parliamentary time was also occupied with issues of maternal and child health. Concerned over what he saw as the unhealthy condition of children in the City area attending schools like St. Mary's, Wesley Hall and St. Leonard's, he told the assembly: *"anyone who is not actually purblind can see that the children of these schools are deteriorating in physique. They exhibit symptoms of tonsillitis, adenoids and decaying teeth."* O'Neal was especially worried by the high rate of deaths among pregnant women and infants. He told the House: *"They have forgotten the great test of the condition of a country, and that is the test of the maternal death rate. When you find the death rate amongst mothers going up by leaps and bounds, you conclude that there is something wrong in this country, that there's great suffering...The mother is sacrificing herself for her husband and for her children."*

O'Neal was quite aware of the kind of people whom he was up against. He knew they had no interest in anything other than their own welfare. In fact, he referred to them as parasites: *"...the animal that sits on another animal's back and sucks its blood; he who draws much wealth from a country, does no work, and has to be kept up by the labourers of that country is the parasite...They would rather continue to make large investments abroad while those who earned the money for them are today in misery and starvation..."*

O'Neal's programme was endorsed, albeit secretly, by no less a person than the Governor, Sir William Robertson. In a classified memo to the Colonial Office in 1926, he said the *"(Democratic) League's programme has little in it to which exception can be taken – improved wages and conditions of life for the labouring class; proper sanitation, compulsory education and matters of that kind."* The Governor went on: *"unless employers and the government come to realise that conditions must be improved and reasonable demands satisfied, adherence to this or perhaps other more revolutionary societies (groups) may become more general...."*

Clearly unimpressed by the leadership of the planter-government, two years later Governor Robertson was at it again: *"...Progress and improvement in any direction is slow in Barbados with its oligarchical government, disguised as democratic, intensely conservative, steeped in the tradition of objection to dictation and suspicious of suggestion."* Nothing justifies the Governor's harsh condemnation of the planter-merchant government more, than their response to a 1935 proposal for the construction of a sanitary facility at the Holetown Post Office. The proposal was turned down on the basis that it might create *"a precedent"*!

Confronted, on one hand, by an oligarchy with a callous disregard for the welfare of anyone but themselves, and a suffering mass of people, on the other, O'Neal had premonitions of social ferment, and in a warning that would be prophetic, made the following comments to the House in 1935: *"Those of us who live in Bridgetown know that there are many people coming to us every day who obviously are starving, who obviously require food and clothing,...Unless the Governor and his committee take the greatest possible steps in this matter, grave trouble is brewing in this country."* A mere two years later his prophesy came to pass as riots erupted in Barbados, sparked by the deportation of a militant labour leader named Clement Payne – about whom we shall hear later.

Like his predecessor, Samuel Prescod, O'Neal did not live to enjoy the delights of retirement. He died ten days before his 57th. birthday, perhaps another martyr for the cause of the poor and down-trodden in post-Emancipation Barbados.

Clennell Wickham (1895 –1938)

With his kindred spirit gone, it was left to Clennell Wickham and the Herald newspaper to carry on the struggle on behalf of the under-classes. Wickham, who served with the British West Indies Regiment during World War One, teamed up with O'Neal on his return home from the war in 1919, even as he waged his own campaign in the pages of the Herald.

When the League secured its first electoral victory in the election of Chrissy Brathwaite to the House of Assembly, Wickham was ecstatic: "*I must salute the new spirit which is upon the waters. It is the most happy augury for the future welfare of the island. It means that in the days to come no man will be allowed to walk into the lobby of the House of Assembly and hang up his hat. He must be carried on the shoulders of the people.*"

There was no streak of timidity in his commentaries on the ruling oligarchy. In one of them he said of the elected members of Parliament: "*There is no sense of duty to the individual or the island as a whole. There is no sense of responsibility for broad and reasonable treatment. There is merely a sense of class.*" He was equally harsh with the merchant-planter class for their exploitation of black labour: "*The employer who pays a young woman eight pence a day is responsible before God for any line of action she may adopt to supplement her wages…That a grown man should have to work for nine hours a day for one shilling…is monstrous. It is a crime…*"

Some might consider his analysis of race in Barbados still partly accurate, even in 21st. century Barbados. "*The entire social and economic structure of Barbados is founded upon distinctions of colour. It is not the same thing as race hatred. It is one of the features of Barbados and other British colonies in which African slaves were brought to labour for white masters, that there should be so little real, personal animosity between the two races, in spite of the definite lines drawn socially...."*

The pen was his sword, and he wielded it with vengeance, as in this analysis of the character of S.C Thorne, a planter and Member of Parliament. *"That Thorne was one of the most prominent members of the House of Assembly was unfortunate for the honour of Barbados; worse, he was a perfect mob leader...the most perfect idea of what a representative of the people ought not to be... absolutely and entirely destitute of every vestige of decency in the conduct of public affairs."*

He was not averse to giving compliments, but even with these, his literary flair could not be suppressed. This bouquet he dished out to the then Speaker of the House of Assembly, Sir Frederick Clarke: *"As a man, Sir Frederick Clarke is not without his weaknesses. The ingredient of vanity is very considerable in his composition. The possession of common sense and the position in which he is placed prevent this quality from being harmful to the public...We may ridicule his haughtiness, we may be severe on his vanity, but he can show an escutcheon fair and unsullied; he stands a knight without fear and without reproach."*

His pen knew no boundaries when it came to articulating the cause of the working people. Among its targets: Governor, Sir Charles Obrien. In an open letter to the Governor, Wickham chided the him for sitting on the fence while the ruling minority pushed the people closer and closer to the brink:

"The mass of the Barbadian population is being forced on the rocks ahead...They are not going to submit without a struggle... Nero fiddled, Sir Charles, while Rome was burning. What are you doing while Barbados is starving....?"

But this bold and incisive commentary was taking place in a country with laws of libel and slander that are among the most crippling anywhere in the world. Each time he took up his pen the spectre of a libel suit dangled menacingly over his head. It happened in 1930 as a result of an article he wrote that was critical of a Bridgetown merchant named Walter Bayley. The jury upheld a libel suit brought by Bayley – whose counsel was Grantley Adams – and that was the end of Wickham's association with the Herald.

After the disaster of the libel suit he migrated to Grenada and continued his involvement in journalism, but his days would be cut short there. He died in 1938 at the tender age of 42. The iniquitous, plantocratic society that Barbados was up to the mid 20th. century had claimed another daring son of the soil. He has not been named among the national heroes – opinions differ on the status of his contribution. The only memorial to him is an inscription bearing his name and that of our next radical, T.T Lewis, on the Wickham & Lewis Boardwalk in the capital, Bridgetown.

Of Wickham, it could be said that words were his tools, and he wielded them like cudgels in the cause of the poor and helpless. He dipped his pen in acid and seared the flesh of the ruling elite. In the end he fell victim to that odious bit of legislation on our statute books, then known as the Laws of Libel and Slander (now the Defamation Act), that has hung over the practice of Journalism in this country, like the proverbial sword of Damocles, in its quest to protect the reputations of the rich and powerful.

Atholl Edwin Seymour ("TT") Lewis in 1946

T.T Lewis (1905 – 1959)

110

But black and coloured people were not the only ones stirred by the infelicities of pre and immediately post-Emancipation Barbadian society. The name Atholl (Edwin Seymour) Lewis, a white Barbadian man of working class background, is listed among the pantheon of warriors for justice and social advancement. Popularly known as 'T.T Lewis', he came to public notice in the early 40's when he was elected to the House of Assembly as representative for the City of Bridgetown.

At various times in his political career he was associated with mass-based parties, but regardless of party affiliation his focus in Parliament was the same: improvement in the lives of the ordinary folk. His foremost passion was universal free education, this in an era when those who dictated public policy considered this idea neither possible nor necessary. Listen to him in a presentation to the House in 1943:

"I think we should say that we must have compulsory education and not say that we cannot afford it. We ought not to have people growing up without a modicum of education; that is disgraceful". And again in 1944: *"There should be free education in all the schools – elementary as well as secondary".*

Very much ahead of his time: free education as a policy did not come for another ten years, and universal free education for another twenty.

But T.T had other causes, too. He threw his support behind efforts to make the voting franchise less restrictive, and campaigned against what was then known as the Occupancy Tax. This was a tax, payable to the Vestry, on people who rented a house, calculated on the amount of rent they paid. As a result of discussions between T.T and the Mayor of Bridgetown, Ernest Mottley, the tax was abolished.

T.T also played a big role in the formation of the Clerks Union of which he became President in 1948. At that time Bridgetown Clerks were predominantly 'Poor Whites' and coloured people who suffered with depressed wages and bad working conditions. When the Clerks complained about their poor wages, Lewis told them that until they came together and formed a union they would never be treated better.

Quite naturally, his advocacy in and out of Parliament en-deared him to blacks and poor- whites, a level of popularity that was matched in the reverse by the resentment in which he was held by the planters and merchants. But, as always, the trump card lay with the latter group and they chose to use it in 1949, the year after he joined the mass-based Barbados Labour Party (BLP), by dismissing T.T from his job at the Central Agency.

It was an act of victimisation that would lead to one of the largest industrial demonstrations in the island's history. The BLP leader, Grantley Adams, jumped to the defence of Lewis, rallying his supporters in Queen's Park, where he threatened to shut down businesses in Bridgetown and halt the reaping of the sugar cane harvest. Adams followed up this rally with two protest demonstrations through the streets of the city, attended by thousands of mostly black workers. The protest succeeded in getting Lewis a severance pay out. Viewed at face value, it was a paradox of unrivalled proportions that at a time when black peo-ple were being ground into the dust by a powerful, white power structure, that the largest public protest would be in support of a white man.

But like Prescod, O'Neal and Wickham, Lewis' time would be limited. He died in 1959 at the age of 54 while in St. Lucia to attend his daughter's wedding . His great nephew, Gary Lewis, in a biography called *White Rebel: The Life And Times Of T.T Lewis*, gives this account of his last moments:

> *"On the day of his death, he awoke as usual, and after breakfast, went for a stroll, and on his return, sat down with a copy of the local paper and his ever-present com-panion, a lead pencil. As he was reading and underlining, he slipped away into that other world which is never far from each one of us. He died as he had lived: reading, not-ing, underlining, preparing to defend."*

He did not fit neatly into the pattern of radical politics of the day but, like all those who loved justice and despised oppression, he was moved to act on behalf of the poor and powerless; and he did it in spite of his colour.

Clement Payne (1904 – 1941)

The turbulent thirties of Caribbean society would throw up the last of the great radicals. The mid to late 1930's was generally a time of social upheaval in the Caribbean. The Great Depression was on and this made the already harsh living conditions of the working people even more unbearable. A vicious combination of low wages, high unemployment and high cost of living was wreaking havoc on the labouring class. Consider, for instance, that in Barbados wages had hardly moved from the level where they were at emancipation in 1838, one hundred years previous! And from Jamaica in the north to Guyana in the south, people were moving to vent their feelings.

The chain of events might be said to have begun in Trinidad in 1933 with a hunger march in the capital, Port of Spain. The march was organised by a group calling itself the National Unemployed Movement which was agitating for relief work for the unemployed, and the restoration of controls on rent which had been abandoned. A similar march was undertaken the following year.

Then in 1935 the militant labour leader, Uriah Butler, led another hunger march to Port of Spain. Butler's militant agitation among the workers brought him into conflict with the authorities, and in 1937 he was arrested and charged with sedition and with inciting a riot. When he failed to turn up for arraignment Police tried to arrest him, triggering violent protests and riots among his supporters. Over in British Honduras – now Belize – workers were also in protest mode, demonstrating and striking against unemployment. A group of unemployed workers known as the Unemployed Brigade staged a march against the lack of work. At a meeting with the Governor, a delegation from the group's leadership told him the workers were starving because their men couldn't find work. They secured a promise of relief from the Governor.

The story was much the same in St. Kitts in 1935. Sugar workers were making their feelings known about the unjust wages they were being paid. The already low wages had been reduced twice in the previous five years. Protest action in the form of strikes came to a head with a massive demonstration at one plantation, leading to stone-throwing and gun-fire. So intent were the protestors to make their point that not even armed Police under a British Army Major could get them to disperse. The militia was called and the Riot Act read. At the end of it all three people were dead and eight injured.

In St. Vincent, the trigger was a plan by the colonial authorities to increase duties on a number of consumer goods – against strong opposition from the people – in circumstances that were already hard on the mass of people. Trouble erupted on the morning of October 21st. 1935 when the Governor of the Windward Islands was chairing a meeting of the Legislative Council.

An angry crowd bearing sticks and stones gathered outside the court house where the meeting was being held. The angry protestors vented their feelings with slogans like *"We have no work"*; *"We are hungry"*; *"We can't stand any more duties on food and clothing"*. The Governor adjourned the meeting, and as he and other members were leaving the building, members of the crowd set upon them, striking the Governor, and the Attorney General who drafted the bill for the increased duties. Armed Police arrived, read the Riot Act and fired on the protestors, killing one person and injuring others; but this did not stop the riots from spreading to other parts of the country, where utility wires were cut and bridges destroyed over the next two days. The authorities brought in military volunteers from neighbouring islands and a British war ship to suppress the violence.

The pattern of social ferment extended to the then British Guyana on the South American mainland, and to Jamaica, and even to non-English-speaking territories like Cuba and Martinique. What we have here is a series of people's uprisings as if originating from the same source. And yes: there was a common source. That source – in the case of the Anglophone Caribbean was a minority clique of British-descended planters and merchants basking in a life of tropical bliss, while the people's mouths were white and dry.

The Barbados story, then, falls into that matrix. The local catalyst was a man called Clement Payne, born of Barbadian parents living in Trinidad. He came to Barbados, saw the plight of the poor, and mounted a series of public meetings to agitate against the wrongs and motivate the people to become organized. Payne was no stranger to radical politics, having been a disciple of the militant, Trinidadian labour leader Uriah Butler. Butler was born in Grenada, but moved to Trinidad as a young man to work in the oilfields. A Garveyite, he would become a powerful labour and political leader in his adopted home, the man at the centre of the labour troubles in Trinidad in 1937. This was the kind of political and ideological baptism from which Clement Payne emerged before he arrived in Barbados. In fact, some believe he was sent to Barbados by the Trinidad branch of the Garvey movement, the Universal Negro Improvement Association, known as the UNIA.

It was as if the Barbadian masses were waiting for someone to ventilate their grievances. Large crowds attended Payne's public meetings in Golden Square and the Lower Green hearing him admonish them to organise themselves and fight against the conditions under which they lived. His slogan was: "*Organise, Educate, Agitate, but do not Violate*".

His platform was, to a large extent, an extension of those mounted by Prescod, O'neal, Wickham and Lewis. He flayed the planter-merchant elite and the oppressive laws they inflicted on the people – like the Masters and Servants Act of 1840 which prevented workers from offering their labour freely to the highest bidder.

But Payne was also concerned about other things – like the Barbadian predilection for religion, and the inadequacies of the education system. He thought Barbadians concentrated too much on religion and too little on industry and economy, and that the education system needed to expose children to personalities and things from the Caribbean. He was especially passionate about organizing among the working people, pointing them to the example of the dominant class: *"The Chamber of Commerce and Provision Dealers are all organized. Organize for the sake of your children. The foreparents of Governor Young and Fletcher and the Chief of Police thought their sons would one day come out to rule us, as they have paved the way for their children. Let us do the same for ours."*

And that's what he tried to do, setting about to organize a labour union which was to be known as the Barbados Working-Men's Progressive Association. His memoirs chronicle this part of his Barbadian experience: The mission was *"to organize the working people of Barbados. This I went about with my best zeal and interest, and I got the help and support of a good many eager workers who were only too willing to see the masses receive a proper political education. From amongst them I selected the most capable speakers and began my campaign of organizing."*

Well, of course, it didn't take long in those days for the ruling elite to deem anyone who dared to challenge the existing order, as a trouble maker, and Payne was soon branded with that label. The Police kept virtual round-the-clock surveillance of him, something to which he was moved to make reference in his memoirs: *"I have been shadowed and suffered intolerance from the Police department. I am not a fascist, a communist nor a Bolshevist. The department has started a war against me. Detectives follow me daily and even if I take a lady friend, the Detectives are there also. I am harassed by Major Goddard, Plunketts and the Detective Sergeant."*

For four months the Police attended his meetings and took notes – until the authorities decided they had had enough. They trumped up a charge: that he had lied to Immigration at the seaport when he arrived, by saying he was born in Barbados.

The truth is that Payne thought he was born in Barbados, because his parents were Barbadians; and he himself lived in Barbados for part of his early life. He was fined ten pounds, but appealed against the judgment. In the interim he held a public meeting and planned a march to Government House, the residence of the Governor. During the march he and some of his protesting followers were arrested for failing to disperse. He won his appeal against the false declaration charge but was ordered deported anyway, and secretly put on board a boat bound for Port of Spain.

It was an emotional Payne – if his memoirs are anything to go by – that sailed out of Barbados on that hapless day: *"Remember to keep the light always burning. Continue to hold mass meetings. Organise, educate, agitate, but do not violate. With these words I retired to my cabin with a feeling that could hardly be expressed, but with a heart and memory of the love, gratitude and high esteem given me by the working-class man and woman of Barbados."*

But as he sailed away from Barbados on the "Lady Nelson" Payne was blissfully ignorant of the explosion that was occurring back in Bridgetown. When news of his deportation became widespread, his supporters vented their anger by overturning and setting fire to vehicles and smashing store windows. The violence spread over the next four days to the country areas, where potato fields were raided. The Riot Act was read, and with that, it seemed, the Police thought they were given licence to shoot at anything that moved.

A virtual shooting frenzy ensued, in which some very innocent persons going about their business were killed. In Suttle Street a young man lay on the ground, blooding pouring from a bullet wound in his side. Another young man from St. Thomas doing business in the city was similarly snuffed out.

A female vendor with a tray of fruits on her head took what she didn't know would be her last walk along Swan Street. A Police bullet sent her crashing to the ground, scattering her fruits through the street. These unfortunate persons were going about their business, completely unaware that their fate lay in the trigger-happy hands of the next Policeman to set his eyes on them. It was nothing short of naked, cold-blooded murder, sanctioned by a power structure that placed little to no value on the lives and welfare of African people.

The local authorities immediately commissioned an investigation into the rebellion. The Governor, Sir Mark Young, appointed a three-man commission headed by Sir George Dean, a retired Chief Justice of the Leeward Islands. It rooted the revolt in the depressed conditions of the people, pointing to poverty, unemployment and lack of grassroots organization. This was followed by another inquiry with a broader mandate, appointed by the British government. The West Indian Royal Commission was set up in August 1938 to investigate and to make recommendations on the social and economic conditions in the region.

The Commission was led by Lord Moyne – formerly Walter Edward Guinness – and among its members was the General Secretary of the British Trades Union Congress, Sir Walter Citrine. Between November 1938 and February 1939 members of the commission visited Britain's Caribbean colonies, investigating conditions in housing, agriculture, health, work and other areas.

Its findings were a complete vindication, not only of Clement Payne, but all of the other martyrs who preceded him: Samuel Prescod, Charles O'neal, T.T Lewis and Clennell Wickham. It took note of the depressed conditions in which working people in the colonies lived. Neither was it impressed with conditions and practices in the labour market. The lack of representation for workers; unsafe working conditions; discrimination against female workers in pay and the use of child labour – against which Duncan O'neal had campaigned – all came under the commission's critical scrutiny.

The commission made a number of recommendations to address the ills mentioned above. Among them were the expansion of the voting franchise and a lowering of the qualification for membership of the legislature to enable persons other than members of the planter-merchant class to sit in that chamber; the formation and registration of trade unions; the provision of unemployment insurance; the establishment of labour departments and wage boards to oversee the fixing of wages; the provision of workers compensation and routine factory inspections to reduce accidents.

The Commission also addressed the question of social recreation, recommending that facilities be widely established to provide opportunities for recreation for the working people. As a result of this recommendation the Barbados Welfare League, the antecedent of the Welfare Department, was set up, and a number of Social (community) Centres were constructed and used for such events as dances, tea meetings and Services of Song (a now defunct Barbadian social event involving choir singing, eating, drinking and speechifying).

The idea of a federated Caribbean was one which the Commission embraced. It suggested this as an ideal which the British government should pursue, and recommended as a start, a federation of Grenada, St. Vincent, St. Lucia, Dominica Antigua, Montserrat, St. Kitts, Nevis and Anguilla. Over time, many of these recommendations were implemented.

He may have sparked a conflagration, but Clement Payne's short-lived campaign to uplift the down-trodden masses of Barbados was not in vain. For out of the innocent blood of a poor, vendor woman and an innocent young man and the 12 other persons nakedly slaughtered by the Police, came a new and better order, the benefits of which are still with us today. The events of 1937 were, indeed, the catharsis that led to a brighter day for the mass of Barbadian people.

Organizing for Change – Politics and Labour

Charles Duncan O'Neal's Democratic League of the 1920's was probably the first, grassroots political organization in Barbados. But it was the formation of the Progressive League in 1938 that can be credited as the foundation of mass political organization.

At the centre of this initiative was a man called Wynter Crawford, a newspaper Publisher, labour leader, and party leader who bestrode the political stage from the 1930's to the 1960's. Crawford was approached by a representative of an organization of prominent Caribbeans living in the United States called the West Indies Defence Committee, formed in the wake of the labour revolts of the 1930's.

The Committee was interested in assisting grassroots organizations in the region, and sent an emissary named Hope Stevens on a regional tour. When he visited Barbados, Stevens met with Crawford, who suggested assistance with the formation of a political organization. That body became known as the Barbados Labour Party. Its first executive committee consisted of Chrissie Brathwaite, a black businessman, in the post of President; Grantley Adams, (who was out of the country) as Vice President and Edwy Talma as Secretary.

The party's name was subsequently changed to the Progressive League, because some thought the original name had militant overtones. This change was later reversed.

But less than a year later the party had an internal conflict leading to a split into moderate and radical factions. This development thrust Grantley Adams – a moderate – into the leadership position. An Oxford-schooled Lawyer, Adams would continue at the helm of the party for the next three decades, establishing himself as the primary advocate for the working people during the period.

The League contested its first parliamentary elections in 1940 capturing five of the 24 seats at stake. Adams, who had already been elected was re-elected. In 1946, through a coalition with Wynter Crawford's West Indian National Congress Party, the Barbados Labour Party (the League had reverted to its original name by then) was able to wrest control from the planter oligarchy for the first time and, in fact, banish for all time the spectre of planter-merchant domination of political power. From then on, its success at the polls was virtually guaranteed. Having snatched power from the clutches of the oligarchy, the party was able to implement several measures to uplift the lives of the working people. It built roads and houses, established Erdiston Teachers Training College, expanded educational opportunities and started the process of free secondary education with the building of modern secondary schools. The racist politics of the old oligarchy having been effectively put to rest, all of the goals for which Prescod, O'neal and the other radical martyrs had fought, were finally being realized, and Barbados was well on the way to its present status as a democratic state, with the welfare of its people at the centre of its politics.

But it would only be a matter of time before another split within the B.L.P. As in the previous instance, it was the party's moderates against its more radical membership. Just under 30 members of the radical wing held a meeting on the night of April 27, 1955 to form what they called the Democratic Labour Party. Among them was the man who would eventually emerge as the leader of the party, Errol Barrow, the dominant figure in the politics of the 1960's and 70's, who first served as Premier, and then Prime Minister after he led Barbados into independence.

The party managed to capture four seats, representing just under 20% of the vote, out of 16 candidates, in its first election contest in 1956. It fared much better in the next poll in 1961, in fact garnering a majority of the seats to capture the government, though it got fewer votes than the BLP. After a hat-trick win in 1971, it lost to the BLP in 1976. This alternating pattern continues to the present.

The next major organizational thrust was the formation of the Barbados Workers Union. The BWU is a direct product of the 1937 people's rebellion. The report of the Moyne commission which investigated the revolt had recommended the legalization of trade unions, and in 1939 a trade union Act was passed. The union registered on October 4th. 1941 as an arm of the Barbados Progressive League, with Grantley Adams as President and Hugh Springer as General Secretary.

It started out with three divisions. These were ship Carpenters, the Barbados Foundry Mechanics and Central Mechanics; but it quickly blossomed into a national organization representing sugar workers, Dockers, Bakers and factory Engineers. There was a change in leadership in 1947 when Hugh Springer quit the post of General Secretary to take up the job of Registrar of the University College of the West Indies – later the University of the West Indies. He was succeeded by his assistant, Frank Walcott who acted in the post until his appointment the following year. Walcott would remain in the post for the next 44 years, functioning as the de facto head of the union. He developed a reputation as a formidable negotiator who was not reluctant to tell it as he saw it. Under his leadership the union's membership expanded to include government workers and clerical and utility workers. He developed an international reputation as a trade unionist, serving in high office with such bodies as the International Confederation of Free Trade Unions, the American Institute for Free Labour Development, the Commonwealth Trades Union Council and the International Labour Organization. But his two greatest legacies are the Barbados Workers Union Labour College and the Mangrove housing development. The Labour College was opened in 1974 on ten acres of land at Mangrove, St. Philip, where the housing development is also located. It is a residential institution, offering education for workers and trade union Shop Stewards in industrial relations and related subjects.

Another change in the union's leadership would come in 1954 with the resignation of its President, Grantley Adams, who was to be Premier of Barbados under a new ministerial system.

The 1960's brought turbulence to the affairs of the union. It came in the form of the so-called Windfall issue. The returns from the sugar crop in 1963 had been higher than expected when the union negotiated on behalf of the sugar workers and it initiated additional negotiations which were successful in securing a portion of the bonus for the workers. The controversy erupted when the union proposed to reserve part of this additional money for a fund for the benefit of the workers. When the enabling legislation was introduced to the House of Assembly, the official Opposition party, then led by Grantley Adams, strongly opposed it and mounted a campaign for full payment to the workers. Eventually, the union gave in and dropped the plan for the fund.

On the militant front the union has had its share of strike action. They began with strikes at the Central Foundry and the Barbados Foundry in 1942 and in 1944, and include the 13-week Advocate (newspaper) strike, the longest in the history of the union, strikes against the Hotel Association, the Provision Merchants and Commission Agents, Clarke and Tucker in the early 1970's and the 1981 David Giles strike, in support of a dismissed Shop Steward at the Barbados Telephone Company.

It is an indisputable fact that the union has made a significant difference to the lives of the Barbadian worker over the years. Quite apart from securing better wages and conditions of work it was able to play a role in the passage of pro-labour legislation. Among these the Workmen's Compensation Act of 1943, the Protection of Wages Act of 1951, the Holidays with Pay Act of 1952, the Severance Payment Act of 1973 and the Employment of Women Act of 1976 which introduced maternity leave.

Political organization was by no means limited to the three entities discussed above; over the years various other parties and trade unions emerged, some more lasting than others. But the formation of the Barbados Labour Party, the Barbados Workers Union and the Democratic Labour Party constitute seminal events in the evolution of modern Barbadian society.

Adams, the Moses of the People

Among the pantheon of leaders and activists who bestrode the Barbadian stage in the post Emancipation period is one Grantley Herbert Adams, the island's first black head of government, or Premier, as the title was then. And as we learnt earlier he also distinguished himself as the first President of the Barbados Workers Union. He was a product of the black, privileged class – the son of a school Principal, who attended Harrison College (the island's 'top' secondary school), won a Barbados scholarship and studied law at Oxford University in England. On his return from England he established what would become a successful law practice.

Sir Grantley Adams

It was his election to the Vice Presidency and later Presidency of the Barbados Labour Party and subsequent leadership of the Barbados Workers Union that propelled him to political stardom. And what a star he became, earning the sobriquet "Moses" among the people, and rising to become a member of the Governor's Executive Committee in 1942, Leader of the House of Assembly in 1946 and then Premier of Barbados heading a full ministerial government in 1954. He was first elected to the House of Assembly in 1934 as the representative for the rural parish of St. Joseph, and gave unbroken service in parliament up to 1958 when he left to take up the Premiership of the West Indies Federation.

His public profile as a defender of the people might also have been boosted as a result of the 1937 revolt: he represented Clement Payne, the man at the centre of the revolt, on his appeal against conviction for allegedly making a false declaration to Immigration and appeared before the Moyne Commission appointed by the Colonial Office to look into the region-wide unrest. Armed with the powerful leverage he had as government leader and trade unionist, Adams set about the task of bringing hope to the black masses of Barbados. Under his watch several pieces of pro-labour legislation were introduced – some of which were mentioned previously – bringing improved working conditions and other benefits to the working people. In the social arena, there was significant reform and rehabilitation, particularly in education, health, housing and road construction. It was during his tenure, too, that the island's lone, public hospital, the Queen Elizabeth Hospital, and the Deep Water Harbour were built. But the highlights of his tenure were the introduction of Universal Adult Suffrage in 1951 which consolidated black control of political power. In 1958 Adams gave up the leadership of the government to take up the post of Prime Minister of the West Indies Federation, based in Trinidad. When the Federation collapsed in 1962 he returned to Barbados and was re-elected to the House of Assembly in 1966, assuming the role of Leader of the Opposition. Four years later he resigned from politics. He died the following year at the age of 73 and was buried in the church yard of St. Michael's Cathedral.

But even though Adams' place among the builders of modern Barbados cannot be disputed, his political career remains steeped in controversy. His accolades as the saviour of the black masses in the immediate pre-independence period continue to be over-shadowed by his failure to identify with the radical politics of the times, his conservative sentiments and his ruthless dealings with some of his contemporaries in the political movement. One of his critics is the head of the left-leaning People's Empowerment Party and Clement Payne Movement, David Comissiong, who charged him with seven *"deadly sins"*, in a newspaper column under the banner of the PEP:

"For several decades now we have heard much about the virtues of Sir Grantley Adams, but Christian theology tells us that for every virtue there is a parallel sin. And so, we now reflect on the'seven deadly political sins of Grantley Adams as follows:-

No. 1 *– Adams' first political sin was to devote the early part of his career to an unrelenting and deliberately obstructionist attack on Dr Charles Duncan O'Neal, the leading progressive and anti-racist reformer in 1920's Barbados. Adams willingly allowed himself to be used by the racist white plantocracy to besmirch O'Neal's reputation, and to help defeat candidates of O'Neal's **Democratic League** in the 1929 general election.*

No. 2 *– By 1930, Clennell Wickham and his **Herald** Newspaper had emerged as the most articulate critics of the oppressive and racist Barbadian oligarchy. This all ended, when Adams undertook to represent Walter Bayley, a wealthy white merchant, in a vindictive libel lawsuit against Wickham, and secured punitive judgment that caused the closure of the **Herald** and the bankruptcy and exile of Wickham.*

*No. 3 – In 1938, Chrissie Brathwaite, John Martineau, Wynter Crawford, Edwy Talma, Hugh Cummins and Philip Payne formed the **Barbados Labour Party** (BLP), under the presidency of Brathwaite, and subsequently invited Adams to join them in the post of Vice President. The BLP...and its trade union arm, the BWU, were rapidly developed, largely through the efforts of General Secretary Herbert Seale. Within the space of one year, Adams manufactured a crisis in the organisation, and attacked, ousted and virtually destroyed Brathwaite, Martineau and Seale.*

*No. 4 – By 1948, the newly established **United Nations** organisation was playing a critical and vibrant role in challenging colonialism - including British colonialism - and the British Colonial Office decided that they needed to respond by arranging for a black man from one of the colonies to speak at the UN in defence of Britain's colonial policies. The black man they settled on was Grantley Adams; and Adams - the first black man to address the UN General Assembly – outraged the progressive international anti-colonial movement with a shameful speech in defence of British colonialism.*

*No. 5 – In the early 1950's Guyana was leading the anti-colonial, nationalist movement in the West Indies, and by 1953, the then multi-racial **Peoples Progressive Party** – led by Cheddi Jagan and Forbes Burnham – had been elected to office. The British colonial masters responded by suspending Guyana's constitution, and by sending warships and soldiers to invade Guyana and to imprison Guyanese activists. Adams supported all of this, by sending the following cable to the British Government:-*
"Our experience of Jagan and his sympathisers leads us to feel that....the British West Indies is.... likely to be harmed by that sort of person. However much we must regret suspension of the constitution, we should deplore far more

the continuance of a government that put Communist ideology before the good of the people."

No: 6 – *The labour activists and leaders of the West Indies established a dynamic and powerful movement led by the **Caribbean Labour Congress** (CLC) - an umbrella organisation which became a member of the **World Federation of Trade Unions** (WFTU) in 1945. However, by 1950, the American and British imperialists had decided that the **WFTU** had to be dismantled, and that socialist trade unions and trade unionists were to be removed from the West Indian labour movement. Once again, Adams - who was President of the CLC - did their bidding, engineering the destruction of the CLC and the substitution of a subservient American dominated **Caribbean Congress of Labour**, and even secured the expulsion of "radical" trade unionists from his own BWU.*

No: 7 – *As early as the 1930's, the anti-colonial, nationalist activists of the West Indies had established a progressive agenda for the region, in which the establishment of a multi-territory 'Federation' was put forward as the major plank upon which self government, independence and a planned regional economy would be built. However, the British-loving and trusting Adams and Norman Manley (Jamaican leader) took over effective control of the West Indian progressive movement in the 1950's, and, under their Anglophile leadership, the British Colonial Office was permitted to negatively transform the West Indian concept of "Federation" into the non-independent, glorified Crown Colony that was foisted on the West Indian people in 1958. Not surprisingly, this British concocted Federation collapsed in 1962, and the Caribbean anti-colonial and integration movement was severely damaged."*

He was definitely the poster boy of colonial subservience in the Caribbean; but Adams was by no means singular in this respect. His was a mental condition that was replicated throughout the British Caribbean and still exists even to this day – but we shall explore that later.

In 1998 the government of Barbados named Grantley Adams one of ten national heroes. His picture is on the one hundred dollar bill, and the Grantley Adams Airport is named after him, as is the Grantley Adams School in St. Joseph. These are among the memorials to the man called the Father of the Nation. That he harboured colonial values, spurned the radical movement and acted less than charitably to some of his associates cannot be disputed, but his contribution will forever occupy an important place in the annals of Barbadian and Caribbean history.

The Father of Independence

If July 26, 1937 is a landmark in Barbadian history, then November 30, 1966 must be the signature of modern Barbados. That's the date on which Barbados formally ended 339 years of British colonialism and became an independent nation. The man who spearheaded this move was Errol Walton Barrow, previously mentioned as a bomber with the British Air Force during the Second World War, and personal navigation officer to the Commander-in-Chief of the British Army at the Rhine between 1940 and 1942.

Rt. Exc. Errol Barrow

As Prime Minister, he headed the list of proud Barbadians who watched as the Union Jack was lowered and the blue, gold and black colours of the Barbados flag – the Broken Trident – took its place. Now a national hero and acclaimed as the Father of Independence, Barrow's (then) left of centre Democratic Labour Party captured the reigns of government in the 1961 general elections, an event that would serve as a major, developmental catapult for the island. The party retained the government for three five-year terms, losing to the (then) right of centre Barbados Labour Party in 1976. The D.L.P recaptured the government in 1986, but the following year Barrow collapsed and died at his home.

The northernmost tip of the island, the parish of St. Lucy was the place of his birth, on 21 January 1920. His father was The Rev. Reginald Grant Barrow, a Bishop of the African Orthodox Church in the United States, and his mother, Ruth (nee) O'Neal, sister of Charles Duncan O'neal.

When he hung up his wings at the Royal Air Force, Barrow enrolled in law school in England and in the London School of Economics, graduating successfully from both institutions in 1949 and 1950 respectively. His tenure in office is associated with such credits as universal free education (there was already partial free education), the introduction of national insurance and social security, school meals, industrial development, improved health services and expansion of the tourist industry.

In the context of a post-colonial, conservative Caribbean, Errol Barrow was a visionary – sometimes maverick leader, and from hind-sight it is not difficult to see why he felt the need to sever ties with Grantley Adams. Adams was the typical, colonial subject. His perceptions of himself and of Barbados were almost entirely rooted in the island's status as an appendage of Westminster. It is reported that many African leaders were alarmed at his speech to the United Nations in support of British colonialism, at a time when the movement for independence was approaching its zenith. Barrow's speech in Parliament during the debate on the independence resolution in 1966 was the complete opposite in tone:-

"There are some people in Barbados who would want to tell you that there is no such thing as colonialism and that we are British subjects, and that we are happy to be called British subjects. But the worst thing about colonialism is this: these islands in the eastern Caribbean only began to get off the ground since they were taken over by democratic governments ... which are responsible to the people. No one is going to be content to be treated as second class citizens

*in perpetuity. No one is going to be content to sit down in-
definitely and watch places like Gambia, Togoland, Malta
and even the Cook Islands...being represented and sitting
around the United Nations table."*

This was quintessentially Barrow philosophy. He was speaking at a time when the notion of Britain as the "Mother Country"
was pervasive among Anglo-Caribbean people and when independence was viewed with more than a little scepticism among
Caribbean people. Indeed, some British-descended Barbadians
chose to migrate to Australia and elsewhere, rather than live
under an independent Barrow government. I remember once
having a conversation with a national of the Cayman Islands,
one of the most conservative of Caribbean countries, and asking
her why her country had not sought independence – I was flab-
bergasted when she told me they had decided to **"remain loyal
to the mother country"**! Many years later, today, they are still a
loyal colony of the British.

Barrow would have none of this colonial infatuation. He considered himself and every other Caribbean person an independent individual, equal in every sense to their British counterparts.
We might even say he was not a great fan of the British, if some
of his words in the 1966 parliamentary Independence debate are
anything to go by:

> *"Colonialism is the reason for the present impasse in
> West Indian Affairs, and we cannot afford to wait. I am
> not going into a recital of what the British have done and
> what they have not done. Their relation with our people has
> not been a happy association. It has been a very unhappy
> association, and it is regrettable that we will have some of
> the down-trodden, who feel that they are now slightly privi-
> leged, fighting on the side of the people who perpetrated all
> these acts of inhumanity against our people.*
>
> *"...When you talk about political immorality, you have
> to understand that there is a country* (Britain) *which has*

ruthlessly taken hold of the economy of other countries, people who are more benighted than ourselves, and less advanced in what they choose to call a civilization. They have murdered, de-tribalised and suppressed their religious activities...forbidding them to use their own language. You cannot be surprised that the residual effects of that kind of harsh treatment must still be manifested in the behaviour of some politicians of the colonial territories today."

A believer in the unity of the Caribbean, he was one the prime movers in the formation of the Caribbean Free Trade Area, known as CARIFTA in 1965. CARIFTA later evolved into the Caribbean Community and Common Market, again with Barrow and the then Prime Ministers of Guyana, Jamaica and Trinidad & Tobago in the lead. His belief in regionalism transcended the petty insularity and xenophobia which traditionally have plagued inter-island relations and which, to date, have frustrated every attempt at regional unity. In fact he played a major role in the failed attempt to federate the islands of the eastern Caribbean after the collapse of the West Indies Federation. In a parliamentary speech to approve the report of the East Caribbean Federation conference in 1962 he voiced his thoughts on regional integration:

"Anyone who does not understand the economic, political and geographical background of the West Indies will not readily appreciate why these islands should want to come together in a federal system of government. If there were one area which a federal system of government eminently suits, it is the eastern Caribbean...We are therefore bound together by some ties of consanguinity, it is true, but we are bound together by similar conditions and similar economic backgrounds more than anything else."

But perhaps he was at his most eloquent on the subject of Caribbean integration at the Caribbean Community heads of government conference in Guyana in 1986, the year before he died:-

> "*If we have sometimes failed to comprehend the essence of the regional integration movement the truth is that thousands of ordinary Caribbean people do, in fact, live that reality every day. In Barbados our families are no longer exclusively Barbadian by island origin. We have Barbadian children of Jamaican mothers; Barbadian children of Antiguan and St. Lucian fathers. And there is no need to mention Trinidad and Tobago which has always been tied to us, not only by the inestimable bonds of consanguinity, but by the burgeoning cross fertilization of cultural art forms. We are a family of islands nestling loosely under the shelter of the great cooperative republic of Guyana. And this fact of regional togetherness is lived everyday by ordinary West Indian men and women in their comings and goings.*"

What a terrible repudiation of this noble, regional spirit it was when in 2009 a government led by the party he founded presided over the mass deportation of Guyanese immigrants working in Barbados. The Guyanese (mostly of Indian ancestry) were here to take advantage of work in the agricultural and construction sectors, and from all indications were making a valuable contribution to the two sectors and to the economy as a whole. But in one of its first acts after coming to office in 2008, a DLP government, led by the late David Thompson, who succeeded Barrow in the rural constituency of St. John, had them repatriated.

It was yet another manifestation of the great philosophical divide between Barrow, on the one hand, and on the other, those who took over the party he founded – persons for the most part devoid of any deep philosophical convictions, and still firmly wedded to traditional conservative values.

Barrow was fierce in his defence of Caribbean sovereignty and dignity, sometimes to the point of risking animosity between himself and other national leaders. Just after his election victory in 1986 he referred to the then American President as *"that cowboy in the White House"*. Ronald Reagan, an Actor who had played in many western movies, was an extreme right-wing leader who was quick to attack and invade other countries. He had already attacked Libya and invaded Grenada. Barrow was highly offended by the latter action and condemned fellow Caribbean leaders who supported it.

In fact, in another clear example of the gulf between him and party, when a resolution in support of the invasion was presented in the Barbados House of Assembly, the DLP, then in opposition, supported it, with Barrow out of the country. But on his return he lost no time in voicing vigorous condemnation of the American action and the involvement of Barbados in it. Clearly not a fan of Reagan, he took a swipe at the then Jamaican leader, Edward Seaga, over the latter's cosiness with Washington: *"Mr. Seaga thinks that the solution to Jamaica's problems is to get President Reagan to play Santa Claus. I do not believe in Santa Claus."* He was speaking at a time when many Caribbean people did believe in the American Santa. The conventional wisdom then was that the Caribbean was in America's *'backyard'*, and as such were protectorates of this great, rich nation, with the right to hold out our begging bowls to Washington.

Barrow would have baulked at the notion that his country was a *"back-yard"* dependant of the United States, as so many Anglophone Caribbean people seem to regard their countries. People actually declare with little compunction that we are in the United States back yard. Listen to him as he addressed a conference on Caribbean American relations, in Miami in 1986:

> *"It is dehumanizing and false to view the Caribbean as potential American problems. We are peoples with an identity and a culture and a history – the parliament of Barbados will be 350 years old in 1989; we don't need lessons in democracy from anyone. However severe the economic difficulties facing the Caribbean, we are viable, functioning societies, with the intellectual and institutional resources to understand and grapple with our problems."*

135

No backyard mentality there. Four years earlier he had spoken in a similar vein at a press conference:-

"We here in the Caribbean should settle our own problems, whether they be political problems or whether they be economic problems. We do not have any right to our independence unless we are prepared to settle our economic problems without going cap in hand to other people, joining in their sterile ideological disputes, even with some of our own brethren – running cap in hand begging them for money. No one from outside the region should be able to come in here saying they are settling disputes in the Caribbean."

He was equally opposed to the militarisation of the region by the United States after the 1979 coup in Grenada, when the U.S, fearful about the spread of communism in the region, orchestrated the formation of something called The Regional Security System. The armies of RSS member nations took part in periodic exercises with U.S troops in Puerto Rico, much to Mr. Barrow's chagrin:

"My position remains clear that the Caribbean must be recognized and respected as a zone of peace...Puerto Rico has become a launching pad for neo-colonization of the region. We have seen it used as a base for a number of military exercises whose purpose is clear...I have said, and I repeat, that while I am Prime Minister of Barbados, our territory will not be used to intimidate any of our neighbours, be that neighbour Cuba or the United States."

But it was the famous *'mirror-image'* speech, delivered in the 1986 election campaign, the year before he died, that has become his epitaph. The speech amounted to a fatherly scolding of Barbadians for the low esteem they have about themselves and their country. It reflected, once more, the philosophical chasm that existed between Barrow and his people.

"I want to know what kind of mirror image do you have of yourself? Do you really like yourself? There are too many people in Barbados who despise themselves, and their dislike of themselves reflects itself in their dislike of other people.

You so much despair of this society that your greatest ambition is to try to prove to the people of the United States Consulate that you are only going up to visit your family....And you are surprised when the people at the United States Embassy tell you that you do not have a strong reason to return to Barbados.

Your ambition in life is to try and get away from this country. And we call ourselves an independent nation? When all we want to do is go and scrub somebody's floors and run somebody's elevator or work in somebody's store or drive somebody's taxi in a country where you catching your royal when the winter sets in?

What kind of mirror image do you have of yourself? Let me tell you what kind of mirror image I have of you. The Democratic Labour Party has an image that the people of Barbados would be able to run their own affairs, to pay for the cost of running their own country, to have an education system which is as good as what can be attained in any industrialised country, anywhere in the world.

In the state of Texas, the government of that state has asked to make the teachers pass an examination to see if they can read and write! The gentleman of the Texas teachers' union came on the news and he said that he was proud of the result because only eight percent of the teachers couldn't read and write!

If Reagan (then U.S President) *had to take the test, I wonder if he would pass. But this is the man that you all say how great he is for bombing the people in Libya and killing little children....This is the man that you all go up at the airport and put down a red carpet for, and he is the President of a country in which in one of the more advanced and biggest states eight per cent of the teachers cannot read and write, and he feels that they are better than we. And you feel that we should run up there and bow.*

What kind of mirror image do you have of yourself? When a government steals from people in the way of consumption taxes and takes that money and spends it on their own high lifestyles, and unnecessary buildings, then that government not only has contempt for you, but what is most unfortunate, you have contempt for yourself, because you allow them to do it.

What kind of mirror image do you have of yourself when you allow the mothers of this nation to be beasts of burden in the sugarcane fields? In Mexico where people suffer under a lower standard of living than in Barbados, they use donkeys to freight canes out of the fields; in Antigua, they use a small railway; but here the mothers of the nation are used as beasts of burden. What kind of image do you have of yourself?

I lived in a little country when I was young, the Virgin Islands. That is a small country. But there is another small country. That country has 210 square miles; it is 40 square miles bigger than Barbados. If you took the Parish of St. Philip and put it right in the little curve by Bathsheba that would be the size of the country of Singapore.

But you know the difference between Barbados and that country? First, Barbados has 250,000 people. You know how many people Singapore has on 40 more square miles? Over two-and-a-half-million, on an island just a little larger than Barbados.

They don't have sugar plantations; they don't have enough land to plant more than a few orchids. They don't have enough land to plant a breadfruit tree in the backyard and nearly every Barbadian has some kind of fruit tree in the backyard. They have developed an education system but they are teaching people things that are relevant to the 21st century. They are not teaching people how to weed by the road. They are in the advance of the information age.

But you know the difference between you and them? They have got a mirror image of themselves. They are not looking to get on any plane to go to San Francisco...The government does not encourage them to emigrate unless they are going to develop business for Singapore. They have a mirror image of themselves. They have self-respect. They have a desire to move their country forward by their own devices. They are not waiting for anybody to come and give them handouts. And there is no unemployment. Is that the mirror image that you have of yourselves?"

Barrow's unconventional behaviour reflected in his personal life. This was a man who could be seen pushing a trolley in a supermarket; who went into the cane fields with a machete in a practical show of empathy with those who undertook the arduous task of reaping the sugar cane harvest; a man who was at home sharing lunch in a chattel house with an ordinary, country woman. Was he a maverick? In the context of post colonial Barbados, definitely.

PART 2 - THE LEGACIES

Economics

It would have been remarkable if the experience of enslavement and colonialism did not leave lasting impressions on Barbados and Barbadians. It did so in a massive way. Indeed, not even the visionary leadership and maverick philosophy of Errol Barrow were enough to transcend it. It was under Barrow's leadership, we must remember, that an independence constitution was framed with the provision that the Queen of England – rather than a Barbadian – be head of state.

Admittedly, he had in his coterie such conservative monarchists as James Cameron Tudor, an Oxford-educated man whose hallmark was his apish feigning of English speech patterns and his infatuation with the Queen and others members of the British Royal family. Tudor wielded considerable influence in the DLP. But it would seem logical for Barrow to be opposed to the notion of a British citizen holding the office of head of state of Barbados, given his expressed views on colonialism. I'll return to this subject later.

The most glaring legacy can be found in the socio-economic status of the island – of every Caribbean island with a history of British colonialism. These islands are perceived and are marketed for tourism purposes as tropical paradises, which they might very well be to visitors lounging on white, sandy beaches or snorkelling with turtles in ultramarine waters.

But a trip inland will soon bring a measure of soberness to the tropical euphoria. The journey, for the most part, will be on narrow, winding roads. There are few roads on which you can

drive for more than a minute without encountering a curve –
those who laid out the road network clearly did not have motor
vehicles in mind. If the journey is at night you might find yourself
driving in darkness on some rural roads – street lighting is sparse
in the country. The view along the way will probably include
what might appear to be caravans to the uninitiated visitor. They
are actually chattel houses made of timber, resting on a stone
foundation. They are a legacy in themselves of post Emancipation Barbados when the landless ex-slaves lived on plantation
land. The moveable or chattel nature of the houses meant that
they could be dis-assembled and re-located.

In more distant times (previous to the 1970's) they were
accompanied by outdoor booths, sometimes called out-houses,
which served as pit toilets. Plumbing would consist of a single,
outdoor pipe with a brass stop-cock. Those without the means
of installing their own pipes would draw water in buckets from
communal pipes in districts throughout the country. The chattel
house may range in status from dilapidated shanties to beautiful,
architectural show pieces.

Still a prevalent form of housing in rural and even urban
areas, they are increasingly being replaced by stone houses with
in-door plumbing, a reflection of the rising standard of living
that has been going on since independence.

The legacy of enslavement and colonialism is never more
dramatic than in the distribution and control of wealth between
black and white Barbadians. The sharp disparity between the two
groups that characterized the pre and immediately post Emancipation eras continues to this day – that's in spite of seven decades
of black government.

There are those who will argue that, in fact, we have seen
that turn-around; that black people now control the corridors of
power in Barbados; that we now live in nice houses with indoor
plumbing, and drive expensive automobiles. But those of us who
are more concerned about the substance than the surface, will
bemoan the sad fact that more than a century and a half after
emancipation, sixty years after adult suffrage – yes, with black
people in the corridors of power – black Barbadians are still

largely confined to the position of consumers, with no significant wealth-generating mechanisms. Yes, we drive good cars and live in fine houses which we buy from other people, but big business and real estate and the ownership of wealth remain largely with the white segment of the population.

So that the first decade and some of the new millennium finds the vast majority of Barbadians, the people who built this country, still in the position of consumers of other people's goods and services – servants, promoted from the field to the office, but remaining largely outside the circle of big money and economic power.

Like gaping spectators, we can only look on and admire the Millennium Heights and the Royal Westmorelands and the Port St. Charles-es and other big projects undertaken by the other five percent of our population.

In the year 2016 it is impossible for me to go to our capital city, Bridgetown, the centre of commerce, and point randomly to a store or other business owned by a black Barbadian. There are no black-owned car dealerships, banks, distribution houses, department stores, – this, in a country where 90% of the population are black. These businesses are exclusively in the hands of Barbadians of British, Indian and other racial backgrounds. The largest restaurant chain is owned by a Barbadian of Syrian origin; the largest department store, now a public company, was founded, and continues to be run by Barbadians of British ancestry; so is the largest construction company and the largest real estate company and the largest insurance company. And the list goes on.

It's probably a Caribbean phenomenon; there is no where else in the world, of which I know, where you will find the majority population in an inferior wealth ownership position – certainly not to the extent you will find in Barbados and other former British Caribbean colonies. So that 178 years after the abolition of slavery, seven decades after the introduction of black government and well over half a century after independence the economic status of the African man and woman in Barbados, vis-à-vis his European counterpart has undergone no fundamental change: white Barbadians, as they did in the period of enslavement and after, still dominate ownership of big business while the black majority provide labour and a consumer base.

There are obvious historical reasons for the advantage which white Barbadians enjoy. They wielded political power up to about the mid 20th. century and used it unabashedly to advance their own interests and retard the progress of the black population. In his book, *"Panama Money in Barbados – 1900 - 1920"* the American historian, Bonham Richardson, gives us a clear example of the latter. Barbadians working in the Canal Zone were sending back home good money which was being invested in Friendly Societies (a kind of financial cooperative).

> *Richardson writes: "The sudden black control of more cash than ever before represented an obvious threat to white officials, especially because of the temporary control of large sums of money by relatively few friendly society officers. What if an island-wide friendly society movement were to coalesce black savings into even fewer hands? The implications of such a prospect required little imagination. Widespread and growing financial strength among black Barbadians, hitherto distributed as small sums in individuals hands could...rapidly be focused toward a takeover of traditionally white resources. **Even the land itself might be purchased with pooled friendly society money!"***

Well – what have we got here? The unthinkable has raised its ugly head: black people in Barbados are now actually in a position to buy large plots of plantation land. We all know that land is wealth; and nobody knew this better than the Barbadian planter class. So it was obvious that something had to be done to prevent this catastrophe in land ownership from taking place. And that's where that invaluable tool known as law came into play.

The 1905 Friendly Societies Act was to be the vehicle of this legislative tool, to nip in the bud, any notion that black people would become big land owners in this country. The Act ends with a critical proviso: "*Nothing shall authorize a benevolent society to hold land exceeding one acre in extent.*" So, in effect: '*you might have a lot of money, but you can only buy one acre of land*'.

So, then, the advent of black government may have changed the complexion of Parliament, but it did little to alter the equation. Black leaders in this country have been unquestionably weak on the subject of racial equality, cowed into silence and inaction by the fear of the racist bogey. We did have one commission on racial reconciliation, but this turned out to be yet another window-dressing exercise devoid of any serious objectives. The Press got copy, the Lawyers collected their fees, a report was published and that was the end of it.

With their historical head-start, the white community consolidated their dominance of commerce, trade and industry. So advantageous is the white skin in Barbados that even descendants of what we call "*poor whites*", those Irish – sometimes Scottish – indentured servants who were banished to the Caribbean to work as labourers, have often been able to climb the ladder of economic success. An oft-told story tells us of one of them who journeyed, in 1921, from the eastern parish of St. John to Bridgetown with a mule, to establish a meat shop, which later blossomed into the multi-national we know as Goddard Enterprises. Another white Barbadian, also reputed to be of "*poor white*" origin, sits on top of the largest construction company in Barbados, which has investments in almost all areas of physical development in Barbados.

His brother heads a group of 13 wholly owned and 17 joint venture companies in Barbados and other parts of the Caribbean. Since there has never been any black business in Barbados of equivalent magnitude, the question to be answered is: 'why'. Are black Barbadians less industrious and enterprising than whites? Are we less intelligent? Is it that we are a lazy people? White business people in Barbados do not take kindly to the suggestion that they have had a racial advantage, but the evidence of this is incontrovertible. For unless black Barbadians are intellectually inferior to white Barbadians, or are lazy and lacking in the spirit of enterprise, we can only conclude that something is working for whites that is not working for blacks.

One person who recognized the value of the white skin in Barbados and used it to his advantage was the German business-man, Walter Mattheisen, who came into Barbados some time in the 1980's on a business mission. To cut to the chase, Mattheisen used his racial capital to gain the confidence of lending institu-tions before fleeing the country, his pockets lined with thousands of dollars in borrowed money.

He was quoted as saying that Barbados is a white man's country – that all it took was one phone call for him to get things done. Well, Mattheisen certainly did get many things done – sev-en million dollars of them, before he fled to Britain from where he was able to beat an extradition order. But in 1935, long before Mattheisen's visit, the Scottish-born, South African Historian, William Macmillan, came to Barbados and concluded that it was *"the most exclusive and colour-conscious Caribbean colony."* So that when J.N Goddard embarked on his epic journey into Bridgetown to seek his fortune, he had much more going for him than a mule.

This is not to negate the hard work which he must have put into his business – a successful business demands hard work, but in the context of a racially motivated Barbadian society, it must have helped that his skin was devoid of melanin and his hair straight. By contrast, black entrepreneurs who ventured into the arena found themselves struggling against the odds in a system that appeared to be putting obstacles in their way.

As a television Producer with the state-owned Caribbean Broadcasting Corporation I once did a series on black business in Barbados, the aim of which was to tell the story of what black business people were experiencing. In almost every case that ex-perience included obstacles securing the necessary funding from finance houses for their businesses, or some effort on the part of white business persons to retard their advancement.

We have already dealt with the legal encumbrances placed in the way of itinerant vending from the early 18th. century onward. This hostility to black enterprise continued right down to the present in one form or another. Indeed, in his book, *Business in Bim*, Historian Henderson Carter, identifies race and class as major factors militating against black enterprise. He writes:

> *"Even if through hard work and sacrifice a worker was able to establish a fledging enterprise, he/she came face to face with the spectacle of race and class prejudices which were critical features of the social landscape during the first half of the 20th. Century. From the days of slavery, race represented a defining element in the social life of Barbadians. Whites were accorded special status on account of their skin colour and wealth, coloureds were next in the preferred group, with blacks falling way behind.*
>
> *With these prevailing attitudes it was extremely difficult for blacks to establish business enterprises to compete with white owned and run establishments."*

Notwithstanding the difficulties, the spirit of enterprise was still able to find fertile ground in the minds of many black Barbadians. In 1911 a black company called Stuart and Sampson established itself on Roebuck Street as a grocery and provision dealer.

Another black entrepreneur, James A. Tudor, subsequently joined the band of Roebuck merchants as a wholesaler and operator of retail shops. These were two of the so-called black merchants of Roebuck Street who thrived at a time when the odds were heavily stacked against black entrepreneurship – but they did so in special circumstances. For instance I am told that Tudor got help with start up capital from a white benefactor.

How terribly disappointing that more than a century later, with black Barbadians in control of political power, black enterprise should still be the Cinderella of business in this country. Indeed, far from encouraging black enterprise, the ruling class and black elites persist in harassing and berating sole traders like street vendors. The treatment of these small traders must constitute one of the biggest failings of black political leadership of the post Emancipation period.

Here are enterprising working-class people who create a livelihood for themselves, but who, instead of attracting the encouragement of the political leadership, are made the victims of their own industriousness – hounded like wild animals, driven hither, thither and yon, just as they were under the old planter-merchant ruling class. These self-employed citizens are a benefit rather than a nuisance to the society. They make fruits, vegetables and other products available at good prices and they help to raise the employment graph. They do not deserve the harassment visited on them by the Police, every 18 months.

One of the most poignant images etched in my mind is a newspaper photograph of a Police vehicle, with what might very well have been exhibits in a street vending court case, fully visible. Not guns, nor marijuana plants, nor stolen goods – just ripe plantains. Some industrious citizen had gone out and bought food with the intention of earning something to put food on her own table, and this country was dragging her before the Court like a common criminal with her produce as exhibits.

They say the more things change the more they remain the same. It may seem like a contradictory statement, but there's a truth in it that is reflected in the social realities of modern Barbados. Political power has passed from the old mercantile-planter class to a black professional class, but many of the social systems, values and sometimes prejudices of the previous era have filtered down to the present.

The deceased, African American scholar, John Henrik Clarke (1915-1998) left us the following bit of wisdom: *"The events which*

John Henrik Clarke

transpired five thousand years ago, five years ago or five minutes ago, have determined what will happen five minutes from now; five years from now or five thousand years from now. All history is a current event." The present is nothing more than the tail end of the past. The two are inextricably linked.

But none of the above should be interpreted as suggesting that white Barbadians – advantages notwithstanding – do not make a valuable contribution to the economy of this country, and have not contributed to their wealth by hard work. We just need the pendulum to swing a little faster towards the rest of the population. They, too, want the opportunity to work hard creating wealth for themselves, their families and the community at large.

Is it too much to hope that one day we will be blessed with political leaders imbued with enough sense of history and vision to recognize the dire need to redress the economic imbalances of the past and finally bring reparations to the people whose unpaid sweat built this country. Will we see the day in Barbados when the sons and daughters of slaves will rule the commanding heights of the economy, as majority people do all over the world? I am not holding my breath for that day. The pigs are very much in control of the farm and striding elegantly on their hind legs.

Living Outside Our Skins

Wow! Imagine trying to condense the psychological legacy of slavery and colonialism into a section of a chapter of a book. It is like trying to get the proverbial camel through the eye of the needle. Let me begin by declaring that the average Barbadian does not have a clue about the true scale of the devastation wrought on the minds of African Barbadians during the periods of enslavement and colonial rule.

It is something of which the Martiniquan writer, Frantz Fanon, was fully conscious when he wrote: *"Imperialism leaves behind germs of rot which we must clinically detect and remove from our land, **but from our minds as well**."* It is my contention that the vast majority of our people have not even reached the detection stage, furthermore begun the removal of the germ of which Fanon speaks.

The pre-Emancipation period was a time of the worst form of exploitation, brutality and subjugation of African people in Barbados, examples of which were dealt with earlier. The imagery of power, authority and legitimacy impressed on the African mind was exclusively white – the Governor, the Parliamentarian, the Plantation Manager, the Merchant, the Priest. This contrasted sharply with the definition of the African as less than human – chattel or moveable property. The equation did not change to any significant degree in the period immediately following Emancipation in 1838 and even later into the 20th century. The centre of the world for Barbadians was still white.

As a primary school boy, I sang the British national anthem and British folk songs, like The Bluebells of Scotland, London Bridge Is Broken Down, Old Folks at Home and Bobby Shaftoe – all quite nice songs but songs grounded in the experiences – real or imagined – of people in Scotland, England and the United States. Where were the songs that spoke to the rhythm and culture of the Caribbean – Pack She Back to She Mamma, Every Time Uh Pass, Cocoa Tea, Linstead Market? They were there, but regarded with the same contempt with which we treated every other indigenous form of expression.

The books we read told stories of white people in a different environment and climate. So we would read about snow and spring and summer – never about flying fish or cricket or carnival. On November the 5th. we celebrated Guy Fawkes Day with "starlights" and mini explosives which we called bombs; and when members of the British royal family visited we lined the street in droves as if the Messiah, himself, had returned to Earth.

The Barbadian writer, Austin Clarke, summed it all up aptly in the title of his celebrated novel, *Growing Up Stupid Under the Union Jack*. This colour-tainted socialisation has done untold damage to the self confidence of the average African Barbadian, who, today, is a victim of an inferiority syndrome that manifests itself in virtually all areas of expression.

For what should have happened at independence – but did not – is a programme of psychological redirection, recognising the damage done by slavery and colonialism, and the need to fashion in the minds of the people a new vision of themselves. Instead, we were content to have a national anthem and a flag and a seat at the United Nations. All of the systems, values and traditions of the colonial period remained intact. The much quoted *"friends of all, satellite of none"* statement of the then Prime Minister, Errol Barrow, to the United Nations assembly in 1966 may have been reflected in foreign policy, but in every other way Barbados remained very much a satellite of Westminster. Barrow, himself, in spite of his nationalist rhetoric, did very little to address the problem, even after the establishment of the state-owned CBC radio and television.

So that in an independent Barbados, every November we have a ceremony in Heroes Square honouring the heroes of someone else's wars. In a similar vein we have a festival celebrating the arrival of the first British settlers. Our sense of history and the experience we under-went as colonials is so muddled that we don't even understand we are in fact celebrating an event that led to the enslavement of our fore-parents.

The organizers of the festival try to justify it by saying it's the origin of modern Barbados, as if the start of modern Barbados can be divorced from the circumstances of that origin. The Holetown landing is a historical fact, but how do you celebrate something that led to the awful experience that was plantation slavery in Barbados? It is akin to the people of South Africa having a festival to celebrate the arrival of the Boers.

What we have here, in fact, is the oppressed assuming the persona of the oppressor, weeping when he weeps and celebrating when he celebrates. It can only be described as a phenomenon, for the oppressor and the oppressed cannot have the same attitude to each other's triumphs and tribulations. How can two people facing each other on opposite sides of a fence have the same view?

This assumption of the colonizer's persona is at the heart of Frantz Fanon's seminal work, *"Black Skin, White Masks"*, a study of the black man/woman in a white culture, who, out of a sense of inferiority, will imitate the dominant white culture. This denial of self in favour of white Anglo-American norms and culture can manifest itself in something as simple as the way we speak and the terms we use. Barbados is a tropical country with bright, sunny weather almost all through the year, yet, somehow, I hear people using the word *"summer"* in reference to local seasons. We have *"summer camps"* and talk about things happening in the summer. But when is summer in Barbados if you have warm, sunny weather all year round? When does it begin and when does it end? And what are the features that distinguish it from autumn or winter?

This donning of white masks is never more bizarre than at Christmas, when, in the torrid heat of the Caribbean you will see men dressed in thick, woollen, red and white suits, complete with beard and woollen hat, pretending to be Santa Claus. In fact, so deeply have we internalised the reality of our European and North American neighbours that one of our musical groups has a Christmas song with the words "*although there is no snow or sleigh bells to be heard....*" Well, we don't have snow in the Caribbean, so our Christmas cannot be defined by snow, like that of other people.

Many years ago at what would have been the start of summer in the northern hemisphere, I heard a local radio broadcaster exclaim with more than a little glee in his voice "*It's summer!*" It was the kind of excitement you would expect from someone who lived in a cold climate and was happy that the warmth of summer had finally arrived. In North America and Europe when you say '*summer*' people have a clear idea what time of the year you are talking about, and what are the features of that time. In Barbados summer has no distinctive features. We do have a dry season and a wet season, but our day temperatures hover around 80 degrees Fahrenheit (26 Celsius) all year round; and except for those periods of the rainy season when we experience overcast conditions, it's blue skies and bright sunshine. How, then, should we relate to the concept of summer?

It gets even more bizarre. The story is told that during the reign of Jean Claude Duvalier in Haiti, his wife Michele would hold parties at which she would have the air conditioning set at very cold temperatures to enable her female guests to wear their mink coats. It must really be an extreme case of mindlessless when you go the extent of copying things that have no practical application to your own environment. We don't see ourselves as being at the centre of the world and therefore we ape those whom we consider to be at the centre.

These days we have "*kids*" instead of children. Why? Because that is what we hear white people in North America calling them. And people are telling us about Halloween, something that has never been part of the Barbadian tradition. The mentality of the average Barbadian today is one of subservience to the white cultures of Europe and North America. It is from these cultures that we look for leadership and precedence. A Barbadian artiste may have zero talent in Barbados but if propelled into stardom on the North American music scene is suddenly celebrated as a national hero and given the keys to the city. The practice is not very prevalent now, but many years ago our sports teams would give themselves names that have no resonance with anything pertaining to Barbados: Youth Milan and Lakers and Hadleighs.

Nothing sums up this sense of inferiority like the popular phrase "*little Barbados*". Barbadians of all strata just love this phrase, used mostly in the context of some noteworthy achievement of either the state or a Barbadian citizen. For instance, if a Barbadian is elected to head some international organization, someone will be moved to note that "*little Barbados*" is heading this or that organization, the underlying thinking being that this small country is holding a position normally held by big (and may I add 'white') countries. Faulty thinking, this is, for the very simple reason that intellectual ability has no natural correlation with the size of the country from which you come. The brain of a Barbadian is no smaller than that of an Australian or a Russian. If you think you're a Lilliputian then everyone else will seem like a giant.

The area of speech is a particularly interesting study with regard to this Barbadian inferiority syndrome. The official language of Barbados and other Anglophone Caribbean countries is English, but throughout the region a form of English dialect is widely spoken.

Linguists have analyzed this dialect to be a marriage of west African and English language systems. For example, someone might tell you in dialect "*I gih (give) she three mango*", the equivalent in English being "*I gave her three mangoes*". The difference between the two, apart from the spelling of the word '*give*', is the absence of a distinct plural form of the noun, a distinct form of the objective pronoun and a distinct form of the past tense in the verb.

But far from a corruption of the English, the dialect version is using a west African grammatical system in which there is sometimes no difference in form between singular and plural, present and past and subject and object. With regard to the lack of a plural form, as the late University of the West Indies Linguist and author of the "*Dictionary of Caribbean English Usage*", Richard Allsopp, once told us, the Africans figure that if they tell you *"two mango"* you would have to be a fool not to know that two means more than one. The other differences can be deduced from the context of the sentence. What a far cry, this analysis, from the general view of dialect – especially among the educated, upper classes – as a bastard form of English to be treated with contempt, if not disdain.

A grotesque form of this dialect is often presented in radio and television commercials, short stories and comic monologues by upper class Barbadians bearing working-class character names like Lick Mout' Lou, Lottie (gossip-mongers) and Market Vendor. Speaking in abnormally loud voice, these characters perform highly caricatured representations of the dialect, the entertainment being, not what is said, but the language form used. Once again, we seem to have a Caribbean peculiarity here, because I am not aware that there is anywhere else where people laugh at the way they speak naturally. Humour is more about the use of metaphor and double entendre and mis-interpretation rather than the language used to achieve this. In Barbados one word in this dialect caricature is enough to evoke peals of laughter.

Of course, the implied message in all of this is that English, the language of the colonial *'master'*, is the respectable standard; the local vernacular, an inferior – even comical – version spoken by the *'natives'*. In some strange way the purveyors and consumers of this dialect comedy appear not to understand that they **are** the natives who speak the vernacular on a daily basis.

So that to speak *"well"* in Barbados is not to communicate effectively, but to moderate the Barbadian accent to the point of sounding like a half-baked English man or woman. It is the mode of speech of some broadcasters, public speakers and persons with anglophile tendencies.

This desire to mask the Barbadian accent can turn up some really curious pronunciations. People will round off the 'R' in 'Barbados' and give you something like 'Bawbados'. I've also observed this rounding off with the word 'welcome', to something like 'WOLcome', and in words like 'boys', pronounced more like 'bueys'. The 'O' is pronounced with a more closed mouth, the fear being that if you open the mouth too wide you will sound like what you are – a Barbadian.

Masking is also reflected in the accenting of the first syllable of words, an Anglo-American linguistic trait. One particularly obtrusive example is often heard in the mis-pronunciation of the word, 'conDOlences'. In an effort to sound linguistically correct, many Barbadians will pronounce that word 'CONdolences' – emphasis wrongly placed on the first, rather than the second syllable. The most bizarre example of this practice is a favourite word of our Sportscasters: "DE-fence" instead of "de-FENCE". You de-FEND someone; you don't DE-fend them.

When I was growing up I would often hear my mother say what a great speaker the late James Cameron Tudor (Cabinet minister in the Errol Barrow government) was. Mr. Tudor, an Oxford University graduate, was the son of James A. Tudor, one of the black merchants of Roebuck Street we spoke of earlier. When he spoke, he could easily have been mistaken for an emissary from Westminster. Like most other Barbadians, my mother interpreted his affected accent to be good speech. After all he was not speaking like one of us; he was speaking like the white people from England.

People always marvel at the speed with which Barbadians who visit England or North America adopt the speech patterns of those regions. In previous times, a Barbadian would return home from a six-month trip to England or the United States speaking with a feigned British or American accent. In fact, we don't even have to travel; the Bridgetown Taxi Drivers will invariably use a North American accent when hailing white visitors they believe to be prospective clients.

It never seems to occur to these persons that the people they are aping never try to speak like us, however long they've been living in the Caribbean. Why? Perhaps they have a lot more confidence in themselves and don't see the need to ape others.

This bias is especially noticeable in the choice of Radio Broadcasters. Radio Programme Managers in these parts seem to think they have found the prime candidate when someone turns up with an English or North American accent, and they see absolutely nothing wrong with inflicting these persons on the Barbadian ear. Let us contrast this with what obtains in England and North America: all of us know that no one with a pure Caribbean accent would ever be hired on a mainstream radio station in those regions. They would consider – and rightly so – that the Caribbean accent would be too hard on their listeners' ears.

Of course, nothing said here is meant to suggest that Barbadians should not have the ability to speak English, which, after-all, is virtually the language of the world and the language in which we do written communication. Facility with English has enabled thousands of Barbadians to migrate to England and North America and make a better life for themselves without any language difficulty. Which is why I never get the point of these periodic debates we have over the use of dialect. In a sense we are a bilingual people. We speak the vernacular and we speak English. One doesn't prevent you from speaking the other. When all is said and done language is a medium of communication; it was not meant to be a symbol of status as the pro-English lobby seem to believe. It is precisely because of this perception of English and the vernacular as symbols of status that we get the oft-repeated statement that dialect is alright, but "*it has its place*". Those who repeat this statement never go on to say what that place is, but it may be safely deduced that what they really mean is that English is the language of respectability, to be used on formal occasions, whereas the vernacular should be restricted to everyday talk and grotesque comedy.

This preference for the colonial standard, regardless, is at its most ridiculous in the case of dress. The tropical Caribbean is the last place on planet Earth you would expect to find people dressed in heavy jackets and stockings, with day temperatures in the eighties. People from temperate climate visiting us for the first time are simply amazed to see women wearing stockings and men in heavy jackets and ties in the kind of heat we have.

One of my nieces, visiting from England, once remarked, with more than a little bewilderment in her voice, that she couldn't believe it when she saw a man in a jacket. She never thought that in a climate as hot as ours people would be wearing clothing designed to keep you warm. The British brought the jacket and tie with them when they came here. As everyone knows, they really do need jackets and ties over there. But in the torrid temperatures we have in the Caribbean it is the quintessence of absurdity to be walking around decked in a shirt, a tie to choke off what little air might still get in, and then a heavy jacket over it all. It is painful to watch men attending a funeral in the mid-afternoon heat, sweating in black suits. Even the animals seem to be coated according to the climate in which they live. The Polar Bear in the icy regions has a much more furry coat than the brown bear, and the Barbados Black Belly Sheep has much less wool than its counterpart of colder climes.

After all these decades of sovereignty, can't we muster enough confidence to determine our own form of dress? We have designers who could easily come up with a design for formal Caribbean wear. In fact, back in the 70's there was a movement away from the traditional suit to the more environmentally-friendly Shirt-Jac suit, a short-sleeved, collared shirt with matching trousers. Progressive leaders like Errol Barrow, Forbes Burnham of Guyana and Michael Manley of Jamaica wore shirt jacks, while the more conservative ones kept on their jackets.

Errol Barrow and Michael Manley in shirt-jac suits

It was a change that could have been the beginning of a process leading to a new standard for formal men's wear in our region. But the vision and self-confidence for that was lacking. Some men stuck rigidly to their European winter suits and those who were minded to change didn't want to feel odd, and eventually reverted to the status quo. Tradition can often get the better of logic and common sense.

The epitome of this Barbadian fascination with over dressing is an annual pilgrimage on Christmas morning after religious services, in which scores of heavily clad men and women and spectators descend on the main city park – known as Queen's Park. It is a veritable peacock party, minus the feathered creatures: women in exquisite hats and stockings, and men in suits, gloves and hats, some of them bearing multi-coloured canes. On these occasions it would not be unusual to see a man strutting in a waist-coat and swizzle-tail jacket, all of them seemingly oblivious to the sweltering mid-morning heat, and thinking they look ever so hot.

Barbadian men dressed "to kill" on Christmas morning in the Park

The event commands the status of a national ritual, and is accorded full coverage in the Press, Radio and Television. And the agency for artistic and cultural promotion and development, known as the National Cultural Foundation, has been known to sponsor a competition for the best dressed man and woman. How much more consistent with the NCF's role as a promoter of indigenous cultural expression, if it sponsored a competition for our Designers to come up with blueprints for a national dress that speak to the history, culture and climate of the Caribbean.

A prisoner must be subject to the dictates of his captors. He must eat their food, drink their ales and wear their clothes; but when he becomes free he should think like a free man: making his own choices rather than clinging to the norms of his previous enslaved condition. Black Barbadians achieved that freedom 178 years ago on August 1st. 1838. Why are we still behaving like slaves?

If You're Black Stand Back

But perhaps the worst victim of the chains of enslavement and colonialism is the racial self-esteem of the African Barbadian. It would probably not be a reckless statement to say that the average African Barbadian regards his blackness as an affliction which he would readily jettison if it were possible. In these islands the less you look like an African the more appealing your appearance is in the eyes of yourself and others. We are the only racial group that uses our colour as a term of abuse – "*The black bastard*". Presumably, a white or brown-skinned bastard is more acceptable than a black one. On the other hand, a beautiful African sister would be called "*a lovely, black woman*". Of course, the adjective, "black", in this case, while purporting to be positive, is really there to suggest to us that black women aren't normally beautiful.

This negative attitude to the black skin correlates with a similar negativity in black Barbadians to any suggestion of an African identity. It is an incontestable fact that black Barbadians and other black Caribbean people were imported to this region from Africa during the Trans-Atlantic Slave Trade, but, with few exceptions, there would be howls of protest if you dared to call them Africans. In this case, negative self-esteem combines with ignorance and negative, mass media portrayal of the African continent.

The customary response is to retreat into nationality: "*I aint no African; I is a Barbadian*", as if Barbados is not made up of people of different races. The irony of it is that the same people would have no difficulty referring to someone born in Barbados of Indian parents as an Indian, or to a Barbadian with Chinese parents as a Chinese. Or sometimes they might retort by telling you the Africans don't like us, and when you question further you realize that they've never even met one, furthermore visited Africa. The black Barbadian will try anything to repudiate his African identity. Of course, it would be dishonest to pretend that black Barbadians are of pure African ancestry. There has been some European infiltration; but no one can deny the predominance of Africa in our racial and ethnic identity. When we embrace that we embrace ourselves.

Even as I write, my attention is drawn to an article in the Trinidad Express newspaper dated Feb 7, 2014, under the caption, TOO DARK FOR PM? The article quotes a former MP and Senator for the opposition People's National Movement, Fitzgerald Hinds, as saying there were elements within and outside of the party who thought the current party leader, Keith Rowley, was too dark skinned to be Prime Minister.

Keith Rowley

Said Hinds: "*Shocked as I was, I went to a number of my colleagues, inside and outside of the PNM, and asked them if they think like that or if they had ever heard anything like that. And to the man and woman, everybody said they heard it before.*" (Take a break from reading, pour a strong rum or brandy and compose yourself).

Yes, this is the Caribbean in the 21st. century, a place where lightness of skin tone and hair texture can, sometimes, determine your fortunes in life, as incredible as that may sound. How is it possible for intelligent people to be considering someone "*too dark*" for a leadership role – or any role? Since when does lightness of skin equate with intelligence? In my own profession it is common practice to favour light-skinned female presenters over darker ones. The people at CBC (Caribbean Broadcasting Corporation) were unshakeable in their love of people with pale skins and foreign accents. The fact that sometimes the requisite skill in presenting was absent didn't seem to matter. Indeed, in a few cases the newscast might well have been mistaken for someone telling the story of Goldilocks and the Three Bears – but the Presenter was fair skinned and nobody cared about anything else.

This obsession with Caucasian-type features is quite serious in the Caribbean. In a predominantly black region, the vast majority of our "*beauty queens*" are girls with fair skins and semi-straight hair; there are virtually no pictorial advertisements featuring women with an obvious African appearance – all fair, with straight or semi-straight hair; black musical artistes making music videos nearly always choose fair-skins with long, flowing hair – never anyone looking like their mother or sister. In these parts the pale skin is, to the prevailing notions of beauty, what the white skin is to business opportunity.

Quite recently, a skin-bleaching practice was reported in Jamaica, in which girls – and I understand some men – would bleach their skins with a commercial product. Jamaica, of course, is the home of the so-called "*browning*" (a fair skinned woman). In this overwhelmingly black country the "*browning*" is like the pearl of great price to any man who gets one – the equivalent of the "*red pole*" in Barbados. It is impossible to over-state the strength of this indoctrination with Caucasoid prototypes of beauty. The concept of female beauty fixed in the minds of our people makes no provision for women with dark skins or hair that is less than semi-straight. In these parts a woman need not have any particularly exceptional features to be "*beautiful*", once she has a fair skin and long, straight hair.

With this blue print for female beauty indelibly etched in their minds, black women devote considerable time and resources to altering their natural appearance. When I was growing up all the girls would straighten their hair with a hot iron; these days they are actually buying straight hair imported from India and wherever else and weaving it into their own. A black woman with long, flowing hair is the equivalent of a white woman with thick, woolly hair.

But in recent time more and more black women have been demonstrating some comfort with their natural hair, opting for braids and other natural styles. It is an awful plight to suffer when you have to spend your entire life trying to look like someone else.

In the old, colonial days when we had visits from female members of the British Royal Family – the Queen, herself, or Princess Margaret – they would choose a girl from one of the mostly white schools to present the Royal visitor with a bouquet. Here is this Royal visitor coming to a predominantly black country and the only person they can find to present her with a bouquet is someone looking like her. Surely they (Royals) must have been thinking: why didn't they send me one of the little 'native', black girls. Caribbean children are imbued with this anti-black, pro-Caucasian prejudice from an early age and by the time they become adults it's almost part of their DNA.

The now outdated doctrine of white supremacy held that the European race was superior to all others, and as such had the right to dominate them. Millions of people have been murdered, enslaved and otherwise dis-advantaged because of this doctrine. When we buy into the highly fallacious and nonsensical notion that the beauty and worth of an individual may be determined on the basis of his or her approximation to European features and values we are implicitly buying into racism.

Concerns with the outward appearance command a significant portion of our energy, time and resources. But like the Preacher in the biblical book of Ecclesiastes, I will summarize it by saying "*all is vanity*". For he who is in search of beauty must

Look beyond the shallow skin
To the invisible soul that lies within
For what is beauty, if not the warmth and love
That radiates from the human heart
It's nourishing virtues to impart.

The Monarchy

The most embarrassing manifestation of the inferiority syndrome lies in our constitutional status. Half a century after the attainment of independence, the Head of State of the sovereign nation of Barbados is a foreigner residing four thousand miles away in Buckingham Palace, who has no kinship with the people of Barbados. It never ceases to boggle my mind how our otherwise intelligent leaders could have agreed to this constitutional monstrosity and maintained it for all these years.

For surely no self-respecting country wants to have as its Head of State someone other than one of its citizens. I suspect that is why all of the former British colonies in Africa and Asia chose to have their own heads of state. In fact, of the 15 independent countries outside of the United Kingdom with Queen Elizabeth as Head of State, nine are in the Caribbean. Of the others, three – Australia, Canada and New Zealand – have a common ethnic and cultural affinity with the people of the UK. In other words there are only three other countries outside of the Anglo Saxon world that have opted to retain the British sovereign. Those countries are Tuvalu, the Solomon Islands and Papua New Guinea. To their eternal credit Guyana, Trinidad & Tobago and Dominica displayed the political maturity of an independent state and severed their colonial ties with the British Crown in favour of republican constitutions.

The Barbados Labour Party, under the leadership of Owen Arthur, did flirt with the idea of establishing a republican form of government, setting up a commission to hear recommendations on constitutional change, and making republicanism a part of its platform for the 2003 general election. The proposed change also formed part of the National Strategic Plan 2005 – 2025, as cited below:

"We, a people steeped in tradition and cautious in our approach to change, are now being called upon to modern-ise our Constitution, cast off the last vestiges of colonialism and take full responsibility for ourselves as a Republic with a Barbadian Head of State, and with the Caribbean Court of Justice as our own highest court of appeal."

Well, lofty wording notwithstanding, the plan was never pursued, allegedly because of the urgency of getting the Caribbean Single Market & Economy (CSME) implemented. To this day the CSME is still not fully functional. Those of us familiar with the strangle-hold of Westminster's chains on the minds of Caribbean people will be forgiven for being a little doubtful that this republican plan represented any genuine intention to change the constitution of Barbados.

For the same Owen Arthur it was, whose party re-named Tra-falgar Square in Bridgetown and pledged to re-locate the statue of Horatio Lord Nelson – which statue remains in place up to now. Arthur is not alone in this diffidence when it comes to severing ties with the Monarch; the late Jamaican leader, Michael Manley, also placed it on the cards in 1977; and the current Prime Minister, Portia Simpson Miller, did so in 2012. Today Jamaica is still bow-ing down to the Queen. In Barbados, the issue was put back on the table, with the announcement by Prime Minister, Freundel Stuart, that he intended to sever the last remaining constitutional link with Britain by 2016, the 50th anniversary year of independ-ence. Mr. Stuart said he found it awkward in the year 2015 to have to stand up and pledge allegiance to the Queen. Well, apparently not awkward enough, for the Prime Minister's office later refuted international Press reports that Barbados intended to ditch the Queen, saying he was giving 'his personal opinion.'

The reluctance to ditch the British monarchy, like the fasci-nation with European values and notions of beauty, is all bound up in our unconscious embrace of white supremacy. Inwardly, many Caribbean people unconsciously believe in the superiority of the European. There is nothing in the United Kingdom named in honour of Barbados or any Barbadian, yet in Barbados we have a Queen Elizabeth Hospital and a Princess Margaret School and a Royal Barbados Police Force. We even have a President Kennedy Drive. These are all people and institutions that have contributed absolutely nothing to the advancement of Barbados. There is no good reason why anything in this country should be named after them.

The republican debate in Barbados can be a very polarized one, pitting progressive, Pan Africanist forces against a small conservative group – mostly whites and Afro-Saxon blacks – committed to maintaining the island's traditional links with the British Crown. Because there can really be no valid reason why an independent country should have a Head of State from somewhere else, and moreover, one that is determined by birth.

The arguments in favour of the monarchy can often be manufactured and downright illogical. The monarchists' case is almost limited to Barbados' political stability (which monarchists attribute to our ties with the British Crown) in comparison with republics like Haiti or "crime-ridden Jamaica". One white, radio talk-show host even suggested on one occasion that we needed the Monarchy because it promotes good values and standards.

Ooooh! Yes, it can get as absurd as that. I think, perhaps, he might have meant standards other than those pertaining to marital stability and fidelity. And then there was the popular argument that if we became a republic we might end up like the republics in South America. I thought that one had become extinct until I heard it being regurgitated by one of our erudite citizens who had recently received a Knighthood. He fears that if we change our monarchical status we will become like the Latin states. He did not elaborate on that point leaving me completely at a loss, since I am aware that nearly all – if not all those states are now stable democracies. I guess this is all part of the illogical thinking I referred to earlier.

Let me share a response I gave in the Barbados NATION Newspaper of May 19th. 2011 to columnist, Lowdown, who advanced some of these arguments. The Nation captioned my article ROLLING UPHILL WITH LOWDOWN.

There's nothing like the word 'republic' to send shivers of fear down the spines of the most conservative elements among us. So embedded are they in their Westminster constitutional nest that they are prepared to throw facts, common sense and logic through the window in order to preserve the status quo.

How else can we account for the highly illogical arguments advanced by the Nation week-end columnist, Lowdown, in response to the views expressed by Sir Frederick Smith, in favour of republicanism? Let's quote him (Lowdown): "Perhaps our unparallel history of parliamentary democracy, our traditional respect for law and order, our present and former outstanding leadership have lulled Sir Sleepy [sic} into a false sense of security....Did he see Guyana, once a respected parliamentary neighbour being turned into a chaotic failed state by just one republican President?...Did he ever think an American presidential candidate would 'tief' (steal) an election? These are the hallmarks of too many a republican government."

When goat dung wants to roll it will surely roll uphill (Barbadian proverb). *Mr. Lowdown, a well-known goat farmer, must know that very well, for the above represents a desperate attempt by goat dung to roll uphill, quite contrary to the laws of gravity, common sense, logic and everything else. Let's start with this "unparallel history of parliamentary democracy". Would this be in reference to the establishment of a parliament in 1639, to which only a privileged, tiny minority could be elected – a parliament that would, for the next 300 years, preside over the affliction of the broad mass of people of this country?*

Yes, I think this is the parliamentary democracy he's talking about. And who would want to experience the political turbulence that came with the Guyanese republic? Our dear Queen may not have any power, but the mere fact that we know she's there sitting dutifully on her golden throne is enough to stop our leaders from indulging in any foolishness. We shouldn't pay too much attention to monarchical Grenada under the Gairy regime - the beatings, imprisonments and murders of political opponents and the rigging of elections. Those things must have occurred at a moment when the sovereign had vacated her throne to attend to personal matters.

The same must be said for the political tensions that led to the murders of hundreds in monarchical Jamaica during the 1980's. These occurrences are deviations from the norm. We had a similar situation farther a-field in the monarchical Fiji Islands in the late 1980's in which a series of coups overthrew the elected government and established a republic. Political turmoil like these only happen in monarchical states when the sovereign vacates the throne temporarily.

As we continue our roll uphill, let's ignore all of the good, stable republics in the world – places like Dominica, the Dominican Republic, United States, Germany, France, Ghana, Kenya, Malawi, the Netherlands, India, Singapore et al. We will roll uphill with those bad ones; our dear Queen must reign over us forever. Long may she live!

A republic – as defined by the dictionary – is a state in which supreme power is held by the people and their elected representatives, and which has an elected or nominated president rather than a monarch. Such a constitution is completely independent of the values, traditions and ethos of a society. It certainly wouldn't make a country suddenly become any better or worse.

There must be an uncontrollable yearning somewhere deep in the human psyche for the surreal – things that take our senses away from the normal and towards the fanciful. How else can we explain the ease with which so many, otherwise normal people would buy into the notion that there are special beings on earth, who, based purely on the accident of their birth, are superior to us – people to whom we must bow down and make obeisance, and whose every utterance and action commands the attention of the rest of us, commoners? I mean – this phenomenon called royalty is a veritable case study in mass brainwashing. How is it possible to convince intelligent people that there are human beings who came into the world in the same way we did, who have the same physical characteristics, who commit the same sins as we, who don't have wings nor halos, but who command our awe and admiration at every turn? It boggles my mind.

If the British think this is a tradition of theirs they need to hold onto at all costs, well so be it, but it really does not reflect well on the intellect of the rest of us to be buying into this medieval foolishness. There *are* no special human beings; we are all equal in status before God, and it borders on idolatry for us to be bowing and scraping before fellow humans. Why, even the British, themselves, are divided over the usefulness of this institution, even though a majority favour its retention.

For example, an editorial in the London Observer, re-printed in the NATION newspaper on September 10th. 2000 asks the question: "*But what does it say about...us that in the first year of the third millennium Britain still selects its Head of State by birth certificate.* The paper opined: "*The monarchy remains symbolic of privilege over people, of chance over endeavour, of being something, rather than doing something. We elevate to the apex of our society someone selected, not on the basis of talent or achievement, but because of genes.*"

Back in Barbados, on February 25, 2012 in one of its regular newspaper columns David Comissiong's People's Empowerment Party raised questions about the effectiveness of the Queen as Barbados' Head of State. The party said in part:-

"*The person who holds that office should be someone who is truly representative of what is best and most noble about the national population, and who is capable of serving as a symbol of national unity and inspiration.*

Can Queen Elizabeth II, an English woman who lives thousands of miles away from Barbados perform this critical function for our nation? Is she representative of our best and most noble Barbadian characteristics? Does she touch our Barbadian souls, and inspire and motivate us? Do we see her as a symbol of our unity as a people?

The answer to all of these questions is a resounding NO ! She does not, and she cannot – no matter how many native Governors General are appointed to be her representative in Barbados, nor how many times she sends her son to visit Barbados. And so, if there is no one who is effectively performing the crucial functions that are required and expected of a Head of State, can we truly say that Barbados has a Head of State?

But Barbados does need a genuine Head of State. Oh, what a great benefit it would be to our nation if, in these trying times, we had in place a native son or daughter that we all admired and respected, and that we all played a role in selecting and elevating to the high office of Head of State.

It is time for us to stop making mock sport at ourselves. It is time for us to discard old, obsolete, social arrangements that are holding us back, and that are doing damage to our children's psyches. It is time for a native Barbadian Head of State that is selected on the basis of a system that provides for input from all of the citizens of Barbados, and that is insulated from partisan politics."

Concomitant with the absurdity of a distant foreigner for Head of State in an independent country is the maintenance of an equally absurd system of imperial honours. I bow my head in absolute shame every year when it is announced that this or that Barbadian has been awarded the honour of Commander of the British Empire or some British Knighthood in the Queen's New Year's honours. How do you accept an invitation to be a commander of an empire that enslaved, brutalized and exploited your foreparents? The bones of Bussa, Washington Franklin, Nanny Grig and all the other martyrs of the 1816 slave revolt must be reeling in their graves. And in the context of the history of Barbados and the Caribbean what is a knight? The symbolism clearly does not have any historical nor cultural relevance to our society. Why are these things not patently obvious to the political leaders of the Caribbean?

Back in 1980 Barbados instituted its own honours, but guess what the highest honour is called: the Knight of St. Andrew. Even when we professed to be going on our own we didn't have the confidence to let go of Westminster's apron strings and be original. What betrays our lack of sincerity in the creation of national honours is the fact that our governments still recommends citizens for receipt of honours from Buckingham Palace. Again the only progressive views on this question are coming from the People's Empowerment Party. Here is what the party had to say on this matter of imperial honours in an article dated October 31st. 2012:

> *"As the world sinks deeper and deeper into a civilizational crisis, sensible and forward-looking Barbadians are earnestly trying to find within our Barbadian society and polity tangible evidence of an authentic sovereign national culture and spirit upon which we can construct a strong and credible response to the encircling gloom.*
>
> *And it is because the Peoples Empowerment Party (PEP) is so profoundly invested in this national mission that we cannot help but publicly deplore the fact that outstanding citizens of our country are still receiving and accepting such "honours" as 'Order of the British Empire' (OBE), or are receiving knighthoods that are dished out as part of the Queen's birthday honours.*
>
> *What kind of psychological foundation are we setting for our nation when we do our most outstanding citizens the disservice of making them "members" and "commanders" of the abomination that was known to history as "the British Empire"?*
>
> *Any historian worth his salt will tell you that the British Empire was arguably the greatest criminal enterprise in history. Its beginnings can be traced back to the Third Crusade of 1188, when King Richard I of England led a*

mercenary army to the Middle East and captured and pillaged Cyprus and the town of Jaffa.

But perhaps a more poignant starting-place for us black folks would be the year 1564 - the year in which Queen Elizabeth I provided John Hawkins with a 700 ton ship and sent him to the West Coast of Africa to burn and destroy the towns and to capture black men and women and reduce them to slavery.

Indeed, the trade in African human-beings provided the British 'kleptocracy' (headed by its various kings and queens) with a springboard to launch its piratical activities into the rest of the African continent, the Caribbean, North America, Australia, India, China, New Zealand, the Middle East, the islands of the Pacific, and the list goes on.

This thing called "the British Empire" was a transnational racket based on organised theft, racism, murder, genocide, mass kidnappings, forced labour, and virtually every other criminal abuse known to mankind!

How can we therefore build the new national society – the "new Barbados" - if we continue to psychologically anchor our nation to institutions that are so anachronistic and alien to our best interests, as the British Monarch and her Empire? The PEP says that the time has come for Barbados to do away with OBE's, CBE's and with the British monarchy! The time has come for us to self-confidently build our own civilization and forge our own future!"

To its credit, the PEP, through its umbrella body, the Clement Payne Movement, has instituted an annual award in the name of this national hero, called the Clement Payne Award. An award that bears the name Clement Payne ought to command far greater prestige than any Knight or Dame of St. Andrew or St. George.

The author (3rd. from right) as he received the 2007 Clement Payne Award, with joint recipient Kathleen Drayton

I was privileged to receive one of those awards in 2007 for my work in broadcasting. It is an award named after a genuine Barbadian hero, an award rooted in the history of my people, not in some irrelevant, colonial tradition. I am proud to be associated with the heroic contribution of Clement Payne.

The bones of all the great martyrs and warriors for liberation from domination and oppression would demand no less than vigorous protest should anyone dare attempt to induct me into any hall of knights.

How dare you call me 'sir'!
How dare you try to brand me with stupid, imperialist accolades – as if Elmina Castle and the Gate of no Return never existed!
As if the brutality of plantation servitude
And the subjugation of colonialism were mere chapters in a Charles Dickens novel.
How dare you call me 'sir'!
How dare you put me in the same bracket as racist murderers like Horatio Nelson and John Hawkins.
The bones of the ancestors cry out at this abomination

*And the dust of the Amerindians is bestirred with
consternation.
Your masters' knights galloped in shining armour, brandish-
ing spears with which they pierced the souls of defenceless
peoples, and trampled them into the ground,
All to enrich and expand their great empire,
On which the sun was never to set.
Three centuries on without reparations or even an apology
You want to call me 'sir'.
You want to induct me into their hall of knights, lords and
barons,
Branding me, like they did three centuries ago with a hot
iron –
The children of freedom must never adorn themselves with
the accolades and badges of the oppressor nor bow down to
him.
How dare you call me 'sir'!
How dare you brandish colonial symbols in my face,
Disrespecting my sovereignty, ignoring my history.
Before Westminster, there were pyramids and Nile Valley
and ancient Ghana
Before their Knights, Barons and Lords we had Pharaohs
and Chiefs and Queens.
So don't **ever** call me 'sir'!
I will not be decorated with the badge of imperialism
Nor the trappings of colonial subservience.
For I am a man – no longer a slave.
FREE AND LIBERATED FROM THE CHAINS OF YOUR
MASTERS' COFFLES!*

The taint of the honours system is not just its affront to our
sovereignty; it is in the blatant abuse to which it has been subjected by politicians. A national honour is supposed to be an
accolade for meritorious service to your country – i.e. service
outside of normal expectations. In the Barbadian tradition, you
can fairly well predict that when one party holds the reigns of
government its tribal icons will be among those high on the list

for honours. These and other awardees tend to be just professionals who did nothing more than perform the duties of their job for 40 years at salaries way above the average.

These individuals are certainly not worthy of any national accolade. They did their job and were handsomely paid; they did nothing outside of what they were expected to do. As a keen follower of national affairs, I'd be hard-pressed if asked to say what some of our top honours recipients did to be so honoured. I really think this honours system is an extension of the classism that is at the core of British society. Their heads of state are determined by birth, rather than the people; then they have all these special people called Barons and Dukes and Duchesses and Earls who are supposed to be superior to the average British folk – people whose only claim to specialness is that they were born into some wealthy family. That wealth, of course, might have come from the sweat of our enslaved fore-parents working for no pay on a plantation in the Caribbean. This is the kind of society our leaders are following so slavishly.

So that for me, Clement Payne was a worthy candidate for the honour of national hero: he went outside of the ordinary to try to open the eyes of the people of Barbados to the unjust system under which they were suffering, and to organize them to resist it. He, himself, was a victim of the system because of his activities, and the events spurred by him led to a better deal for the people of Barbados. Samuel J. Prescod and Charles D. O'Neal went outside their comfort zones for the upliftment of the people. What a contrast to our be-knighted 'honourable' party faithfuls and professional elites who enjoyed the best the society has to offer, with little – sometimes no sacrifice.

The colonial dependence displayed in our choice of head of state and national honours is reflected in the response of some regional countries to the Caribbean Court of Justice. In 2001, the countries of the Caribbean Community established their own final court of appeal, obviating the need for us to go to the British Privy Council. The court has an original jurisdiction for matters pertaining to the treaty governing the Caribbean

Community and an appellate jurisdiction as the final court for member countries.

Well, guess what happens: initially, only two members of the Community, Barbados and Guyana, signed onto its appellate jurisdiction – the number since increasing to three with the accession of Belize. To be fair, there were constitutional hurdles in the way of immediate accession for some countries; but in other instances the hindrance was a reluctance to break with the Privy Council. Some individuals openly declared their preference for the British Privy Council; others expressed doubts about the impartiality of the Caribbean Judges. No doubts about the judgments of the English Lords – perhaps they are infallible. The most pointed expression of lack of confidence in the CCJ has come from Jamaican attorney Hugh Wildman, a former senior prosecutor who has served across the Caribbean. He actually declared that Caribbean Judges were incapable of delivering judgments that are equal in quality to those of the Privy Council. Mr. Wildman urged regional governments to be careful in moving to replace the Privy Council with the Caribbean Court of Justice (CCJ).

Hugh Wildman

"I am not confident or comfortable that we are going to replace the Privy Council with a court of equal standing in terms of erudi-

tion. It is my considered view that the quality of the judgments given by the Privy Council are far superior to what we are seeing in the region and for that matter what we are seeing coming out of the CCJ," Wildman told a Gleaner Editors' Forum held at the newspaper's offices in central Kingston.

Wildman's views mirrored those of the former leader of the conservative Jamaica Labour Party, Edward Seaga. Speaking as Leader of the opposition back in 2000 Seaga gave this assessment of the move towards a Caribbean Court of Justice:

> "There has been no more sinister attempt to subjugate the rights of the people to justice that is pure and not perverted than this attempt to unleash on an unsuspecting people a lesser breed of justice which can be moulded in the shape of the political will."

Justice that is pure versus a *"lesser breed of justice"*. What a pitiful case of mental slavery. Well, the Privy Council might be the purest form of justice for Mr. Seaga, but the signals coming from London suggest that they would rather we got out of their hair and go with our lesser breed of justice. In 2009 the President of the United Kingdom Supreme Court dropped a bomb-shell, bringing to pass the fears expressed by the late Errol Barrow in those famous words: *"We will not be caught loitering on colonial doorsteps after closing time."*

Reports from London quoted Lord Nicholas Phillips, as saying that the Law Lords on the Council, were spending a 'disproportionate' amount of time on cases from former British colonies. He raised questions as to whether some of the cases coming before the Council really needed to be heard by Britain's most senior judges.

Lord Phillips indicated his personal preference to see a reduction in the number of appeals from Commonwealth

Lord Nicholas Phillips

countries. He was concerned that the law Lords were spending as much as 40 per cent of their work time on appeals from the Caribbean and other Commonwealth countries. *"It is a huge amount of time. I personally would like to see it reduced. It's disproportionate,"* he said. The British Jurist argued that in an ideal world Commonwealth countries would establish their own final courts of appeal, instead of relying on the Privy Council.

The unthinkable has actually happened: The British are telling us *'your welcome has expired; get out'.* The vast majority of so-called Commonwealth countries did not wait for this indignity to be inflicted on them; they went ahead, like sovereign states do, and established their own final courts: Guyana in 1970, Ghana in 1960, Nigeria in 1963, Australia in 1986, Canada in 1888, India in 1950, Malaysia in 1978, Pakistan in 1950, Singapore in 1994, Sri Lanka in 1972, Hong Kong in 1997, Zimbabwe in 1980, and South Africa in 1950 – and the list goes on. What do the leaders of all of these countries know that some of us in the Caribbean don't? Perhaps they know that a sovereign state ought to stand on its own feet rather than seek to hang on to the coat-tails of Westminster.

The human brain, unlike the computer, is capable of independent thought. But we often forego this wonderful ability and behave like programmed computers or animals motivated by instinct. Growing up in rural parish of St. John provided me with a first-hand view of animal life and behaviour. One of the things I noticed about animals – especially chickens – is that if you kept them encaged for a long enough period they would become conditioned to that environment to the extent that even if you opened the door they would not venture outside. I have vivid recollections of chickens (or fowls as we called them) peering curiously out of an open coop, but never venturing outside. Their minds would have become so accustomed to imprisonment they wouldn't know what freedom was.

And so it is that nearly two centuries after freedom from slavery, and half a century after the end of colonial tutelage the good people of Barbados are peering cautiously, like caged chickens, through the door of freedom, their vision of themselves and

the world still circumscribed by the strands of mental bondage.
What a lamentable state of affairs. It makes me want to

weep for my people –
Still jumping at the crack of the Master's whip 178 years after
the fact.
The chains have been broken, but the prisoner remains
shackled,
Walking diligently in 'superior' footsteps
Like sheep following the trail of the shepherd.
I weep for my people –
More than half a century after the vote
Still peering cautiously from the open cage
Unable to take the flight of freedom over these fields and hills –
Free, but enslaved –
Proclaiming nationhood, but pledging allegiance to Massa, his
heirs and successors.
The trident is broken, but the prongs remain firmly in place.
Emancipate yourself from mental slavery and
Stop loitering on colonial doorsteps after closing time.

I weep for my people –
Still living in the shadow of the old great house –
Exuding fear and trembling at the sound of the master's voice:
"Yes, master, your servant heareth."
The spirit of servitude safely nestled in the bosoms of free men.
I weep for my people –
Forever labouring; never rising to the commanding heights.
Sweating in the chain-gangs of concrete plantations –
Creators of wealth but victims of poverty and debt.
The actors have changed but the roles remain the same:
Saxon power and control; African labour and dependence.
I weep for my people –
Consummate consumers – basking in the glory of the latest
BMW;
Slurping on noodles at Chinese restaurants – "I love Chinese
food" –

Or, heads bowed like sheep, buried in the keypads of iPods,
Samsungs or tablets –
Buying, buying, buying; never controlling; never owning.
I weep for my people –
The lost children of great civilisations,
Basking in blissful ignorance of a glorious ancestry;
Despising and rejecting their true identity,
Preferring to be clones of their oppressors rather than Ashanti
Princes and Princesses –
"I en no African; I is a bajan."
Black men with the tar of Africa dripping from their skins
boasting of Scottish blood;
Yearning to be knights and dames of St. Andrew and St.
George.
I weep for my people.
Indoctrinated with alien notions of beauty,
They baulk at their mirror image –
Black sisters flaunting blond wigs and Caucasoid hair.
I cry when I see black brothers swooning over 'red poles' and
'brownings' –
Mulatto girls for music videos and advertisements, instead of
Nubian princesses –
Mirror, Mirror on the wall, who's the fairest of them all?
Beauty from the master's mirror.
I weep for my people
When I see them decked in wintry garb and roasting in the
tropical sun –
Strutting their neck-ties and collars, coats and tails
Like pea-fowls at the peacocks' party –
The threads of winter without the snow.
Look how they spurn the vibrations of the African drum for
the stiffness of the Master's quadrille and the Latins' salsa.
Monkey see; monkey do.
I weep for my people –
Stripped of the confidence to affirm and celebrate their culture
Spurning the traditions of noble ancestors
And latching onto the whims and fancies of outsiders –

Cornflakes over cornmeal,
Croissants instead of cassava,
Television soap operas that mimic the rich and famous instead
of the sights and sounds of Kingston, Bridgetown and Port of
Spain.
I weep for my people
When I hear them speak in the tongues of aliens, aping the
accents and terminologies of foreigners –
Yankee twang and hip-hop talk.
I weep when I see them skinning and grinning at the nation's
language,
Making mock-sport at the idiom of the ancestors –
"The dialect is too sweet – but it has its place."
I cry for my people.
How I wish they would throw the shackles , fly the coop and
soar like eagles.
Break forth, my people, and spread your wings unto the
heavens!
Soar! Soar!
Rise to the ends of the earth and claim the fron-
tiers of freedom!
FREEDOM!
FREEDOM!
FREEDOOOOOOOM!

Westminster's Choir Boys

For obvious reasons, the Westminster parliamentary model is the system of choice for Barbados and other Anglophone Caribbean countries. In the case of Barbados we have a parliamentary tradition – as was mentioned earlier – that is one of the oldest in the western hemisphere. I think we can now safely say that we are a parliamentary democracy – with a bicameral legislature, comprising a lower House or House of Assembly, (equivalent to Britain's House of Commons) and a Senate, (equivalent to the House of Lords). The House comprises 30 elected members representing the equivalent number of constituencies, and the Senate, 21 appointed members. The ruling party appoints 12 members to the Senate, the opposition party two and the Governor General (representing the Queen), appoints seven, referred to as *"independent"* Senators.

In concept, the Senate is a review chamber, re-examining legislation and resolutions emanating from the House, endorsing those with which it agrees and rejecting those which it opposes. It should be noted that when a measure is rejected, it is sent back to the House with recommendations for change – which may or may not be accepted – but after that the Senate has no further say in that measure. In fact, in its 50-year history the number of measures rejected by the Senate can be counted on one finger – yes: only on one, single occasion. This chamber, then, has functioned as nothing more than a rubber stamp for the ruling party and there's a strong body of opinion that it is just a colossal waste of public money and should be abolished. How do they justify keeping a review chamber that in half a century has expressed an independent opinion only once?

As a source of news – when I was a Reporter in the 1980's – the Senate was never an assignment to which you looked forward with any degree of eagerness. Its *"honourable members"*, largely made up of rejected election candidates; senior Barbadians, steeped in conservative values and just plain, old party hacks, engaged in a weekly rehash of matters debated and passed in the House previously. The speeches were mostly mundane - no unexpected challenges; no innovative ideas on any issue. At the end of the tiresome sitting all matters dealt with are passed. And for this, members get to take home a not insignificant, pension-able stipend at the end of each month.

Parliamentary procedure is patterned after Westminster, down to the black robes worn by officers of the Parliament (they've now discarded the wigs) and the use of the title *'honour-able member'* in reference to MP's and Senators. In the House, the Speaker presides over proceedings, assisted by a Deputy Speaker and a Chairman of Committees. In the Senate the chief presiding officer is the President, who's assisted by a Deputy President.

Today's Parliament represents a revolution in the history of governance in this country. It has moved from an undemocratic institution controlled by a plantocracy for their own interests, to one controlled by the black majority, serving the needs of all. It has had its highlights and its "low-lights" over the years. Heading the list of highlights, of course, is the passing of the Representation of the People (Amendment) Act of 1950 which gave the unconditional right to vote to every Barbadian adult. Among the other high points: the passing of the Trade Union Act of 1940; expansion of free education to universal status in 1962; the resolution taking Barbados into independence in 1966 and the Tenantries Freehold Purchase Act of 1980, which gave plantation tenants the right to buy their lots at the nominal price of ten cent a square foot. These tenants are the descendants of the enslaved who were permitted to rent their spots, on condition that they gave their labour to the plantation. The Act, which came into being during the Tom Adams regime, represents the only form of reparations ever made in respect of slavery in Barbados.

On the negative side we had one of the most outrageous assaults on the freedom of the people in the provision of the Barbados Defence Force Act banning the wearing or possession of any camouflage material. This embarrassing piece of legislation was also introduced during the Tom Adams era, ostensibly with the aim of preventing persons from impersonating members of the Barbados Defence Force. It is easily the most irrational, ill-conceived piece of law ever enacted in this country. Can you imagine that someone arriving here from abroad with a toddler dress in material with one square inch of camouflage could find themselves in trouble with the law?

One of our Designers, Rhaj Paul, has undertaken a campaign on Facebook against this stupid law. Says Paul: *"The civilians, from children to adults, who actually use the camouflage pattern in a safe, fashionable, stylistic way that in no way represents impersonation of military personnel, are being treated like criminals. This draconian law itself is a crime against conscience and common sense,"* I endorse his views entirely. Impersonating a member of the security forces is one thing; using camouflage material as a small part of a design is quite another. It takes a paranoid mind to confuse the two.

But the lowest of the low points was unquestionably the unceremonious cutting of funding for university education by the DLP government in 2013. Grappling with the economic melt-down which followed its election to office in 2008, the party founded by the benefactor of universal free education in Barbados, Errol Barrow, simply announced one day that students would have to pay their tuition costs from the following year. In one fell swoop one of the pillars of Barbadian society was partially dismantled – no discussion, no consultation on alternatives, nothing. The University, parents and students were all left scrambling to see how they would deal with this unexpected bombshell deposited in their laps by the Minister of Finance.

Confronted by the dire consequences of his government's rash action, the Minister of Education announced plans for a bursary programme to help students cope with the expense they would now have to bear, only to be rebuffed by the Minister of

Finance, who tells him he has no money for such a programme, and that in future he should refrain from implicating the Ministry of Finance in expenditure without first ascertaining that the necessary funds are available. It was an awful case of administrative bungling, fraught with negative implications for the future of tertiary education in this country. The fall-out was immediate and dramatic. At the end of the university's matriculation exercise in 2014 enrollment had fallen by 34%. The reduction in some faculties was so significant that there was talk of dropping courses and cutting part-time Lecturers.

There was widespread condemnation of the funding cut; but the most biting attack came from no less a person than the Principal of the Cave Hill Campus, Professor Sir Hilary Beckles. He described the move as a catastrophe and said it had set back the campus by 20 years. Beckles lamented that after years of investment from private enterprise and international donors that was used to build a modern state-of-the-art internationally competitive institution, the Cave Hill campus had now suffered a *"tremendous setback"*, returning to mid-1990's enrolment levels. He denounced the cut as an attack on working class women, noting that 75% of the students affected were young women, some with children, who were looking to higher education to improve their lives. The leading Caribbean academic was further concerned that the government's action could lead to what he described as an intellectual recession, as exemplified in what he saw as an existing poverty and looseness of thought in the society.

Of course Beckles knew that in these Caribbean parliamentary democracies you don't criticised anything done by the ruling tribe; but having just been appointed to a more senior post within the regional university system he probably reasoned that he was on safe ground. The response was as predictable as it was caustic. The Prime Minister, a lawyer, himself trained at the U.W.I, flayed Beckles, accusing him of disrespect and *"descending from Mount Olympus"* to preside over an alternative government.

The cut in university funding was not only an assault on a major plank of social policy, it was a betrayal of a pledge the ruling party, itself, made to the Barbadian electorate previous to the 2012 election. The party gave the assurance that despite the increase in costs, university education would remain free to Barbadians. A spokesman for the party said the DLP would meet "*every possible commitment*" to Barbadians attending the UWI. He added: "*There is no person or institution or political party in this country that can challenge or contradict the absolute commitment of the Democratic Labour Party to public education in this country*".

An educated population is the springboard for the advancement of a country. Errol Barrow knew this – the visionary that he was – and in 1962 he abolished tuition fees which were still being charged by public secondary schools. He wanted to ensure that the sons and daughters of Agricultural Workers, Maids and Gardeners had an equal chance at education. Until recently, successive governments have managed to maintain that concession. It is a measure of how far removed they are from his thinking that those who took over the party he founded could so cold-bloodedly attack this pillar of his legacy.

In these parts, some of those who offer themselves for public office may be as motivated by the desire to serve, as they are by the temptation to profit from the flesh of the fatted calf. When it comes to securing their well-being and that of their families into the future, our political office holders are not at all hesitant. We've only got to take a look at the generous separation packages these '*servants of the people*' have sat down and voted themselves. Barbadians were shocked recently when the amazing details of these packages were publicised in the Press by one of our Trade unionists and social activists, Caswell Franklyn. Franklyn, who's the founder of the recently launched Unity Trade Union, has been a fearless campaigner against the many social infelicities in the Public Service and government.

In an exposé, published in the Press on June 29, 2014, Franklyn demonstrated in indisputable terms the shameless actions of politicians over the years in feathering their own nests, while depriving ordinary Barbadians of the little benefits they enjoyed. Following is an edited version of that article:

On March 1, 1969, a piece of legislation, entitled the **Retiring Allowances (Legislative Service) Act**, came into force. It was quickly followed on March 27 by the **Pensions (Prime Minister) Act**. Those two acts have put in place a regime which ensures that former parliamentarians, who qualify for pensions, would be set for life. Ordinarily M.Ps qualify, at age 50 years, for a pension after a minimum of eight years' service. The original legislation made them pensionable at age 55, but a 1989 amendment reduced the qualifying age to 50.

I must point out that the eight-year minimum and the age restriction do not apply to the Prime Minister. The holder of that office qualifies for a pension of two-thirds of his salary in less than an hour. Section 3 (1) of the **Pensions (Prime Minister) Act** states, in part:

"Every person who, having been appointed Prime Minister on or after the 30th November 1966, ceases at anytime after such appointment to be Prime Minister shall be paid a pension under this act with effect from the date on which he ceases to be Prime Minister."

Put simply, a person who demits office at any time after being appointed P.M is immediately pensionable and becomes entitled to receive a pension of two-thirds of the highest annual rate of salary. At current rates, a former PM would be entitled to a pension of $11 287.53 per month. However, if he opts for a gratuity and a reduced pension, he would be entitled to receive a tax free gratuity of $423 282.50 and a reduced pension of $8 465.65 per month. (Wow! Imagine getting a pension of eleven thousand dollars after holding the job for one hour! Doesn't get any better than that).

After the politicians effectively set themselves up for life in 1969, they went about systematically dismantling the pension entitlements of most other public servants. They started with the most vulnerable by amending the **Casual Employees Pensions Act** to prevent persons who became casual employees after July 1971 from receiving *a pension. Hereafter, they were required to rely on National Insurance or make private arrangements for any additional benefits that they may require.*

Also, the retirement age for casual employees was increased from 60 to 65 years, with a provision that existing employees could opt to retire at the later time on condition that service after the workers' 60th birthday would not be taken into account in computing their pensions. After dealing that knockout blow to casual employees, the next assault on the pension entitlements of public workers came in 1975. Government amended the various pensions acts so that workers entering public service employment after September 1, 1975 would continue to be pensionable but that their Government pensions would be reduced by the amount that they receive from NIS (National Insurance Scheme). In essence, the people at the bottom of the public sector pay scales would no longer get a pension from the Treasury. And to strengthen my point about being elitist and self-serving, that reduction did not apply to MP's, Judges and the Governor-General....

In 1978, the Tom Adams administration abolished the contributory pensions that would have benefited the widows and children of deceased public officers, on the basis that NIS made provisions for survivors' pensions. However, in 1985 Tom Adams died, and it was discovered that there was no provision for a widows and children's pension in the **Pensions (Prime Minister) Act**. *Rather than send his widow to NIS, as Adams had done to other public servants, his former colleagues introduced legislation to provide a non-contributory pension for the PM's widow and children and gave it retroactive effect. Mind you, the then DLP Opposition supported the bill.*

This apparent conflict of interest was at its most blatant when our honourable parliamentarians voted themselves a ten percent increase in parliamentary salaries in 1991, ahead of an eight percent cut in the salaries of public workers and parliamentarians, as the country grappled with a difficult economy. In effect, when government workers are taking home eight percent less salary, parliamentarians were taking home two percent more.

The obvious conflict of interest in legislators voting salaries and benefits for themselves, which the Barbadian parliamentarians appear not to recognise, is taken care of in other countries by the appointment of special committees to advise on parliamentary salaries and allowances. In Britain, there is the Independent Parliamentary Standards Authority which not only sets MP's salaries but establishes and monitors expenses for Members of the House of Commons.

In Australia, there is the Salaries and Allowances Tribunal which has responsibility for both determining and recommending rates of remuneration for the Governor, Members of Parliament, Judges, Magistrates and other top state functionaries. New Zealand has a Remuneration Authority for the same purpose; and closer to home there's the Salaries Review Commission in Trinidad & Tobago and the Parliamentary Salaries Review Committee in Jamaica. It is patently unacceptable that our legislators should have the power to set their own terms and conditions of service in the outrageous terms described by Mr. Franklyn.

We've settled down to government by two alternating political parties: Grantley Adams's Barbados Labour Party and Errol Barrow's Democratic Labour Party. So what is the distinction between these two political parties? Why should we choose one over the other? The truth is that they are both chips off the same block; the Democratic Labour Party originated as a break-away faction of the Barbados Labour Party back in 1955. The Barbadian electorate has no real philosophical choice between the two of them. They are both centrist parties, committed to a mixed economy and the preservation of the traditional Barbadian way of life, with a strong aversion to change, especially change that threatens any aspect of the island's colonial legacy. They win and lose elections based, not on principles of governance, but on personality and the mood of the electorate at the time. Indeed, so philosophically homogenous they are that MP's elected on one party's ticket have been known to cross the floor to join the other party. The classic case of this floor-crossing is that of the MP who went back and forth from party to party. If the party to which he was affiliated did not form the government he would simply cross over to the other side. If there is any difference, it is that the Barbados Labour Party has shown itself to be a better manager of the economy and the state as a whole than the DLP after Errol Barrow.

Generally, after three terms the people are ready for a change. That change is decided by a minority of voters outside of the two major political tribes whose voting patterns cross party boundaries. But it is simply amazing that you would have people unswervingly committed to these parties, who cannot tell you what are the core values and principles of the parties. They've never had a political philosophy nor principle in their life, except the principle that whenever an election is called their party is the one for which they should vote. For them, it is enough to put on party colours and wave their banners from the bandwagon at election time. The one redeeming factor in all of this is that we have kept political party rivalry within non-violent limits, unlike what has happened elsewhere in the Caribbean, where election violence – including murder – has been known to occur.

But perhaps the most pernicious factor in the practice of political tribalism in these islands is the nepotism and victimisation practised by those holding the reigns of office. It is a given that operatives of the ruling party will use their positions of power to secure jobs in the public service and state corporations for supporters of the party holding office, members of their family or friends; and sometimes to block the hiring of those from the other side. In extreme cases persons from the opposing party who are already in positions may be dismissed or be denied a renewal of contract.

The blatancy with which this sometimes occurs can be shocking, even to those of us familiar with the culture. In some cases people are placed in positions for which they are clearly unqualified and for which they have absolutely no previous experience.

This partisan recruitment is at its worst in the periods leading up to an election, when statutory corporations and other public agencies could find their payrolls bloated with potential voters. In one notorious case involving a shameless betrayal of trust, the payroll of a statutory corporation was packed with scores of workers leading up to a general election; the ruling party campaigned on the promise that it would not lay off public workers despite a major depression in the economy – in fact a senior member of the party was most emphatic in his assurance of this:

"So all those people out there who are holding on to a job, the difference between you having that job and you not having that job is (the Democratic Labour Party) winning the next Government..." Well, that was on the election platform. The electorate, in their infinite wisdom, returned the party to office, and the following year three thousand public workers were sent home.

Those of you who are horrified at the impropriety of all this might be better able to put it in its true perspective when you understand that Barbados, for all its much touted history of parliamentary, Westminster governance, has no laws governing integrity, transparency, accountability nor conflict of interest. The politician with power in Barbados is as free and unfettered in the distribution of largesse as the king in his kingdom. This fact must have been foremost in the mind of one of our political leaders when he made what is now known as *'the fatted calf'* speech at a party conference, just before a general election.

"We have learnt our lesson as a party. The fatted calf...will be slaughtered and shared among those of you who have stood this course. The fatted calf will be slaughtered and shared among those of you who have fought the battles and who would have won for us a glorious victory at the polls."

Well, you couldn't want it clearer: the fatted calf – i.e the resources of the state – will be used to reward those who helped the party to victory. Many years before that a member of parliament from the opposing party then in control of the fatted calf, spoke in a similar vein, declaring on the floor of parliament that even anyone with a name bearing the initials of the opposing party, would starve (while his party held the political reigns). Admittedly, it was an angry outburst from a particularly rambunctious politician, but at least the notion of a fatted calf must have been an idea in his head when he spoke.

Not surprising, then, that Barbadians – especially those working in the government service – are highly guarded about their political allegiances. They know only too well that sometimes the small-minded tribal zealots who wield power can cause damage to their livelihood. No one knows this better than Cecil Foster, the now Canadian-resident Barbadian author, who was forced to leave Barbados in the late 1970's under the then Tom Adams government.

Tom Adams

Adams, who was Prime Minister from 1976 to 1985, was easily the most vindictive of Barbadian leaders, and – not surprisingly – the most despised. He was notorious for his victimization of those who crossed his political paths and also had a reputation as an abuser of women. As a young Reporter with the Barbados Advocate newspaper in the late seventies, Cecil Foster, would have done just that. And having committed the unpardonable sin, Foster soon realized that his employment prospects in Barbados were suddenly curtailed.

Cecil Foster

He migrated to Canada where he became a successful author and university Professor. Foster's story is replicated in the experiences of Adrian Sisnett and Mohammed Saied, both Reporters at the state-owned Caribbean Broadcasting Corporation in the 1980's. Their sins were the same: the stories that flowed from their Journalistic pens offended Caesar. One day they were summoned to the Manager's office consecutively and handed dismissal letters. Then there was the case of the Guyanese-born Journalist, Rickey Singh, resident and working in Barbados at the time of the United States invasion of Grenada in 1983.

Rickey Singh

Singh was almost singular in his opposition to the invasion, which was orchestrated by Adams and the late Prime Minister of Dominica, Eugenia Charles. His principled stance may have earned him the respect of many, but it caused great offence to Adams, who lost no time in having Singh's work permit revoked. Foster, Sisnett, Saied and Singh – four cases of which I know, but undoubtedly there are others, innocent victims of an immature politician, intoxicated with political power.

His death, in 1985, allegedly of a heart attack, brought joy to the hearts of many. Fate had finally ridden them of the great serpent. The story is told of the woman who called the radio talk show host and proceeded in a very calm voice to lavish praise on how well the funeral ceremony had turned out, only to shock the host with the words: " *there's only one thing: it should-a* (should have) *happen' ten years ago*".

Another story talks about the elderly man with a bent posture who went to view the body. With hands clasped behind his bent back he peered into the casket bearing Adams and walked away with the words: "*I only come to make sure de bitch dead in truth*". These comic diversions ought not to distract us from the fundamental point in all of this: that here we have a political system that is not hesitant to flaunt its adherence to Westminster parliamentary democracy, with all of the history and respectability that come with that, but which in practice can function more like a tyranny, apparently with the full blessing of the society.

For in none of the cases of victimization I mentioned do I recall a word of protest from any branch of civil society – the Church, Unions, Press, NGO's – all silent. Westminster parliamentary democracy for us, then, must not be confused with what may obtain in Britain and elsewhere. Our leaders wear the same wintry garb as their English counterparts, follow the same parliamentary procedures and attend the same Commonwealth conferences, at which they speak the same rhetoric, but if we look beneath his robes we would find that the Emperor is stark naked.

The Bajan at Heart

The warmth and colour of the tropical Caribbean finds a perfect match in the personality of Barbadians, easily among the most affable people anywhere. It's a match that has redounded to the benefit of the island's all important tourism industry. The thousands who visit our shores, mostly to seek refuge from the ice of the northern winters, experience the tanning rays of the sun, the cooling breezes of the trade winds and the blue waters of the Atlantic Ocean, but will almost invariably speak of the friendliness of the people.

There is a certain openness in the personality of Caribbean people – though I suspect some of the friendliness of which visitors speak may have to do more with a certain awe with which black Barbadians regard white people. If you want to see a black Barbadian in his element (speaking very generally here) watch him as he entertains his white tourist friend in the local rum shop with his Barbadian friends present. The only thing his exuberance will not permit him to do is jump over the moon. I once watched in amazement as a local fellow tried to help two white male shoppers find a product in the supermarket. The two shoppers had apparently asked him where they could find the product. Well, he not only helped them, but the eagerness and anxiety with which he did so must have left them spell-bound.

Whatever his motivation, the friendly *Bajan* is definitely a fillip to the Barbadian visitor experience, a fact borne out by the many compliments from visitors to the island. It is a trait with historical links to the African continent. Barbadians who visit west Africa are often struck by the similarities in the culture and demeanour of the people. We may not be aware of it, but the soul of Africa, transported across the Atlantic with our fore-parents, is as alive today in Barbados as it is on the continent.

The best representation of the Barbadian spirit can be found mostly – but not exclusively – in the village life of rural Barbadians. When I was growing up in the eastern parish of St. John there was a community spirit and neighbourliness we took for granted. We knew everyone in the district by name; we played together, visited our neighbours' homes and shared food. People greeted each other with a warm (Good) "*Morning*" or "*Hello*" whether you knew the other person or not. In more distant times, those who didn't have refrigerators nor telephones would go to the homes of those who had to ask for some ice or a telephone call. It was an exemplification of the brotherly love which Jesus Christ admonished us to have for our neighbours, and it came from the Barbadian soul.

You can imagine the shock when people left our shores and migrated to England to find that, not only did neighbours not know one-another, but would actually pass one another without so much as a grunt. To the Barbadian that was the height of impoliteness – or "*un-mannerliness*" as it is deemed here.

Conversely, the British visitor to the island may be taken aback at the infrequency in the use of phrases like "*please*" and "*thank you*". Many Barbadians, without the slightest intention of being rude or impolite, will often omit them from their average interaction with one-another, while accepting them from others.

I know this claim will raise the ire of Teachers and aficionados of etiquette, but it is a cultural trait which cannot be denied. Barbados does have a culture – contrary to what some Barbadians believe – and that culture carries with it its own form of etiquette.

The notion some have that you can send someone to Switzerland to bring back a code of etiquette for the Caribbean is fundamentally flawed, for the very reason that you are dealing with two almost totally different cultures. An elderly Barbadian woman wanting help with a heavy basket may turn to a young man and say "*Gih muh a lift wid this basket here, son*" (*Give me a lift with this basket here, son*). The young man helps her lift the basket to her head and when it's settled she simply says *"alright"* or *"good"*, and they both go on their merry way. Notice the complete absence of *"please"* or *"thank you"* in that exchange, and yet the young man does not feel offended. He's not offended because he recognised the *"please"* and the *"thank you"* in her tone. Good manners are often communicated in tone and behaviour; they are not limited to words.

There is also an understanding in closely-knit societies like ours that the granting of simple favours is not governed by formalities. I daresay in Switzerland it might very well be unthinkable to ask a total stranger to help you lift a basket. Maybe because Switzerland is in Europe and Barbados in the Caribbean, two different societies. This softness on formalities is not peculiar to us; it also exists in other parts of the world, India, Denmark, Holland and the Philippines. My research tells me that in India you might actually offend a close associate by using words like *"please"* and *"thank you"*. The thinking is *'why are you treating me like a stranger?'* This openness and lack of formality in social relations can work to your advantage sometimes. A Barbadian will not see you in danger and do nothing, whereas our American and European counterparts believe they should mind their own business.

I recall standing in a line at a public place and feeling someone touching my collar. When I looked around it was the person behind me brushing an insect from my collar. She did it without even thinking she needed to notify me in advance. She knew I would be grateful for the gesture once she told me about it afterwards. These are valuable cultural traits we should preserve at all costs. But modernisation and development often cause us to lose some of our traditional moorings, and in Barbados some of the neighbourliness of the past has been lost. It is not uncommon for residents of some of the more recent housing areas – referred to disparagingly as the *"heights* and the *terraces"* – to know their neighbours only by the registration numbers of their vehicles. The mostly middle and upper income inhabitants of these neighbourhoods have resorted to an importation called The Neighbourhood Watch to achieve what naturally obtains in traditional Barbadian villages, where people will keep an eye on the home of an absent neighbour even without being asked – yes, another case of us looking for leadership from abroad.

The friendly, out-going Barbadian personality described earlier can easily mask what really is an ultra conservative – I'm tempted to say closed-minded person. Yes, the two personalities may seem to be at odds; but truthfully, Barbadians are probably among the most conservative, unadventurous people in the world. We do not venture too far from comfort zones. Outside of inter-personal relations, there's an aversion to newness and openness that can be quite resolute. It is, perhaps, symptomatic of this closed-mindedness that in the heat of the tropical Caribbean many Barbadians would keep the windows to their homes closed or just slightly open, even during the day. You would expect, with weather like ours, that everyone would want to have open windows letting in the cooling, tropical breezes. In fact, the opposite is true. If you happen to see a home with all the windows open, chances are it's occupied by non-Barbadians.

Barbados is, after all, the place where a Minister of government boldly declared he would not support gender neutral legislation against domestic violence. Apparently motivated by homophobia, this Minister said he would resign before voting in favour of the legislation, which would protect same-gender couples from violence. How can a legislator tacitly support violence against the person simply because he has a phobia against same-gender relationships and fears the law might apply in such relationships? This is the kind of closed-mindedness of which I speak – although I suspect this example is somewhat of an extreme one.

It is my view that this comfort with the status quo and aversion to change has retarded our advancement as a nation in many different areas. It is the reason why our economy is on the verge of collapse right now for lack of reform; why our judicial system is now bottle-necked, with some cases taking up to seven years before judgement. It is certainly the reason why we remain in the embarrassing constitutional rut in which, as a sovereign state, our leaders must pledge allegiance to a head of state residing at

Buckingham Palace in London, *"her heirs and successors"*. This discomfort with change and openness is as Barbadian as flying fish and coo-coo – the national dish. It is, I suspect, a by-product of the lack of confidence born of our colonial experience.

The Barbadian at heart is also very fascinated with titles and names. This is the place where Ministers of government are referred to by the parliamentary title, *"Honourable"*, even outside of the parliamentary setting where the title really belongs. MC's and other speakers at public functions will invariably refer to Ministers present as *"the Honourable..."* (Ministers around here are very special people even without their titles. There's no social event imbued with greater awe and trembling than one involving a Minister and his Public Service minions).

Academics with doctorates and professorships command their own deference from the general Barbadian populace, who will almost always refer to them as *"Doctor"* or *"Professor"*, even in casual contexts that have nothing to do with their professional disciplines. I could never understand why someone's academic achievements should impose on the rest of us an obligation on how we address them. The purpose of higher education should be to enable us to contribute to meeting the varied needs of the society, rather than to place ourselves on top of a pedestal to be worshipped by lesser mortals. This quest for specialness appears to be particularly rampant among church Pastors, who will appear one morning as *"the Reverend, Doctor"* so-and-so, without the slightest indication as to the source of this new title and the process through which it was acquired. In recent years we've seen a number of these overnight doctors flaunting their new found titles on an all too unsuspecting public. We'd never suggest that they are all suspect; some have, indeed, gone through the rigours of academic study, but others – I make bold to say the jury is still out. Certainly, the paucity of the thoughts emanating from some of these goodly 'Reverend Doctors' are not representative of minds that have gone through the rigours of higher education.

But what a blatant repudiation of the example set by the Master, Jesus, himself, who denounced all the trappings of the social elites of his day. He dressed like the ordinary man; associated with working-class people and went so far as to advise his followers not to address anyone by lofty titles like '*Rabbi*' (Matthew 23:9). Were he with us today I have no doubt he would view all of the titles and other accoutrements with which our academic and religious leaders adorn themselves in a similar light. Jesus was very much about the fruits of the heart; he taught us that our specialness should lie in the virtues of love, justice, humility and purity of life which he exemplified and taught his followers, rather than in the adornment of titles and grand attire. He would definitely ruffle many feathers among the title-hungry class in Barbados if he were around today.

I am a big fan of clause 8 of section 9, Article 1 of the United States constitution.

To quote: "*No title of nobility shall be granted by the United States; and no person holding any Office of profit or trust under them, shall, without the consent of the Congress, accept of any present, emolument, office, or title, of any kind whatever, from any King, Prince, or foreign state.*" So, in effect, all citizens of the United States are of equal status: no Dames, no Knights, no OBE's, no CBE's. Classism, born of titles of nobility and academia, is like racism: both are rooted in the notion of superiority and inferiority of people.

This obsession with status and titles is also reflected in the names we give things and the things to which we give names. There is an institution in Barbados for training in the Arts, named after the late Prime Minister and national hero, Errol Barrow. They could have called it the Errol Barrow Arts Centre or the Barrow Centre for the Arts – anything that rolls off the tongue. They named it *The Errol Barrow Centre for Creative Imagination*. Quite a mouthful. Can't help wondering how imagination can be anything but creative, since the use of the imagination to generate ideas is necessarily a creative function.

It was, no doubt, somebody's attempt to be grandiose and official. Not so long ago we used to have Public Relations Officers, and then someone thought this title didn't have enough mystique and complexity; now we have Corporate Communications Specialists. These are different from PR Officers; they '*specialise*' in '*corporate communications*'. Similarly, there used to be a time when people retired; not any more. Academics and other professional socialites are suddenly being awarded the title '*Emeritus*', which is added to their names.

This is the land of names. There is a highway with three different names – yes. One section is called the Tom Adams Highway, the second is the Errol Barrow Highway, and the next is the Hugh Cummins Highway. Its full name is the Adams, Barrow and Cummins Highway, but Barbadians have shortened it to The ABC Highway. This highway has a number of round-abouts which facilitate intersecting traffic, that were all named after the areas in which they were located. But *in* rushed the naming Czar with new names for these round-abouts. They now bear the names of current and former political leaders and our sporting icon, Sir Garfield Sobers. The big problem now is that whereas we all knew where the Kendall Hill and Top Rock Round-abouts were, we now struggle when we hear of the Edwy Talma and Garfield Sobers round-abouts.

This naming frenzy can get quite ridiculous. We even have boardwalks named after people – the Richard Haynes Boardwalk, named after the late former political party leader and Minister of Finance, Sir Richard Haynes and the Lewis and Wickham Boardwalk, named in honour of T.T Lewis and Clennell Wickham. Why would anyone want to attach someone's name to something as pedestrian as a board walk or a round-about?

But it seems the hospitality I spoke of earlier that is so much a signature of the Barbadian character is doing nothing for the island's customer relations reputation, which is said to be on the lower rungs of the ladder. When it comes to the delivery of service, we are just not there – and this pertains to service across the board. It is the mother of all paradoxes that a people with a reputation for friendliness should also be known for poor customer service. The criticisms may range from rudeness, to failure to engage the customer with a sense of urgency, to failure to acknowledge the presence of a prospective customer, to slowness of service. Gosh! We must be the slowest people on the planet Earth. Everything in this country moves at snail pace.

The problem was deemed to be of sufficient national concern to warrant the creation of a unit to put service on a higher plane. The National Initiative for Service Excellence – NISE, as it's called – is a joint venture of the Social Partners, a coalition of the government, the labour movement and the business sector. As part of its efforts to promote service excellence, NISE has been publishing reports from members of the public about their service experiences. The following small sample from those reports gives a clear indication of the crisis we face in the delivery of service in this country:

My co-worker and I had had an early meeting to start off our day and at its conclusion, we really wanted to get some breakfast. While on the road (I was not the one driving) I called a coffee shop to find out if we could still get scrambled eggs and bacon, as it was about 9.50 a.m. **"If it is still here,"** *was the response from the young lady who answered the phone. I said:* **"Pardon me?"** *She repeated* **"If it still here".** *I told her I was not sure what that meant, I was on my way there and I wanted to know if they were still serving breakfast and whether I could make an order for scrambled eggs and bacon. She told me to hold on and came back and asked: "You want fry eggs?" I said: "No* **I am trying to find out if I can get scrambled eggs".** *She told me to hold on, but did not put the phone on hold as I could still hear...She said to another person:* **"You better come and deal with this call."** *Another young lady came on the line and asked: "How may I help you mam?" I said:* **"I am trying to find out if I can get two orders of scrambled eggs and bacon."** *She asked:* **"Two omelettes?"** *I said:* **"No, scrambled eggs."** *She put me on hold. When she came back she explained that I couldn't get scrambled eggs because they were boiling all the eggs they had left. I said:* **"Fine thank you very much".** *All the while this conversation was taking place we were still driving and were nearly there when I got the last set of information. The ironic thing was that there was a sign outside advertis-*

ing a breakfast special, and at no stage, did she explain to me that there was such and what it consisted of, to see if, perhaps, I would have been interested in that instead. Needless to say, my hunger won't take me there as I was not at all impressed.

Today, I went into...to purchase some items, as well as get some advice on computer parts. I was approached by the most willing and the nicest people you could ever want to be around. They assisted and helped me with everything, giving me advice on what to purchase, actually encouraging me to buy items from the display. Then a senior employee came into the store, and all of a sudden the atmosphere of the store changed. It became full of fear. The guy continued to show me the problems and tried to help me, when all of a sudden she said to him, '**What are you doing?**" I found the tone rude. The attendant replied "**I am assisting a customer with purchasing items and showing him how to work them**". She then proceeded to correct him in front of me, which again I took as being rude to him and to me. She then started to come over to me, and to tell me that there is a cost to what he was doing. This is where I got angry. I explained to her that I didn't know how to set it up and therefore would need that advice, but I was told he could only do it at a price. I continued to ask her stuff about the computer which I had no idea about and she told me not to be silly. At this point another customer suggested that I not respond. I could not help reflecting on the service I received, compared to another couple in the store. I consider the service I received was negative and rude.

(**Letter to government office**) I made a call to... to speak to a person who worked there, not realising it was the wrong depot which I had called. The phone was answered by one of your employees. I said: **Good morning, may I speak to**" (the person's name), but rather than *say that I had called the wrong number, the employee sucked his teeth and hung up the phone in my ear. I was astonished by this behaviour, so I immediately redialled the number. The phone was answered by him after four rings. I said to him: "**That is not the right way to do things**." His reply to me was: "**Carry your....you idiot!**" In an era of Public Sector Reform and the National Initiative for Service Excellence, this behaviour does not reflect the vision of Barbados as the ideal place to do business. It proves that some Government employees do not share the Government's vision. People should always be treated with courtesy when calling business places, but he seemed not to be aware of this.*

A couple of weeks ago I was in the supermarket and in front of me was a tourist . When she got to the checkout, the cashier greeted her saying **"Good morning did you find everything you wanted?"** *The cashier chatted with her all the way through and when she was finished told her to have a very nice day. I was next in line and when I got to her, her face never cracked a smile. I said good morning and she looked at me and just carried on checking my items. So I asked her if she was having a hard day and she said* **"No, I just tired".** *I said: "**You had a nice smile for the lady in front of me and in that space of time you are tired**".*

*She replied: "**That is what we are supposed to do**." I said: "**No you are supposed to be nice to everyone; there is a sign in front of you that says how you should greet the customer**." I have lived overseas for a lot of years and I have been back a couple years and I find the attitude towards tourists and white people is one thing and when they come to the Bajans the niceties disappear. I can't figure out why because I figure service is service. I didn't think NISE came in to being to be NISE to tourists. NISE means NISE to everyone you meet.*

The Barbados Water Authority (BWA) turned off the water in Eversley Road, Brittons Hill, St. Michael. I called the BWA to suggest that they should inform the public prior to turning off the water. I spoke with a representative who said he did not know why they did not inform the public. On Monday, July 3, I called the BWA to offer a similar suggestion. I spoke with a clerk who told me she would transfer me to a senior officer. I spoke to the officer who then asked me why I would link him to the BWA. The officer continued by shouting at me and I asked the officer if he was aware that the working public was responsible for paying him and he shouldn't be speaking to me like that. He responded by saying that the working public don't pay him. I told him I would be going to the media with my story and he told me he didn't care if I did.

A little while ago, I had the opportunity to have a mini-vacation. I am a local and the first thought was to go overseas, but then my husband and I decided to pick a hotel here, one that we had never been to before. We chose to visit the **Butterfly Beach Hotel…** *Our short stay at Butterfly was an absolutely pleasant, professional and truly heart-warming experience! As soon as we entered the doors we were greeted at the reception area by a very pleasant lady who took our information and relayed other information to us. While chatting away with her another lady came to welcome us to the Hotel with a sweet smile and two glasses of juice, I looked at my hubby in shock… We have visited some top end hotels and resorts here on the island and never had we been greeted like this or rather treated like this, as if we were tourists! It was a wonderful first impression! The room was immaculately clean also, and even the maids who were cleaning another room were so friendly when we ran into them outside.*

When we left there was a different lady working at reception but she did not disappoint; she was also very,

very pleasant, as well as the staff at the bar/restaurant. I am sorry for sounding repetitive but everyone was truly wonderful. Butterfly Beach Hotel is truly a diamond right here in Barbados! Keep up the wonderful job you're doing. I can't wait to go back again!

Recently my family and I celebrated a family member's birthday at one of the prestigious restaurants in St Lawrence Gap, Christ Church. From the time we entered the main entrance and were seated we were treated well, but it was Malcolm, our waiter, who made the evening complete. He was attentive, and pleasant. He always approached us with a smile, made valuable suggestions with respect to the menu... When we told Malcolm that it was a celebration, the birthday person received a special dessert platter with **'happy birthday'** *drawn on the platter. At the end of the evening, Malcolm wished us a safe journey home, shaking each member's hand. Thank you Malcolm! Keep up the good work. I am not sure if it is appropriate to mention the restaurant's name – if it is, the restaurant was JOSEF's.*

The last two reports – thankfully – give us cause for hope that all is not lost, and it is still possible to get good service in Barbados. (And oh how shocked we are when that happens) Indeed, many people – locals and visitors – do come away from a customer relations experience with positive feelings, but the incidence of negative encounters is far too high.

The great irony in all this is that we are a country whose primary source of foreign exchange is tourism, a service industry. Indeed, all indications from the website of the Grantley Adams Airport, the island's entry point for air passengers, are that many visitors to our country experience this shabby treatment right at the point where they should be receiving a warm welcome to paradise. The following sample of comments from people passing through our airport should be a wake up call for tourism planners in both the government and the industry itself.

Moseh Dunn (United States) Wed. 27 Apr 2011

I am not going back to this island; they are very rude. The people at the airport look down at you as if they are better than you are…I am a Jamaican born, US citizen. When I handed them my US Passport they smiled at me, they looked me up and down then asked some rude question: what was my reason for visiting and I said vacation. Then he asked if I have any Bob Marley. Now you know what he meant by that comment, That means if I have any weed or ganja. Now I am coming from America, never smoke weed in my life or anything and for this officer to say that to you really spoiled my vacation. Please don't go to this country.

MRS V. Braithwaite (UK) Tue, 3 Jan 2012

My travel experience at Grantley Adams Airport was a FANTASTIC experience that I will never forget. From the moment the plane landed, the welcome staff were there on the concourse to greet you. All the airport staff were polite and very helpful, particularly the security staff. They were exceptional. Regarding the Immigration, some of the staff could do with re-training in basic customer care skills. But apart from that, excellent service.
I would recommend it.

Joe Bloggs (UK) Fri, 6 Jan 2012

I flew into Barbados on the 3rd of January 2012, I am married to a Barbadian citizen and have been for nearly 4 years. I waited for nearly an hour and a half to reach the immigration desk as 4 or 5 planes landed at the same time. When reaching the immigration officer I was greeted with pure attitude. My visit was not a vacation but a move to live on the Island with my husband. Upon reading my *immigration card the female officer more or less growled at me that I would have to come with her, she took me to the holding place and told me to sit and wait. I was asked all kind of personal questions about me and my husband, only to be informed that I needed written confirmation from the Chief (who was away on vacation) to enter Barbados, and without this I would have to return to the UK that same day...In complete shock I asked if they would let me see my husband who was waiting outside for me, but they told me I had no time, that my flight was leaving now and I had to go. I then asked for a quick phone call so I could at least let him know I was alright and I got totally ignored. I was escorted back onto my Virgin flight without my luggage and my husband was left outside without knowing what had happened, he was outside for another few hours before finally finding someone who told him I had been sent back to the UK. No proper explanation has been given to me as yet...but as for the Immigration staff they need some serious training in manners and how to deal with the public; they seem to think they are better than everyone else.*

H. Andrews (UK) Wed, 1 Oct 2014

The rudest airport staff in the world. My parents have been visiting Barbados for many years but refuse to return simply due to the airport experience when departing. As we went through security last month my mother was told to 'get them shoes off'. Why is no one taking charge of this? I think the Airport staff need a reminder that they do just work in an airport and they are required to provide a service. I have to go to Barbados with work but would never choose to holiday there.

C Konig (UK)

I just want to say how excellent the staff at the Airport are. My family were all very worried as my daughter was stuck there and couldn't get on a flight as they were all full. The Airport manager put my whole family's mind at ease by finding out that my daughter had got on a flight. I travel to BGI a lot with work and always find the airport staff to be very friendly and helpful.

Cathy (US) Sun, 25 May 2014

I am a Bajan and sadly what most people on this site are stating is correct. When I come home I find the agents to be rude. I have a hyphenated last name and the last time there a customs agent pointed out to me that it was not necessary to have one and that the dates on my American passport was backwards because Americans do everything...backwards. My last name is none of his business. Anytime I come home I am faced with the sour faced, unwelcoming looks on their face. A Caucasian person may get a smile and welcome out of them. What is more embarrassing is that I brag about my country all of the time and a few people who have visited from abroad have mentioned how rude the customs agents and some workers in stores are and that they would not visit Barbados again because of this. How embarrassing. All I can do is hang my head in shame and hope that the authorities take note of these things and make a change....People visiting should not have this type of rudeness as the first impression of my beautiful country.

As a Barbadian, I am deeply disturbed by some of the comments here. I was especially galled at the experience of Mrs. Joe Bloggs from the UK, who was repatriated because the Chief Immigration Officer was on vacation! (So why didn't they close down the place until he got back, since no one can act for him?) This woman was not even allowed to speak to her husband before they packed her on a plane back to England. How terribly insensitive! For as long as we have people with these experiences at our airport we will continue to see declines in our tourism business.

Of course, the reviews are not all bad, but it's the bad ones that can do damage to our economy. When confronted with negative comments about their country from outsiders some Barbadians lash out in angry defence, sometimes trying to shoot the messenger. But when all the huffing and puffing is done, the stark reality will remain that what we get in the delivery of service in this country is often way below an acceptable standard; and those who manage the industry need to act decisively to arrest this problem.

But perhaps the last place you would expect to experience these negative encounters is in an institution called the Public Service, the various departments of government established to service the needs of the public and do the government's business. The short-comings of this entity are legendary among Barbadians – slowness of service and a chronic disrespect for the very people it was established to serve. This institution is a hang-over from colonial times, with operating procedures and customs that render it more like an albatross around the neck of the nation than a mechanism for responding to the needs of the people. Like everything else left by the British, it has never undergone any meaningful reform over the years, and today it lumbers on – an "*army of occupation*", as the late Prime Minister Errol Barrow, once described it – with all of the expedition of an elephant in labour. Everybody in Barbados knows that if you have business with any degree of urgency about it, the public service is not the place to go. Simple transactions that can be accomplished in a couple of days might well take you several weeks, as letters and files gather moss on the various desks through which they must pass before a decision is made.

Letters to heads of departments from members of the public with concerns are not answered; telephone calls are not returned. I once had some queries about my income tax returns and thought I could write to the head of the income tax office – not once but twice. To this day I have not received a reply to any of the letters. On another occasion I had cause to write to the Permanent Secretary in the Ministry of Finance. Again: denied the courtesy of a response. There is a very real notion among the administrative officials of this institution called the Public Service that they are a cut above the average citizen, and in fact should not condescend to deal with these lesser mortals.

This behaviour is perhaps also symptomatic of a certain lethargy in the Barbadian persona – what visitors euphemistically refer to as our "*laid back*" style. It'll only take you a trip on one of the state-owned buses to recognise this sloth. The simple routine of stopping and collecting a passenger can sometimes become a major production, particularly when the passenger is an elderly person. The bus will come to a halt, the passenger gets in, inserts the fare into the fare box or shows a pensioner's ID, and then, very often, the Driver will wait until the passenger walks half the length of the bus – or perhaps the entire length – and take his/her seat before moving off.

Disembarking is equally laborious: a passenger will ring the bell, and remain seated until the bus virtually comes to a halt before rising – very often, then, using the entrance as the exit, causing further delay if persons are boarding the bus. In all of this the Driver remains stoically silent. Not at all suggesting that we should not be patient with elderly persons who are clearly debilitated, or disabled persons, but the patience exhibited by Drivers to abled-bodied folks often seems overly generous. I can't help but compare it with the sense of urgency I noticed when I travelled on the London buses many years ago.

The buses lost no time picking up passengers, young and old. As soon as passengers embarked – including the elderly – they reached for the hand rails for stability and the bus was gone. The letting off of passengers was done with equal expedition: those disembarking would rise from their seats well before the bus stopped and were ready by the exit to dismount once it came to a halt. Everyone boarded by the entrance and dismounted by the exit.

To this national lethargy I spoke of earlier we might add a certain low-mindedness, as Barbadians would call it – a tendency to be content with the lowest common denominator: not to aim for the best, even when the best is affordable. One of the best exemplars of this is the Ministry of Transport and Works (MTW), the government agency responsible for road maintenance and drainage, among other things. (Perhaps I should point out that these ministerial departments are headed by a minister of government who's responsible for overseeing the business of the department). Everybody knows that whenever we have even a moderate down-pour in Barbados, swimming pools form on our roads, retarding the flow of traffic and putting pedestrians at risk of being splashed. It's as if nobody in the MTW had ever heard the word *'drainage'* before. The problem of drainage in this country is horrendous.

One of the most glaring examples of this problem has been permitted by the authorities to continue for several years now outside a shopping mall, in a suburban commercial area known as Sheraton. A very large pool of water, almost covering the entire road, settles there each time there's a down-pour, impeding traffic flow as vehicles swerve to avoid driving through the pool. The solution? It's probably as simple as digging an extra well or cleaning the existing one, or both. Whatever it may be, the MTW has clearly decided that this is a nuisance with which the taxpaying people of Barbados and the thousands of visitors who make our tourism industry can put up indefinitely.

But when the department does decide to act, the process can sometimes take forever. It is not unusual for repairs to a short stretch of road – say about a half a mile – to take years to be completed. I've been told that in other countries repairs will start one evening and by the next evening half the job is done. Perhaps the comparison is not a fair one; but it is certainly unacceptable for repairs to a half mile of road to take up to four years to be completed, as the stretch of road from Deighton Griffith School to Gall Hill appeared to have taken.

Putting up with public nuisances caused by lethargic government agencies is something to which the people of Barbados have grown accustomed over the years. Ever so often you'll get an eruption of popular indignation in the national arena, but it is usually a nine-day wonder, after which life returns to normal.

A typical example of this is the serious anti-social behaviour of a set of drivers on public transport vehicles known as mini buses and ZR's (registration code) who've been creating havoc on our roads for the last couple decades. These drivers are virtually a law unto themselves, literally doing as they please on the roads. In Barbados these days a long line of slow-moving traffic does not necessarily mean you are in rush-hour traffic; it might simply be that one of these drivers is at the head of the line scouting for passengers or "*killing time*" and driving at ten kilometres per hour, totally unmindful of the inconvenience he's causing all the other motorists behind him.

They flagrantly violate road traffic laws – stopping any and everywhere; they drive recklessly, maiming and killing; they disregard the dress code for operators of public service vehicles; they simply do as they please, if not with the blessing, then surely with the apathy of transport and law enforcement authorities who, up to now, have been unable to reign them in.

The authorities are displaying a similar indifference towards other transgressions of law and public nuisances. It has become a popular pastime in this country for young motor-cyclists to cavort up and down the roads doing dare-devil stunts on cycles which either have no silencers or ones that are modified to shatter our ear-drums with the noise they produce. The Road Traffic Act mandates that motor cycles have silencers.

You are walking along a street and suddenly you hear a deafening roar followed by one of these cyclists zooming past you with one wheel in the air. The noise is so unbearable you instinctively stick your fingers into your ears. Or on a quiet Sunday afternoon the peace of a neighbourhood will be shattered by the deafening sound of one or more of these cyclists riding recklessly up and down. Where else in the civilized world would these nuisances be permitted such free reign?

The traffic laws also prohibit parking on public roads, unless parking permission is indicated, yet throughout the country, vehicle owners routinely use the roads as parking bays. In fact, in some instances a Motor Mechanic will set up his business beside the road, with a series of parked vehicles impeding the flow of traffic. In other countries illegally parked vehicles are towed away; in Barbados this remedy is yet to be discovered. Citizens have complained ad nauseam about these nuisances, and the authorities have simply sat with their arms folded.

Anarchy is a state in which the rule of law is replaced by freedom to act without consequences. The indifference being displayed by authorities in Barbados to these and other infractions of the law places us on the borders of anarchy.

We've coined the phrase *"life in the tropics"* to make light of our lethargic and permissive modus operandi, but increasingly, it's being recognised that this attitude may be retarding the country's economic progress; and no less a person than the island's Minister of Finance is among those voicing concern. The Minister bemoaned the lethargy and low level of productivity in the workforce and warned that this could cause the country to miss out on much needed foreign investment.

We quote him: *"The standards in the high pace environment of the corporate decision making process are shifting upwards at such a rate, that countries such as Barbados stand to lose on impacting and securing top investments, if we cannot raise the quality and speed of our productive output...Several of us in both the private and the public sectors have lamented the general lethargy of our business culture and have all commented and have committed to seeing improvements across sectors. I am afraid however, that this might not be enough."*

Well, we might not only be missing out on foreign investment, but according to a former President of the Barbados Chamber of Industry and Commerce, we're losing out on exports because of tardiness. Business leader, Andy Armstrong, says slowness in reforming our laws is hampering exports to the European Union and North America. Let's add to these voices that of no less a person than Nicole Laframboise, the head of an

International Monetary Fund Barbados team. She cited delays and other problems at the Bridgetown Port as being disadvantageous to businesses and to the island's tax revenue. *"There are significant problems and delays in that and it's also something that's been cited by the private sector as a major impediment,"* Ms. Laframboise said.

Well, if we needed to be persuaded any further let's hear from tourism executive, Roseanne Myers, General Manager of Atlantis Submarines: *"We have to come to the recognition that the length of time we take to make decisions, not only in the public sector...is probably twice as slow as it needs to be. And you can think about every decision that we have looked at in the last little while in Barbados and how long it takes. We're just too slow. A good decision made a day late is not a good decision. I think that is something in our individual businesses that we have to work on."*

The slow syndrome is probably at its worst manifestation in our judicial system. The wheels of justice in this fair land turn at the speed of molasses, much to the disappointment of litigants and accused persons. It is a matter that engaged the attention of the Caribbean Court of Justice in its judgment in the case of Winton Campbell versus the Attorney General. The Court decried the fact that the trial Judge took three years to deliver his judgement, and that the Barbados Court of Appeal took almost four and a half years on the same matter. The CCJ said such delays deny parties access to justice, and undermine confidence in the administration of justice. It suggested that judgments should normally be delivered within three months – six at the most.

Equally outrageous is the case of indecent assault brought by a woman that dragged on in the courts for more than seven years without a hearing, because of the inability of the Police to produce the file. What kind of banana republic are we living in when something as important as a court file can be lost? This is totally unacceptable, and whoever is accountable should have paid the price for this dereliction of duty. What is particularly distressing about the inefficiency and incompetence of the system is that it is largely the poor and underprivileged who suffer the most – people like the elderly man who drew his plight to the attention of the nation via a radio call-in programme. He was injured and incapacitated in an accident in 1988 and attended court 74 times without a hearing. What an awful travesty of justice.

The delays and other inefficiencies of the justice system have not escaped the eye of the Roman Catholic Bishop of Bridgetown. Delivering the sermon at a religious ceremony marking the start of the 2013 – 2014 judicial year, Bishop Jason Gordon lamented the poor state of our justice system. Before an audience comprising the Governor-general, the Queen's representative in Barbados; the Chief Justice and the Attorney general, Gordon declared: "*After 46 years of Independence, when we have the administration of the nation and justice in our hands, in a country where we believe in the rule of law, we have reached this untenable position where the legal system is plagued by reports of lawyer misconduct, poor administration within the registry, including files being lost, delays in the administration of justice, with thousands of cases reportedly being outstanding,*"

The Roman Catholic cleric deplored the denial of justice and violations of human rights incurred when judicial decisions are not handed down in a timely manner, and when persons remain on remand for extended periods of time.

"*It sounds to me,*" he said, "*as if...Mr. McGuffey* (his metaphor for the powers that be*) is large and in charge, not just in the leaders, but at every level of the legal system. This system is not working to bring Lady Harmony* (justice*) to our people...It is tired and needs innovation. Your core business is the restoration of Lady Harmony. Everything you do, must serve this end.*" And to that we can only say "*Amen!*" I daresay Mr. McGuffey has never heard such frank and pointed comments from a member of the Cloth. He (Bishop Gordon) may very well have ruffled a few feathers. I wait to see how many more such functions he will be invited to address.

A functional justice system is one of the cornerstones of a modern, civilized society. It is nothing short of a national scandal that aggrieved persons who turn to the Courts to seek redress should have to lumber through a system for seven and more years before they can have a judgment. Those charged with the duty of administering the system need to rise from the comfort of their cloistered quarters, dash their gowns aside and apply themselves to the task of bringing justice to the people.

Environmentally Unfriendly

The word *'Caribbean'* is loaded with imagery of brilliant sunshine, white sandy beaches, blue skies and refreshing breezes. For many who live in colder climes, a vacation in the Caribbean is an exotic experience of utopian dimensions. To them, it is *'the life'* to sit on a beach, caressed by the surf of the blue ocean, sipping a rum cocktail; or to watch as the golden rays of a tropical sunset slither through the dancing blades of coconut palms. Add to that the endearing smiles of a few black *'natives'* and you are in heaven.

A figment of the imagination, you say? Well, not quite. In fact many visitors to Barbados do have just that experience, natives and all. Kissed by the elements and charmed by the warmth of its people, the Caribbean offers the visitor an experience that is both refreshing and therapeutic, and Barbados has a long reputation in this regard. The enchanting qualities of the island's coastal environment are legendary, good, not only for recreation, but according to historical literature, for your health. In his book, **History of Barbados**, the 19th. century, German-born, British explorer, Robert Schomburgk, had this to say about the therapeutic properties of Barbados:

> *"Barbados is justly considered one of the healthiest islands in the West Indian archipelago...tubular consumption is almost unknown; the distressing...fevers which prevail...in some of the adjacent islands, and which sometimes baffle the Physician's skill, are not met with among the natives of Barbados; on the contrary, those who suffer from such causes are advised to resort to Barbados for restoration of their health."*

Schomburgk's view on the salubrious nature of the Barbadian air was confirmed by another 19th. century writer, The Rev. John Moxly, Chaplain of the British military forces in Barbados. Moxly felt strongly that the Barbadian environment was ideal for recuperation, particularly for persons with respiratory illnesses. It was probably this reputation for healing air that influenced the visit of George Washington – who later became the first president of the United States – and his ailing brother in 1751. On the advice of his Doctor, Lawrence Washington, suffering with tuberculosis, visited the island, accompanied by the teenaged George, staying at what is now George Washington House. The house now enjoys the status of a Heritage site, where visitors can experience a re-enactment of an 18th. century dinner with George.

So that well before the dawn of the 20th. century, Barbadians and visitors were taking advantage of the island's environmental charm, facilitated by the establishment of hotels like Atlantis and Edgewater at Bathsheba and the Crane, St. Philip. The Barbados hospitality and tourism industry was effectively born. Those simple origins have led to the development of what is now the island's principal revenue earner and a significant source of employment.

We may have made an industry out of our natural attributes but many Barbadians still live in blissful disharmony with this glorious environment. Small island people are people of the sea. They fish, they swim, they sail; the sea is an integral part of their lives. They certainly are not afflicted with sea phobia, as many Barbadians and other Caribbean people are.

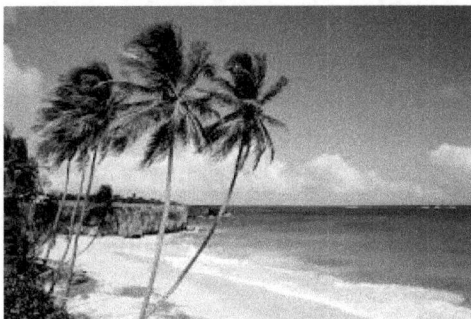

Coconut palms on a Barbadian beach

It is virtually impossible not to see the sea from any point of elevation in Barbados; the big, blue ocean is always there encircling the Barbadian landscape. We literally have no where to run from the sea; and yet if you ask ten Barbadians if they can swim, chances are eight out of them will say '*no*', many of them reciting the national mantra, "*De sea en got nuh back door*" (The sea doesn't have any back door). There is a fear of the sea among Barbadians that is as mysterious as it is unnatural for people living on a small island. It's akin to living on top of a mountain and being afraid of height. I have a sister who has probably never had a sea bath. She has made attempts to do so, but on each occasion once she reaches the beach her fear kicks in and the attempt is abandoned. There's another sister who lives in England but visits quite often. Well, you'd imagine the first thing you'd want to experience, coming from England is a refreshing sea-bath. No: that is never on her agenda.

This disconnect among Barbadians with the glories of the environment is something which the Rev. Moxley observed back in the 19th. century, and which he found quite strange: "*Could but such air, such water, and such natural baths be transported to our English coasts, what multitudes of bathers would enjoy them, while here they are almost unknown and but little availed of.*"

I was always very impressed with the fact that children visiting Barbados from England all had the ability to swim, when we couldn't. Apparently, swimming is an integral part of their school curriculum. I shall put that down to the fact that Britain, having benefited from the proceeds of plantation slavery in the Caribbean, could afford to have swimming pools in schools, whereas we could not. But then, with beaches, in many instances less than half an hour's drive away, we didn't need to have swimming pools in schools. These days we are in an even better position to ensure every Barbadian child knows how to swim, with the existence of The Aquatic Centre, a facility with an Olympic-size swimming poll and a baby pool for children.

Since its construction, scores of Barbadian children and adults have acquired confidence in the water – which is really what being able to swim is, since all animals do float in water.

They have to thank Mr. Maurice Foster whose vision and initiative led to the existence of the Aquatic Centre. The sad truth, though, is that there's still no comprehensive provision in the curriculum of our primary schools for the teaching of swimming. So that out of a population of 280 thousand, a whopping 200 thousand of us (based on my estimation) do not have confidence in water. Anywhere else in the world this would be regarded as a national embarrassment, but in Barbados it fits quite neatly into a general disconnect between the people and their environment, and nobody will bat an eyelash over it. This disaffection also pertains to the use of the sea in other ways – transportation via the sea, for instance, is unheard of in Barbados. With the congestion on our roads being what it is, you would think someone would have seen the economic wisdom of offering a ferry service connecting Speightstown in the north or Oistins in the south with Bridgetown.

A Bermuda ferry

But let's look at little Bermuda. Not only do they have a highly efficient bus service; they also have an efficient ferry service, in which high speed, air conditioned ferries transport locals and visitors between distant points of the archipelago for both pleasure and business purposes.

A similar point can be made for inter-island travel, now retarded by outrageously high air fares. These islands are separated by a couple kilometres of water, yet are largely unconnected by water transport (Among the exceptions, the Bahamas, the Virgin Islands and Trinidad & Tobago). Barbadians, St. Lucians and Vincentians have no access to a ferry service if they want to travel to each other's islands. Elsewhere in the world where island groups exist, sea travel is an integral part of the transport system – the Philippines, Japan and the South Sea Islands.

There's a natural harmony between a people and their environment that seems to elude us. This disunity can sometimes be to our detriment as is so often demonstrated when a tropical hurricane strikes. Situated for the most part in the natural path of most of the Atlantic storms, Barbados and its Caribbean neighbours are extremely vulnerable to a hurricane strike and, in fact, most of the islands have been hit at one time or another. The image of roofless houses, fallen utility poles and flooded neighbourhoods is one with which we are quite familiar. Stands to reason, then, that we must be the most storm-prepared people on the planet.

Surprise! Surprise! We are not. After nearly four centuries of living with storms, we are not prepared in our infra-structure; we are not prepared in our architecture and we are not prepared in our psyche. It baffles me that each year on the approach of the storm season the mass media still finds it necessary to inform householders of the most basic acts of preparation: stock up on canned foods and water; what shelters are available and where; safety precautions in the event of a hurricane. There's very little in our architecture that speaks to the power of hurricane-force winds. Many houses are devoid of hurricane shutters and roof straps. In fact, the roof of choice for many chattel houses is a flat – sometimes overlapping roof. Architects will tell you that the flat roof is more vulnerable to strong winds than the four-hip roof, and when it overlaps it is fair game for a hurricane. No one should be surprised, then, that flying roofs – like fallen utility poles – are so symbolic of Caribbean hurricanes. The question of over land utility poles might be an economic one; underground cabling is recognised to be more expensive to put in place but thus far there seems to be no hurry to implement this, even on a piecemeal basis. For whatever reason Barbados has been able to escape the ravages of hurricanes for a good while now, but the peripheral impact sometimes leaves us with serious flooding.

Our failure to make the connection with the region's status as a storm-proned zone is matched by a similar failure to recognise the economic advantages of the climate in which we live. The economies of Barbados and other Caribbean states are reeling under the burden of energy costs. But while we shell out millions in scarce resources for imported crude oil, sources of natural energy with which we've been blessed by nature go to waste. On an average day Barbados gets about eight to ten hours of sunshine, a huge resource of potential solar energy that largely goes untapped. We have had a solar water heating industry for quite some time now, but the enthusiasm and energy for a greater thrust into solar and other forms of renewable energy that might be expected from a country with our climatic conditions is strangely lacking.

Standing in stark contrast to us is the aggressiveness with which countries in the temperate zone are pursuing the solarisation of their energy supply. Germany, a country that gets no where near the amount of sunshine Barbados does, is at the helm of countries involved in the exploitation of solar energy. The Germans are the world's top installers of photovoltaics (the hardware system that converts solar radiation into electricity) and they are looking to expand production of solar and other forms of renewable energy to 80% of their energy needs by the middle of the century. From just over six percent in 2000 net generation of renewable energy jumped to 30% in 2014. Already, the northern state of Mecklenburg-Vorpommern produces more than 100% of its power needs.

The Australians appear to be equally anxious to tap into the sun's energy-giving potential. Australia is among the leading countries as far as installation of domestic solar systems is concerned, with over one million homes powered by solar energy. And the government is planning incentives to increase that number to two million. Japan and even Britain are among countries looking to the sun for relief from the burdensome cost of fossil fuel and the pollution it causes.

In Barbados we've been regional leaders in the production and use of solar energy for hot water since the 1970's. Statistics for 2009 – the latest available – indicate that there were approximately 50,000 solar water heaters in operation, 75 per cent of them in domestic dwellings. Estimates suggest that the use of these heaters saved the atmosphere from thousands of tons of carbon emissions and, over time, saves the economy hundreds of millions in crude oil imports. Admittedly, we do not have the resources to invest in the technology as do countries like Germany and Australia, but perhaps with the right vision and determination we could have tapped into available sources of funding.

With the astronomical rise in the cost of crude oil and the deleterious impact on the environment and the health of people posed by fossil fuels, importing countries like Barbados have been force to look more towards renewable sources of energy. Under a new Public Sector Smart Energy Programme, twelve government buildings are to be retrofitted with renewable energy and energy efficient technologies, and solar photovoltaic systems installed on all public buildings. Additionally, approximately 25,000 street lights are to be made energy efficient. We were tailor-made for solar energy; we shouldn't be playing catch-up with the rest of the world.

We Culture

So – does Barbados really have a culture? It's a question some Barbadians have asked. Of course, the question doesn't really make sense – at least on the surface of it – since it is impossible to be a people without a culture. Culture is, after-all, a way of life. But the question is not altogether pointless; it has validity on two fronts. In one instance, those who ask it may do so because they genuinely do not recognise what we do and how we do it as *'culture'*. It's like being surrounded by the trees and not being able to recognise that you're in a forest.

Similarly, some say we don't have an accent. St. Lucians have an accent or Jamaicans or Americans, but not we. Because people tend to regard the way they do things as being the *'normal'* way, and the way others do things as being different. Of course, what we don't realize is that other people think exactly the same way about us as we think about them. The question whether we have a culture may also be interpreted as whether we have a culture of our own. There is a notion some have that Barbadian culture is really British culture; that what African culture our foreparents brought with them has been lost.

Nothing could be further from the truth. In fact, while there are definite British imprints, our way of life and national spirit are far more west African in character than British; and this became apparent to me from my first visit to England when I realized that the ethos and mores of the place were quite different from what I knew. The notion, then, of Barbados being a *"Little England"*, as it has been nicknamed, is rooted more in fantasy than fact. This notion is very popular among certain Barbadians anglophiles who would have us believe that everything we have was derived from the British.

We did take some things from Britain, our passion for cricket being one of them. Our adoption of this quintessentially English game produced one of the greatest cricketers of all time, Sir Garfield Sobers. We shall learn more about the cricketing career of Sir Garfield a bit later. Cricket is undoubtedly the national game of Barbados, even though interest in the game has waned in the last few decades. Sir Garfield would have grown up in a Barbados in which cricket was played in every nook and cranny – and even on the beach. As a manifestation of British culture in Barbados it is rivalled only by the Anglican Church.

But the British influence is not the only one shaping the Barbadian cultural landscape. As I mentioned earlier, these days, North American culture can be a powerful magnet for Barbadian and other Caribbean people. It is not unusual to find, in the Caribbean, avid enthusiasts of American country music, complete with boots, hats and studded belts.

Country music is, of course, southern American folk music, very much rooted in southern, white, American culture. Music does have an international appeal – jazz and the Euro classics are two examples that spring to mind. We can also point to Jamaican reggae and to a lesser degree calypso. But it is highly unusual for people from one culture to copy the folk music of another culture and the dress that goes with it. Imagine a group of west Africans, dressed in kilts, playing and dancing to bagpipes – or a group of Texans dressed like Caribbean folk singers doing "*John Belly Ma Ma*". Yes, it would be an oddity. Yet, somehow in the Caribbean we see nothing wrong with copying the intimate cultural art forms of others. In Barbados there are dance companies with some very passionate members who pursue their art with something approximating religious fervour. They are Latin dancers. The choreography, music and dress are unmistakeably Latin, but they embrace them as if they were natural parts of Caribbean culture.

The base of Barbadian culture comes from the African continent. As was mentioned previously, the congenial spirit and sense of community for which we are known is typical of west African society. Every Barbadian who goes there is immediately struck by this and other similarities. African retentions can also be found in our cuisine. The national dish of Barbados, called 'cou cou', is a clear derivative of the west African dish called 'fu-fu', which is also made from corn-meal. Cou-cou (pronounced cuckoo) is made with yellow cornmeal and okra and eaten usually with fish and copious amounts of sauce. The Barbadian conkie, a dumpling, made of grated sweet potato, pumpkin and coconut and steamed in a wrapping of banana leaf is also derived from African cuisine – most likely Ghana, where there is a similar delicacy called 'kenke'. And, of course, like the Africans, Barbadians have traditionally consumed yams, eddoes, sweet potatoes and plantains, although the taste for them among younger members of the society is not as strong as that of the elders.

Barbadian communication – oral and otherwise – also has its share of African influences, some of which we mentioned earlier. We may add to those the dropping of the verb, 'to be' between the subject and predicate of some constructions. Hence in English the sentence: "*the dog is barking*" would be represented in Barbadian dialect as "*the dog barking*". Similarly "*we are having lunch*" would be: "*we having lunch*". This economy with words that is so typical of west African languages also applies to questions. The English practice of inversion is not employed. The Barbadian would say: "*you want a taxi?*" instead of "***do** you want a taxi*", an upward inflection on the word,"*taxi*" making the distinction between the statement and the question.

Outside of grammatical influences there are very few African linguistic retentions. No African languages are spoken – in fact, one of the few African vocabulary retentions is the word "*wunna,*" widely used, almost in its original form, in place of "*you*", second person plural. It comes directly from the word "*unu*" in the language of the Igbo people of Nigeria. It's used interchangeably with "*you all*" – or "*all yuh*", as the Trinidadians would say. Other word retentions are '*warri*' the name of a seed and board game originating in Ghana, once played in Barbados, mostly by older men; and '*susu*', a derivative of the Yoruba '*esusu*'. As in Nigeria, the susu is a rotating savings pool in which participants contribute an agreed sum periodically.

In the area of non-verbal communication, two African re-tentions stand out: the *'suck-teeth'* or *'chupse'* and the *'cut-eye'*. The *'suck-teeth'* is the sound made with a sudden inhalation of air through the mouth with the teeth held close together. It is an expression of anger or frustration. Cutting the eye, practised more by females than males, is a display of contempt or dislike of someone. The victim is given a look of disdain and then, with the eyes closed, the head is turned in the opposite direction – as if to say "*I don't want to see you'*. Very often they are performed simultaneously. It would be considered very rude for a minor to perform either of these acts towards an adult.

But if there's one thing that defines the African spirit in Barbadian and Caribbean people it must surely be the music of the region. The calypso art-form in its various manifestations echoes the drum beat of Africa in a clear and unmistakeable way, imbuing the region with a cultural vibrancy for which we are famous all over the world. There's been a bit of controversy over the origins of calypso in the Caribbean, some crediting Trinidad with taking the lead. In fact, no one Caribbean country can lay claim to originating the music, since it was part of the cultural baggage brought to the region by our African ancestors. So that wherever African people are found in the Caribbean – from Belize in central America to Jamaica and even Guyana – calypso will be found.

It is not readily recognised but Barbadian folk songs like *Millie Gone to Brazil*, *Bromley* and *Pack She Back to She Mah* are all sung in the calypso idiom, as is most of the folk music from the rest of the Anglo-Caribbean. The distinctive rhythm of calypso is caused by what is known as syncopation, the emphasising of a short, normally weak note just before a longer one. Add to this a heavy bass anchor and you have an almost irresistible rhythm. The lyrics, sung mostly in dialect, are normally based on some social event or issue, putting the calypsonian in the role of social commentator.

These commentaries can often be very biting – sometimes too biting for the kind of thin skinned-politicians we have in the Caribbean. Under the regime of the late Tom Adams, some calypsos were banned from broadcast on the government-controlled radio and television station, CBC. They were, for the most part, songs written by the island's foremost calypsonian, Anthony Carter, known by the stage name, The Mighty Gabby. In one of his banned songs, Gabby criticised the establishment of an army in Barbados, asking the question: was it necessary to have so many soldiers in a small country like ours.

Anthony Carter

The song called out Prime Minister Adams for *"buying boots to cover soldier toe"* at a time when unemployment was high and the treasury low. Well, the intolerant Tom would have none of it. CBC was ordered to keep it off the air (Yes, that kind of thing can happen in these islands) Fortunately in more recent times the practice of banning songs has all but disappeared; indeed all of Gabby's music is now played freely on all stations.

The Trinidadian Calypsonian, Historian and Ethno-musicologist, Hollis Liverpool (PhD), locates calypso in the west African practice of court singing by griots (singer/story-teller). Liverpool sees reflections in calypso, of the songs of praise and derision sung by the griots. These include rhythm, the use of call and response in the lyrics, (*the singer calls and a chorus responds*) extemporaneous singing and satire.

Like every aspect of indigenous culture, calypso was regarded, traditionally, with a certain contempt, especially by evangelical Christians, who considered it unworthy of Christian patronage. *"Don't sing nuh (no) banjo in this house"* had become somewhat of a national mantra, representative of those dark days in our history when, as children, we would be reminded of the limits to our enjoyment of this music called calypso. (The word 'banjo' was often used as another name for 'calypso'). This prejudice also extended to radio stations which refrained from playing calypso on Sundays.

In my household a mild form of this bias existed. My parents were members of the Christian Mission; and while they didn't rail against calypso, it was certainly understood that this was not the best kind of music for Christians to listen to. I remember experiencing a disconcerting ambivalence towards the music when I was growing up. On the one hand I am told that this is not good music but on the other when I hear it, it makes me want to dance. I would go to St. John church fair (the parochial Anglican church) and join the crowd of youngsters jumping up to the music; but later on I would feel a sense of guilt. That continued until I came to the awareness that if this music is so irresistible then it couldn't be bad for you. I have enjoyed calypso liberally ever since with the knowledge that this music is no different in moral status from any other music.

It was all tied up in the Eurocentric bias afflicting the society previous to the early 1970's. Up to then we had come to know the arts as Euro-classical piano or violin recitals or – in the case of dance – ballet. The sole counter to this European cultural bias was Elombe Mottley (Baba Elombe Jacuta) the maverick pan Africanist who dared to point a reluctant Barbadian society in the direction of African cultural expression. Elombe established an artistic centre called Yoruba Yard where young people were trained in African dance and drumming. The existence today of African dance companies like Pinelands Creative Workshop, Israel Lovell Foundation and Dancing Africa might well be credited to the seed which he sowed back then.

Elombe was indefatigable in his efforts to wean Barbadians away from their inherited Eurocentric values and instill in them a sense of their African identity and culture. I suspect he ruffled many a feather among the conservative middle and upper classes; but he succeeded in changing the mind-set of many young black Barbadians. I have a strong sense that he was a major influence in my own consciousness and celebration of my African identity.

Elombe Mottley

Not surprisingly, this country has not recognized nor honoured his contribution – far greater, in my view, than those of many of the knights and dames we've had – but in 2011 he was presented with the Clement Payne Award by the Clement Payne Movement for his outstanding contribution to the building of African awareness among Barbadians.

But it was the revival of the Crop Over Festival in 1974 with its annual calypso tents and competitions that elevated the calypso art from the doldrums of popular consciousness. The festival is a modern replica of an ancient celebration marking the end of the sugar cane harvest in the pre-Emancipation times. It was, perhaps, the only high point in the otherwise laborious lives of the enslaved. On the last day of the sugar-cane harvest the plantation overseer would organize a celebration for all parties involved in the harvest. The plantation yard would be decorated with flags, and the Overseer, Book-keeper and workers would all mingle to dance, eat and drink – an early form of rum was the drink of choice on these occasions.

These days Crop Over is more a festival of the arts than a celebration of the harvest. It's revival in 1974 was a strategy by tourism planners to draw more visitors to the island in the slow "*summer*" months. Calypso music is the engine of the festival. It can be heard in the calypso tents (staged performances by calypso-nians at public venues), fetes, the national competitions to choose the top Calypsonians in various categories and, of course, on the day of the grand finale, the street carnival, called Kadooment.

Africa is also very much alive in the Barbadian musical ensemble called the Tuk Band, a group of musicians comprising bass and kettle drum players, a flute or penny-whistle blower and a triangle player. Some believe the Tuk Band has influences from British military music; but the rhythm of the band is very much similar to that of the calypso.

Traditionally, the Tuk Band made its appearance on public holidays, accompanied by any of four masked or costumed characters of west African origins. There is the Mother Sally, a fertility character dressed like a woman with highly exaggerated breasts and buttocks.

Tuk Band

Or you might catch the Stilt-man, known elsewhere in the region as the Moko Jumbie, a character – sometimes masked – dancing on high stilts. *"Moko"* is an African deity and *"jumbie"* is a Caribbean term for *"ghost"*. The Donkey-man and the Shaggy Bear are the other two Tuk Band characters. The Donkey-man is a dancer costumed to look like a donkey. He represents a tribute to the role of the donkey in transportation. The Shaggy-bear is the most enthralling – and for children the most frightening – of the Tuk Band characters.

This masquerader – representing the African witch doctor – comes fully covered in a costume made of dried banana leaves or other plant material. These days the costume is sometimes made of pieces of cloth – somewhat like a rag mat. The distinguishing feature of the Shaggy Bear is his acrobatic movements and facelessness. The costumes, manoeuvres and dance movements of these characters are as entertaining to Barbadians as they are to visitors.

More than three-and-a-half centuries after the traumatic experience of the trans-Atlantic crossing and the ensuing brutality of plantation servitude in the Caribbean, these elements of African culture are alive and well in Barbados, vivid testaments to the enduring bond between the people of west Africa and the people of the Caribbean.

Broadcasting

The crisis we face with the lack of self-confidence and feelings of inferiority was aided in no small measure by the mass media, especially the broadcast media. I take no comfort in saying that, as one who spent the majority of my working life in radio and television; but the stark fact is that for the past eight decades – yes, even up the present, the broadcast media has been feeding Barbadians images and sounds that reinforce the popular belief in the superiority of white, western civilizations. This innocent indoctrination began with the launch of a wired radio service in 1934 bearing the name Radio Distribution (I say 'innocent' because I don't believe it was deliberate).

Its programming was sourced from the BBC and short-wave stations in the United States and Canada. The evolution of the station into Barbados Rediffusion Service Ltd. nearly two decades later in 1951 did little to change the alien character of its programming.

The music was almost totally foreign – American artistes and other "*international*" music stars were standard fare, along with a generous daily serving of Euro-classical music. Of course they did play Caribbean music from time to time. We'd get things like *Caribbean Spotlight* and *West Indian Scene* – cute diversions from the norm into the rhythmic, island music of the '*natives*'.

News from the BBC was a staple – at least six servings a day, starting at seven in the morning. And British comedies like *The Clitheroe Kid*, *My Word* and *Just a Minute* entertained us. For lovers of soap operas there were *Portia Faces Life*, *Dr. Paul*, *Mary Lane* and *Second Spring*, with characters who all spoke like the foreign, white people they were. Those were also the days when the Announcers were all white: Nick Stanford, Bobby Atwell, Jo

Harrison, Irvine Skinner, Olga Lopes-Seale, Frank Pardo, Alfred Pragnell, Jeffrey Weatherhead – and nobody even mentioned the word *'discrimination'*. The people, themselves, were fine persons – I later worked with Autie Olga, Alfred and Frank, and you couldn't want nicer persons; but the society at large appeared to be totally oblivious to the colour factor at play.

In September 1979, the newspaper publisher, The Nation Corporation, purchased Barbados Rediffusion Services Ltd.; and a second radio station called The Voice of Barbados (VOB 790) was launched on May 1st, 1981. By this time the government had established radio and television services, called jointly, The Caribbean Broadcasting Corporation (CBC). The Rediffusion wired service survived until 1997 when a decision was made to close it for financial reasons.

The advent of CBC and VOB ushered in a new era of indigenous programming. Listeners began to recognize more and more of themselves in the offerings of these stations. Although foreign music still dominated, there was a significant increase in the volume of Caribbean music, and talk radio was rooted in local issues. The Announcers got darker – even though they felt obliged to imitate the speech patterns of foreign newscasters.

The establishment of CBC Television in 1964 was especially significant in the context of an evolving colonial society. For the first time, the state had at its disposal – perhaps the most powerful tool of mass communication. I am yet to be convinced that those who set up the station had any notion of this significance. We had established CBC Radio a year earlier, now CBC Television; *'all modern countries have television'* seems to have been the thinking.

I have seen nothing since then to persuade me there was any understanding of the value of television in the work of building a new, national consciousness, in a country emerging from the psychological afflictions of slavery and colonialism, and needing to inculcate its people with values that speak to self-esteem, pride and sovereignty. But as youngsters growing up in the late 60's and early 70's we were excited about this new entertainment option. Pictures like *Star Trek*, *The Saint*, and *Dark Shadows*, captured our fancy and were eagerly awaited week after week. There were a few occasions when we would see images and hear sounds from our own environment, but by and large we understood that this medium was about foreign, white people – the people who really mattered, and not about us.

Those occasions when we saw and heard ourselves were – like the diversions into local music on radio – merely departures from normal programming – quaint interludes, as they were, when the natives got a chance to be on T.V. It could not escape our notice, either, that on those special occasions the medium seemed to have a preference for local persons with skin tones and hair textures approximating those of the foreign, white people.

Those early games shows – *Stump The Panel* and *What's My Line* all had panels who were either Caucasians or were high in Caucasoid features: Pam and Dorielle Went, Frank de Bruno, Anne Musgrave, Bentley Storey, et al. The need for the token black presence on these shows was usually met in persons like Sydney Simmons, Anne Hewitt and the late John Young (these persons didn't offer themselves as tokens; I think that is how they were perceived by the producers of the show). The fact that nobody thought there was anything wrong with this lack of melanin in a country of 90% black people tells us the extent to which whiteness – or paleness of skin – was accepted as the legitimate skin tone for T.V.

In a similar vein, English or North American speech patterns were perceived to be at the pinnacle of the standards scale for radio or television presenters. When I was a Reporter at CBC we had a Barbadian girl with an *'unblemished'* English accent (She was schooled in England where her mother lived) and people almost fell down at her feet in obeisance.

And, of course, they put her on TV to read the news. I personally overheard the station's Chairman pressing the Manager at the time to indicate *"when we going get…reading the news?"* He had obviously initiated the move and was growing impatient. To be fair, I would say she turned out to be a fairly good reader, though this had little to do with her accent. So, with television we were starting out with an addition to the social landscape of our country that made little reference to our environment and culture, and even less to the racial identity of the vast majority of our people. Indeed, we could even say that it promoted the notion of white, North American and European racial and cultural superiority and black, Caribbean racial and cultural inferiority.

The established notion, then, was that radio and television were media through which we were entertained by persons of other cultures, and informed about the affairs of their lives. Their movie stars were our stars; their sporting icons and teams were our icons and our teams and their politics our politics. In fact, it might be said that some people considered us an unofficial state of the U.S.A. Many years ago CBC would sometimes carry a major address given by the President of the United States. I remember on one occasion the Operator at the television master control desk ran a graphic to promote one of these speeches with the words: *"The President will address the nation at....CBC will carry the speech 'live'".* Well, fortunately, not all of us, even then, bought into the notion that we were a de facto colony of the United States, and someone called the station to point out the inappropriateness of the graphic. It was subsequently changed to indicate that it was the President of the United States.

Back then the people at CBC were enraptured by the United States and American television. People would come up with new programmes and simply copy a name from U.S television – CBC Evening News, after CBS Evening News; Morning Barbados after Good Morning America; Cabaret, after the American Broadway shows. When you questioned this apish behaviour you might be told: *"Well, there is nothing new under the sun."* I can only conclude that our American neighbours lived in a sunless part of the world, since they were always able to come up with creative ideas and names for their programmes.

So, as far as television was concerned, we were like fans at a cricket match – mere spectators, looking through a window at the performance of foreigners in the middle. The passage of time has not succeeded in altering this reality to any significant degree. In the year 2016, half a century after the introduction of CBC Television, the face of the station is still largely that of

Caucasians in foreign environments. Up to the year 2014, prime time television viewing in Barbados was dominated, not by images and sounds from Barbados and other Caribbean countries, but by an 'R' rated soap opera called *Days of Our Lives*. Barbadians from six to 96 would watch nightly as the stars of this soap engaged in the most erotic behaviour short of naked sex. When I drew to the attention of the Manager of Broadcast Services the inappropriateness of the time slot given to this soap, her response was that it was a popular programme and that I should supervise my children. Perhaps she was saying it would be alright to air porn at prime time once people supervised their children. Fortunately, the serial was discontinued after its cost became prohibitive for CBC.

Half a century into its existence CBC is a national embarrassment – an enterprise adrift with no sign of visionary leadership nor mission in sight. It is, perhaps, symptomatic of the crisis of management and leadership in which the station finds itself that in the second decade of the 21st. century its programme department is functioning without a budget for the purchase and production of shows. This bizarre circumstance has resulted in viewers without alternative choices having to endure never-ending repeats of programmes, some of them more than 15 years old. Were it not for the Crop Over Festival and the morning chat shows the station's local offerings would be virtually limited to repeats and – believe it or not – social hops and karaoke for the elderly.

How I long for the day when I can sit in my drawing room and see on CBC Television the young and talented musicians of Barbados – the young pianists, organists, saxophonists, vocalists. What a refreshing treat it would be sit and listen to the melodious sounds of choral groups like the Bel Canto Singers, the Cecilian Chorale, the Myriad Singers et al – to be intrigued by a dramatic production by the students of the Community's College's drama department. These artistes are all part of the multi-coloured fabric that makes up the arts in Barbados; and television stations in progressive countries around the world are large consumers of the arts.

Even in those moments when the station has the opportunity to put a local face on the screen – as in fill-time between programmes – the choice, which is largely left to a switcher at a desk, is for some foreign artiste. If it's a Sunday then it will be the cacophonous strains of an African American gospel group. This obtains even in the lead up to the main news at 7:00 in the evening, when the station commands the eyes and ears of the nation. How much more inspiring to sit and be entertained by a talented Barbadian singer, instrumentalist, dancer or poet, rather than an unknown artiste from North America. It still amazes me that none of the station's Programme Directors over the years possessed the vision to see the inappropriateness of airing foreign entertainment at these times of national attention. But such has been the crisis in the management of CBC over the years.

This problem of foreign content has also been engaging the attention of a former head of the National Cultural Foundation. Writing in the daily NATION of November 29, 2001, Antonio Rudder, had this to say about television in Barbados: "*We hardly see anyone who looks like the majority of our population, and when we do, they are cast in questionable or stereotypical roles. What is so wrong about seeking to develop indigenous programming that speaks to Barbadian issues? Why are we facilitating the cultural penetration?*" Perhaps, Mr. Rudder, we should say cultural penetration by invitation; this is certainly not rape. It is very much consensual.

That this grotesque state of affairs could pass before the eyes of our political and social leadership without question speaks to the enormity of the problem confronting us. In effect, we not only had a problem servicing this new medium in a way that was appropriate to our culture, environment and people, but there seemed not even to be an understanding among those with influence and power, nor indeed among the general population, that a problem existed at all. It comes right down, I think, to the national consensus that we are mere appendages of Europe and North American – vessels for the receipt of their music, their images and stories.

Now let us compare that with the attitude of the British to the BBC. If you visit the BBC's website on the internet you get a fairly good idea of the vision which the British have of the BBC's role in British life. But if you wanted it straight from the horse's mouth, listen to the then Secretary of State for Culture, Media and Sport, Chris Smith, as he spoke in the House of Commons on February 21, 2000. *"The BBC is the UK's most important cultural institution…A strong BBC is crucial in ensuring that everyone can have access to information, news, education and current affairs, using efficient, modern methods, so that we can build a society for the 21st. century on the solid foundations set down for us in the 20th."*

So the BBC is at the heart of British life. These are people who obviously believe in their way of life. They have a sense of who they are and are proud of who they are. For them it would be unthinkable to have a national television service that reflected a culture foreign to British society. But in Barbados there is not even a serious discussion about this absence of Barbadian material on television. Not that there hasn't been some talk.

The record will show that there has been no shortage of words by high level personalities both in the government and the broadcast industry, expressing outright support for Caribbean programming on television, or implying such support. A few years ago some of us were encouraged by the idea being advanced in political corridors of having 80% local programming. It was – and still is – an attainable goal, requiring only the will and the resources. Well, it seems this was merely yet another grand idea that would just waft away. Like the idea broached by the leader of the opposition Barbados Labour Party, Mia Mottley - then Minister of Information in the BLP government, for a fund to finance indigenous Caribbean programming. Ms. Mottley was of the view, then, that the programming presently offered on Caribbean TV (*'Caribbean'* here again meaning the English speaking nations) *"has brought a cultural influence that translated into life-styles which place heavy demands on the taxpayers dollars each year to deal with such problems as AIDS, crime, road accidents and drugs."* Given the power and potential of the medium, she suggested the creation of a regional programming fund supported by the public and private sector to finance programming. Well, as if to add fuel to fire, no less a person that the then Prime Minister, Owen Arthur, joined the chorus of those noting the high foreign content in television programming. Mr. Arthur was reported as lamenting the fact that "*a random examination of our television programming will...reveal that we consume 90 percent of programmes with an imported content*," and that "*much of it glorified crime and violence.*"

We therefore have two very influential political persons, a former Minister of Information and a former Prime Minister sending very positive signals about their vision for television programming. It all amounted to what in local parlance we call "*a lot o' long talk*". The blunt truth is that there has never really been any commitment either in political circles nor in the management of CBC to having the station reflect Barbados – like BBC reflects Britain, like American TV reflects America, like Chinese TV reflects China, like Indian T.V reflects India. In fact, many countries simply do not leave it to chance. They enshrine in their broadcasting legislation provisions to ensure that the content of their systems reflects the values and culture of their people. The 1991 Broadcasting Policy Act for Canada, for instance, includes the provisions that:-

"*the Canadian broadcasting system shall be effectively owned and controlled by Canadians...*" and that "*the...system should serve to safeguard, enrich and strengthen the cultural, political, social and economic fabric of Canada* and "*encourage the development of Canadian expression by providing a wide range of programming that reflects Canadian attitudes, opinions, ideas, values and artistic creativity...*" The policy further stipulates that: "*each broadcasting undertaking shall make maximum use, and in no case less than predominant use, of Canadian creative and other resources in the creation and presentation of programming, unless the nature of the service provided by the undertaking...renders that use impracticable*".

The Australians were no less nationalistic in their Broadcasting Act of 1983. The Act mandates the Australian Broadcasting

Corporation to offer "*programs that contribute to a sense of national identity and inform and entertain, and reflect the cultural diversity of the Australian community.*" Oh! that our political leaders could be imbued with a modicum of this nationalist vision.

In the book, "*Television – An International History* " Anthony Smith gives a clear insight into the power of the medium. He writes "*It* (television*) may have aided in the process of disrupting cultures, but it has helped much in the overthrow of tyrannies. It has wantonly manipulated our wants and distorted our true needs, but it has democratized and levelled, opening the eyes of millions to things of which they had been long deprived. It has reflected the ugliness of this century, but taught hygiene to rural and urban poor.*" Smith was obviously familiar with the medium and its ability to influence in the most unassuming way. He writes: "*Beneath the most routine or trivial entertainment, the medium operates as a subtle instructor, with the complicity of the audience.*"

Let's think about those words for a minute. '*Subtle instructor*'; '*disrupting cultures*'; '*overthrow of tyrannies*': we are talking about a fairly powerful force here. Certainly doesn't sound like that inanimate piece of furniture in our drawing rooms, does it?

It is a force of which Antonio Rudder, was all too conscious. Listen to him, writing in the article cited earlier: "*We must never be so naïve as to believe that the entertainment and sporting icons that dominate our screens are culturally neutral. These images serve to shape our tastes, and quietly acculturate our society. As a result, we must re-examine the changed behaviour of our young people in light of the images we continuously feed them.*"

The solution to the problem lies not only in the will, but in the pocket – of the government, that is. It is imperative that the government take an interest in the offerings of CBC, decide on a programming format that speaks to our history, environment and culture and fund the corporation to execute that format. For if we leave it to the whims and fancies of the market there will surely be no change in the status quo. The advertising and commercial sectors have made no secret of the fact that they are not interested in anything but the normal fare: frivolous entertainment that can sometimes be demeaning to us as a people.

In the midst of the deluge of foreign fare we have managed to produce some pretty good programmes, but almost invariably these programmes fail to attract commercial sponsorship. They suffer from two negatives: a negative attitude from an uninterested CBC Sales staff who make little or no effort to market indigenous programmes, and a negative reception from advertisers who would rather put their clients' money into a cheap foreign comedy.

There is no shortage of broadcasting foundations and agencies elsewhere in the world that are dedicated to ensuring that what they get from television is not determined solely by the agenda of big business. In the United States where the free market in paramount, there is a Public Broadcasting Service, a network of more than 300 television stations airing programmes deemed to be in the public interest. These stations do not rely on commercial sponsorship, but, instead, are supported by grants, licence fees and other sources of money.

I already mentioned the BBC. Here is a world-wide broadcaster, funded entirely by the British taxpayer, that is able to produce and air programmes of the highest quality to the people of Britain and the rest of the world. Not even the unbridled, free-market zeal of Margaret Thatcher posed a threat to the BBC, to this day funded from the public purse. What is there about radio and television that not even Margaret Thatcher would want to risk putting them totally in private hands? It's a question on which I would like our political leadership to ponder.

British governments over the years have had a clear vision of the role which they want the BBC to play in British life, and they were prepared to pay for it. They do not perceive the billions of pounds poured into the BBC over the years as wasted money, but as a solid investment in the nourishment of the British spirit. They understand that this is a responsibility which they cannot leave to the purveyors of soap powder, potato chips and fried chicken.

Let's quote from that BBC website I spoke of earlier.

"*The BBC, its broadcasters, producers and programmes are at the heart of Britain's cultural, intellectual and political life. The standards and values we embody endure beyond our programmes…in the digital age the BBC remains committed to public service broadcasting and to a cultural role far greater than the market alone can provide.*"

That is the kind of vision I wish we in Barbados had for CBC: that CBC could be at the heart of Barbadian life, exuding the spirit of Barbados through our music, dance, drama and literature. We must feel sufficiently good about ourselves in Barbados that we want to see and hear more of us in the mass media than we do of foreigners; and are prepared to put the necessary resources in place to achieve that.

But the BBC is four thousand miles away. Let's look no farther than a few score miles to the west of us, to the Helen of the Caribbean, St. Lucia. While in Barbados we have been talking around the issue, St. Lucia has actually done something to put a St. Lucian face and voice on television. A National Television Network, funded by the government has been in operation there since 2001. The NTN was created out of concerns about the preponderance of foreign programming on the regular television systems, and was given a mandate to bring St. Lucians '*alternative*' and '*relevant*' programming.

To quote the then Director of Information Services, Embert Charles, "*When we speak of relevant we mean programming which allows St. Lucians to see images of themselves, as well as (of) other people in the Caribbean and elsewhere who are facing similar challenges, in our common quest for development.*" The network is modelled after a public broadcasting service and its objectives are:

1. to provide alternative programmes in public television
2. to increase the volume of local programming on television
3. to provide opportunities for local producers, communities and organisations to tell their stories through the broadcast medium
4. to serve as a feedback channel for public sector agencies and national organisations.

WESTMINSTER'S JEWEL - THE BARBADOS STORY

The channel, operated by the Government Information Service, also offers quality local productions by independent producers and productions from other Caribbean countries.

St. Lucia, the country that has produced two Nobel Prize winners, has set the lead for the rest of the Anglophone Caribbean in television programming. What do they know that we don't? Well, for one, they know that they cannot depend on private funding to achieve the objectives which they have for television broadcasting in St. Lucia. And secondly, they know that the financial investment which they have made in NTN is a worthwhile investment in their people, which will redound to the benefit of the society as a whole.

The new CBC programming format, then, might very well mirror the St. Lucian model, guided by a policy for national radio and television broadcasting (if one does not now exist) that mandates it to reflect the best of Barbadian and Caribbean life and culture. A CBC that is reflecting Caribbean culture and imagery will choose a Caribbean artiste to fill time between programmes, rather than regale us with videos from Arista Records, or the boisterous strains of some American gospel group, simply because that is what one person at a desk wants to play. Programming on national television cannot be left to the questionable choices of an operator at a desk.

Perhaps it is a reasonable curiosity that in considering the reform of television programming I should begin with what might be considered the least important area of programming: fillers. How could a few minutes between programmes make any difference to anything? Well, it makes no difference to us if we are unaware of the nature of the medium with which we are dealing. If we think we are just filling space with a song, then it makes no difference. But if we understand TV to be the *"subtle instructor"* that Anthony Smith thinks it is – the electronic octopus whose tentacles reach into every nook and cranny of our minds with all kinds of subliminal messages, then everything we put on it assumes importance.

Well do I remember the experience I had in England during a news training programme at the BBC. When I returned to Barbados the thing that I had learnt most – that impacted on me the greatest was not even part of the course. It was the unassuming, inviting manner of British television news presenters. They told the news in moderate tones and with clarity – certainly without the grinning and bellowing to which we have become so accustomed in Barbados of late. It was a style I adopted ever since.

TV is, indeed, the subtle teacher. When we show a preference for Presenters with Caucasian-type features we are teaching our people to have a negative self-image. When advertisers, consciously or otherwise, choose fair-skinned persons for prestigious ads, and black people for ads packaged in grotesque comedy, exaggerated dialect or buffoonery they are doing the same thing. When we reach automatically for foreign artistes to fill programming space we teach people that our music is second class.

When the majority of our programme material comes from North America and Europe we teach our people that these societies are at the centre of the world, whereas our is on the periphery looking in. TV is a wonderful medium in the right hands; in the wrong hands, it is a potential disaster.

The re-directed CBC, I suggest, should be a predominantly – if not totally – Caribbean station. With the existence of Multichoice and other cable services offering international programme options, the need for foreign television fare is adequately satisfied. The station's programming mandate, then, should be to offer programmes of local and Caribbean content exclusively. This objective can be facilitated greatly with the assistance of the Caribbean Broadcasting Union, the regional confederate of radio and television stations.

Through the CBU, member stations can have access to a pool of programmes from within the grouping. This is already happening, but on an all too limited scale. The infusion of Caribbean content in our programming can only help to augment the regional spirit among our people, and negate traditional inter-island prejudices. CBC may also wish to offer incentives for the production of local programmes. These incentives could begin with a warmer reception by the corporation's management to proposals and programmes from independent producers. They are too many stories of independent producers who've been turned away in frustration by the negative, un-cooperative attitude of CBC when they try to sell programmes to the station. Why – as has been happening – should an independent producer have to find sponsors for a programme he's selling to CBC? They don't ask the foreign suppliers to do that. As a matter of policy the station should accept the works of independent Producers, the only criteria being air worthiness and quality.

The existing commercial-public service hybrid may yet continue, with the station providing an avenue for commercial broadcasting – without being dependent on it – while at the same time pursuing a new, larger public service mandate, funded by the state. These are times when state coffers would appear to be low on resources. Well, if money is a problem I would recommend the re-introduction of the television licence fee or some other fiscal measure to fund the public service aspect of CBC.

But it would be like fixing the front of your house and leaving the back in disrepair if we reformed the programming of CBC Television and failed to address the managerial short-comings of the station. In my view this station has never been blessed with the expertise of the best management. This may have something to do with the tribal biases which have traditionally under-pinned these appointments. A minister of government appoints the board of directors and the board appoints top Managers some of whom might be known party loyalists. Over the years the staff recruitment process has been heavily tainted with nepotism and political tribalism.

Positions like those of General Manager, Head of the News and Current Affairs Department and other departmental headships have traditionally been reserved for persons who can command the blessing of the ruling party. And, like other statutory corporations, CBC has been used as a dumping ground by politicians, under pressure to find employment for their supporters. This pernicious interference in the recruitment function has resulted in significant bloating of the corporation's payroll over the years. It is simply outrageous that an operation the size of CBC would have a staff complement approximating 300, as has been known to happen.

This abuse of the recruitment process can sometimes take place in very blatant terms. Someone with no experience in a particular field might be recruited, at a higher level than those who were already on staff. In one particularly notorious case a recruit with neither experience nor competence for the job was brought in, based on inside connections, and proceeded to cause embarrassment to some of us – if not to the corporation's management – with their uncouth behaviour and ungrammatical presentations. In my view it represented one of the lowest points in the half a century of CBC's existence. Naturally, the complaints from viewers and listeners were numerous, but the hands of the management were tied: this individual could not be touched.

In another case, someone with absolutely no experience in television was brought in and placed in a senior position in the television production department. On one occasion this individual, who had never produced a TV programme, was asked to supervise a television production assignment given to Producers. The individual was later transferred to another department more in line with his experience, where he took the job of someone known to be a supporter of the rival political tribe.

The only thing that comes close to the inept management of CBC is the inefficiency of its operations. The station is a veritable broadcasting dinosaur, lagging way behind industry standards in both equipment and methods of operation. It is an incredible fact that independent operators, including individuals, are far better equipped than the national station. At CBC it has not been unheard of for itinerant (ENG) Camera Operators to function without reflectors, headphones, microphones and – yes – sometimes without lights. Archaic editing suites, lacking in basic facilities, poorly equipped studios and dysfunctional equipment are all part of the reality of CBC in the 21st. century. As a national broadcaster, the station is in an abysmal state; and it does not appear as if this condition is causing anyone with the ability to effect change to lose a minute's sleep.

Whenever this matter is discussed among staff, fingers all point in one direction. There's a consensus as to the source of the station's predicament. The big question is: where is the station's management in all of this. My guess would be: sipping palm wine in an oasis, somewhere in the Sahara Desert. It really is a sad state of affairs that a national institution with such potential for social good would be permitted to drift, like a rudderless ship tossed to and fro by the ocean. The people of Barbados, like the people of Canada, Australia, Britain and everywhere else on the planet earth, deserve a national broadcasting service that is well equipped, and run efficiently to represent their reality in this year of our Lord, two thousand and sixteen.

The corporation's radio services have performed slightly better over the period. But while local content has been greater than that of television, the staple fare on the three corporate stations is still music from outside of the Caribbean. Ever so often someone will raise the issue pertaining to the paucity of local music on the airwaves, but things eventually settle back down to the status quo. In recent times there's been an exponential growth in Barbadian and Caribbean musical output.

This new music adds to the large volume of old and not so old Caribbean music already in the libraries of radio stations. It would be an easily attainable goal to have an all-Caribbean station, if anybody thought that was something worthy. But instead, we are regaled with a daily diet of un-Caribbean music including the so-called "*oldie goldies*", the old and supposedly golden music of people from a different time, place and culture.

We may continue to nudge our broadcasters and DJ's about local music, but I sense that the battle against Brook Benton, Connie Francis, Paul Anka and the music of the '*golden oldies*' will forever eclipse Gabby, Bag, Chalkdust, Sparrow and the myriad Caribbean artistes whose music is covered in dust in music libraries across the region. For to all intents and purposes decision makers in our neck of the woods have all but resolved that nothing created by musicians from this region will ever be considered worthy enough to take precedence over the music of North America and Europe. Where there is no vision the people perish, musicians starve and Caribbean radio stations continue to wallow in the oftimes tiresome strains of Paul Anka, Connie Francis, Charlie Pride and Marty Robbins.

But what about talk radio? With three stations at its disposal surely CBC should offer a greater serving of talk radio. I number myself among the many people not terribly entertained by much of the musical offerings on radio, and the repetitive, daily banter between Announcers and fans sending shout-outs to every Tom, Dick and Mary. We would rather sit and listen to a feature about some interesting aspect of Barbadian society or the personal life of someone. Or how about an in depth look at solar and other forms of renewable energy or genetically modified foods and the risks they may pose to our health. The material for a programming format like this is endless: parliamentary debates, lectures, discussions, interviews with elderly Barbadians – these are all alternatives to the profuse diet of music, that are begging for air time on radio. Unfortunately these pleas continue to fall on the deaf ears of programme administrators who are convinced that radio is now about pandering to the lowest common denominator.

But if we are talking about improving CBC there is one word we must use: "*training*". CBC has suffered significantly over the years because of its failure to expose its staff to professional training. The effects of this lack of training is evident whenever we view CBC's local offerings. It could be a newscast consisting of little more than what a politician said today – the predictable line is "*Prime Minister X says*"; a news video clip of two people looking into the camera and shaking hands repeatedly as they pose for a stills Photographer (CBC, you don't pose for television cameras; TV is about moving pictures); an introduction to a news story that is repeated in the Reporters narration or a report that offers no background information on the story – sometimes not even where and when the event occurred.

Whatever it is, CBC staff needs training in it. How often have we sat in our drawing rooms to hear a commentator introduce a Reporter on the scene, only to be disappointed with the words *"we seem to be having a technical problem..."* Sometimes you wonder *'why do they bother to try'*. They have been minor efforts at training over the years. They've brought in professionals from news organizations for short stints, but this has apparently done little to improve things. I, myself, had the benefit of training in television feature production when I was there, at the Caribbean Institute of Media and Communications in Jamaica. CARIMAC – as it's called – offers a range of courses for mass media practitioners, yet CBC has made little use of this training opportunity.

Some have tried to pass on what little knowledge they have to individuals within the organization, but there is a fixation with the mediocre at the place that is so strong an atomic bomb would not be able to change it. Everytime someone dies in a vehicular accident, you can predict what the lead will be: *"Barbados has recorded another road fatality..."* They have been using that lead for the past 40 years, and no amount of advice from anyone is going to change them. As a matter of fact, there are certain stories and leads which I think they should package and put in storage for whenever the need arises.

Every year, for instance, you can be sure to be told that *"Barbadians from all walks of life celebrated the birth of Christ today"*. A modified form of this lead might also be used on Good Friday or Easter. And then there are those non-stories they keep giving us – like the big clean-up after Kadooment, the Crop Over street carnival, or how good – or bad – sales were for vendors at the Oistins Fish Festival. If we can be sure about anything in life it is that we will get those stories from CBC each and every year. My understanding about news is that there must be an element of freshness to it. The collection of garbage after any big public event is a given; it cannot be news each and every year that sanitation workers have done a good job of cleaning the streets after Kadooment. That is what they are paid to do.

Whatever training takes place will probably not change CBC's de facto status as the propaganda arm of the ruling political tribe. Both major parties have treated the station in this way, and the staff – especially the news staff – have bought into this relationship fully. Even a cursory observation of CBC's television news will reveal the obvious bias in favour of events involving Ministers of government or persons associated with the ruling party. Those who have run the news department over the years have been fully conscious of that fact that they must provide coverage for nearly every cock fight sponsored by or attended by the political power brokers. They are so fully aware of the role expected of them that they naturally self-censure their output. I once did a programme on tourism which took a critical look at the industry, with comments from the then Leader of the Opposition and later discovered that a certain political operative had received a call from a Minister of government about it.

In my idealistic ignorance, one day I suggested to my immediate supervisor that she could repeat the programme, only to be told that on the last occasion it caused problems. The programme was a good one; the only reason it couldn't be repeated was that it had content which the ruling party didn't want to hear. The political moguls in Barbados are fully aware of the lack of intestinal fortitude and balls among their minions in the public service and state corporations and they exploit it. When I was a Reporter at CBC I was once called into the Manager's office over a story I wrote from the parliamentary debate on the then fledgling Caribbean Examinations Council. The story did not have inaccuracies; believe it or not, the concern was that it was too critical of the CXC. An opposition member of Parliament had suggested that the Council's exams were too difficult and I had reported what he said. Before me sat the Chairman and the Manager looking for an explanation from me.

What I said to them then is as clear in my mind as if it were yesterday. I disagreed that the there was anything wrong with the story and told them: "*The CXC is a young institution; every criticism, no matter how invalid it may seem, should be highlighted, so that in case there is any validity the defects can be remedied. It is better that way, I think, than for us to set defective moulds which may take decades to correct.*" There was a pregnant silence after that statement and the meeting ended shortly thereafter.

For all the vaunting about parliamentary democracy among the socio-political elite in Barbados this country remains one of the most controlled, undemocratic states outside of extreme totalitarianism; and most Barbadians are blissfully unaware of it.

But how can I write about CBC without relating some of the many comical episodes of my sojourn there. One of my favourites is the news story by a Reporter known to have a penchant for journalistic sensation. Reporting on a house fire one day, he considered it important to inform his listeners, with all of the urgency he could muster, that *"meanwhile at a nearby house a saucepan* (the Barbadian word for 'pot'*) blew up, but fortunately there were no injuries."* When I heard the story my brain immediately went into overdrive trying to figure out how a saucepan blowing up in someone's kitchen could be deemed newsworthy. Well, apparently I was not the only curious one; I subsequently learned that the Chairman of the board was asking a similar question.

Then we had the highly creative, if not extra-ordinary, television report from a female Reporter on a street demonstration. She began the report by singing – yes, that's right; she sang the first line of the chorus to the 1960 hit by Nancy Sinatra, *"These Boots are Made for Walking"*, presumably with video of the demonstrators' walking motions:

These boots are made for walking, and that's just what they'll do one of these days these boots are gonna walk all over you.

It was hilarious. And then we had interviewers who were either ignorant of the subject matter, not as focused as they should have been or, perhaps, just a little witless.

I put it down to lack of focus when the interviewer, having been told that her guest was the leader of a musical quartet later asked him how many members there were in the group. These were all errors of judgment, lack of focus or lack of knowledge, but the faux pas which still boggles my mind up to now is the one in which the commentator on a broadcast of a state visit told viewers that Photographers were taking pictures for PROS-

PERITY. I suppose some of the Photographers might have been hoping to prosper from their pictures, but I doubt that was the line of thinking of our commentator. My bewilderment stems from the fact he was able to confuse 'prosperity' with 'posterity'. The two words are distinctly different both in pronunciation and spelling.

But none of them beats my favourite presenter who persists in asking the wrong questions. Interviewing officials of the ex-soldiers organization, the Barbados Legion, he blurted out in typical cocky fashion: "*Don't you think more young people should be encouraged to join the Barbados Legion?*" Where-upon the guest very discreetly responded with the assertion that the Barbados Legion is an organization of retired servicemen.

That one is in the same league as the question he posed to a guest about the naming of a portion of coastal land we know as Land's End. "*Why is it called Land's End?*" he sought to find out. The guest, with a cheery chuckle in his voice, promptly replied: "*Because it's the end of the land.*" Well, you'd think after this, our very astute interviewer would have learnt his lesson. Not at all. In a subsequent interview with the same guest he sought to find out why the street running right next to Carlisle Bay (*named after the Earl of Carlisle*) was named Bay Street. The guest explained it to him – this time without the chuckle.

But the comic relief CBC has to offer can also come from managerial circles. For the station's 40th. anniversary one Manager came up with the novel idea of laying down forty, enlarged images of human footsteps leading from the main entrance to the building to the gate entrance. The footsteps were not simply painted; they were mounted, and caused considerable inconvenience to motorists traversing the station's front parking apron. I am told a visitor to the station tripped on one of them and fell, and brought a legal action against the station. The '*footsteps*' were subsequently removed.

If, as they say, hope springs eternal in the human breast, then we may yet wait for the day when those wielding political power in our country will be imbued with a vision for CBC. The revamped CBC, liberated from the mismanagement and misdirection of the past fifty years and charged with a new national mandate, will be a blessing to the people of Barbados, a beacon of broadcasting excellence in the Anglophone Caribbean, and will have been worth every penny it took to get it there.

Admiral Horatio Nelson

The Nelson statue in Bridgetown

" *England expects that every man will do his duty*": the rally-ing words of the British war hero, Horatio Nelson as he led his men into the famous Battle of Trafalgar against the com-bined French and Spanish forces on October 21st. 1805. It was a battle that cost Nelson his life, but exalted him to hero status among the British people. News of the victory over the French was greeted with national jubilation back in Britain. Church bells pealed across the country sounding the spirit of euphoria that had overtaken the land. And well might they celebrate for it was a victory that ushered in an era of British ascendancy in Europe and dominance on the high seas.

But the joy was tempered by the loss of the one who made it possible. And from then, every year on October 21st. the great victory of Admiral Horatio Nelson has been celebrated across the United Kingdom. The celebration has been formalised as Trafalgar Day.

The response to Nelson's victory in Barbados was much the same as that in Britain. The planter-merchant class that governed the island clearly harboured a kindred spirit with their kith and kin in the imperial government. That apart, the notion was spread far and wide that Nelson's victory at Trafalgar had saved Barbados from French colonization. One year after his death, they held a memorial service for him at St. Michael's Cathedral in Bridgetown, the seat of the Anglican Church in Barbados, and launched a fund to raise money for the statue.

More than two thousand pounds was collected; and by February 1813 the first stone of the pedestal was in place at a location they would later name Trafalgar Square. The statue, itself, was mounted the following month, 17 years before a similar one was erected in London. And every year since then, on October 21[st,] Barbadians would celebrate the Battle of Trafalgar. The observance was abolished in 1963 by the island's first Prime Minister, Errol Barrow.

Debunking the notion that Nelson and the Battle of Trafalgar had saved Barbados from the French has been a virtual obsession with Barbadian Historian, Trevor Marshall, who has written and spoken ad nauseam on the subject. The following quote encapsulates the audacity and passion with which he approaches the issue: "*The statue of Lord Nelson in Barbados represents the most astonishing exercise in mass self-delusion on the part of the Barbadian white elite of the early 19th. Century...and the most thorough indoctrination of an entire people....*"

So what's the true Nelson story? Nelson, it appears, was in hot pursuit of the Admiral of Napoleon's French Navy, Pierre Villeneuve. His aim was to destroy the French fleet to kill the possibility of a French invasion of Britain. In 1805, Villeneuve, equipped with a fleet of ships and ten thousand men, arrived in the Caribbean, anchoring at Martinique, about a hundred and fifty miles north of Barbados. Marshall notes that on that occasion Villeneuve made no attempt to launch a strike on Barbados but instead sailed north and directed his men in an attack on Antigua before departing from the Caribbean.

In early June 1805, one month after Villeneuve and his men had left the region, Nelson arrived in Barbados in search of the French admiral. He anchored in Carlisle Bay from where he enquired whether the French fleet had passed by the island. With a negative answer he set sail for Trinidad on the same mission and eventually returned to England. Nelson's next encounter with Villeneuve would take place in October 1805 off the Spanish south west coast in the climactic Battle of Trafalgar, by which time – according to Marshall – France was no longer looking to attack Britain.

Nelson had finally gotten his way with Villeneuve and the French fleet, but in doing so he paid the ultimate price. With the rise of nationalist and Pan Africanist sentiments in Barbados over the last four decades, there've been strident calls for the removal of the Nelson statue from the city centre, Marshall's voice being the foremost of those heard.

The Barbadian Historian is not at all enamoured by Nelson's declared support for slavery:

> *"I was bred, as your know, in the good old school, and taught to appreciate the value of our West Indian possessions; and neither in the field, nor in the Senate shall their just rights be infringed, whilst I have an arm to fight in their defence, or a tongue to launch my voice against the damnable doctrine of Wilberforce and his hypocritical allies."*

The *"take-down-Nelson"* lobby has not been without its opponents. Conservationists and others have been making an equally strong case for the retention of the statue in its present location. They argue that the erection of the status – whatever the reason – is a part of Barbadian history that cannot be erased.

So far, successive governments have not given in to the demand for the re-location of the statue. There was some cosmetic window dressing in 1999 when the then government of the

Barbados Labour Party under Prime Minister, Owen Arthur, re-named the square Heroes Square. In fact, on that occasion Mr. Arthur did hint very strongly that the statue would have been removed, but apparently had a change of heart. His words on the occasion could not be faulted for nationalist fervour:

"This National Heroes Square is for our citizens and visitors, who should be aware that we own an indigenous culture of human achievement that stands tall with the whole world." Well today, a decade and a half after, Nelson still stands tall in Heroes Square. Hmm – kind of reminds me of the great election campaign for the Republic of Barbados under the same leader.

To the vast majority of Barbadians, Horatio Nelson is not a hero of Barbados; but the psychological ravages of the imperial system for which he gave his life have worked to ensure that his likeness will remain a feature of National Heroes Square for some time yet.

Strokes of Genius

Rt. Exc. Sir Garfield Sobers

The use of the superlative to describe him has long become trite. But how else would you speak of his exceptional cricketing aptitude. This national hero of Barbados and international cricketing star loomed larger than life on the cricket field.

In a career spanning two decades he literally mesmerized cricket fans and players, from the Caribbean to England to Australia – wherever the game is played – with his cricketing prowess. It was a career that brought him personal fame – if not fortune – and glory to his country. We speak of none other than Sir Garfield St Aubrun Sobers. How could we talk about the history and development of Barbados and fail to mention his name.

In local parlance, his *'naval string'* (umbilical cord) is buried at Walcott Avenue, Bay Land, St Michael, where he shared a home with his mother and five siblings. He lost his father, a Seaman, as a young boy, when his ship was torpedoed by a German submarine during the Second World War. From an early age, Sobers demonstrated a skilful ability with ball games, particularly cricket, football and basketball. But it was cricket that would become the dominant of the three. Owing largely to his cricketing skills and those of his brother, Gerald, his primary school, the Bay Street Boys School, was able to capture the Interschool Cricket Championship for three consecutive years. It was at Bay Street, Sobers remembers, that the foundations of his game were laid:

> *"My brother...was the batsman and I was the bowler. In those days I was inclined to be a little bit scared of the hard ball, so I would prefer to bowl and bat lower down the order. Gerald was far...the better batsman so he was able to handle with the fast bowlers, and by the time I got in to bat only the spinners were on...Playing around the Bay pasture I think that was really where the main foundation of my cricket started – bowling at players like Dennis Atkinson and Roy Marshall and Norman Marshall. It was a very good foundation in those days, and then I went to play for a team called Kent. The boys on the Bay pasture wouldn't pick me. They thought I was too young and might get hurt so when nationals were playing in those days I couldn't get into the team..."*

Well, Bay Street's loss was Garnett Ashby's gain. Ashby, captain of the St. Philip team, Kent, in the Barbados Cricket League (BCL), saw him and recruited him to play for the country team. It was with the B.C.L that he made his Kensington debut, playing against the Barbados Cricket Association. But Ashby was not the only one whose eyes were on Sobers. The then racially exclusive Wanderers Cricket Club, among whose ranks was West Indies test player, Denis Atkinson, sought him out for bowling practice.

Sobers: *"...they used to send down to my home which was about 200 yards away from the ground – they didn't even know my name – and they used to tell the grounds man 'go and get that little, left-handed boy and bring him up here'. And I used to go up there and bowl at them. They used to put a shilling on the stump – and in those days a shilling was a...lot of money, so that used to encourage you..."*

His days of bowling practice at Wanderers exposed Sobers to another pair of eyes. They belonged to the captain of the Police B.C.A team, Inspector and later Commissioner Wilfred Farmer. Farmer offered him a chance to play for Police in the 1951-52 season while he was only 15, and by the following year he was in the Police first division team.

That same year he was called to trials for the 1952-53 Indian tour of the Caribbean and made the team as 12th. man (Reserve). As fate would have it, he got his first chance to play for Barbados when Frank King, West Indies fast bowler for the Test series, was forced to withdraw. And so it was on January 31st. 1953, at the age of 16 that the Barbados' wonder boy of cricket made his first class debut. Batting at number nine, he scored seven not-out in his only innings, but made an immediate impression as a bowler, taking four for 50 and three for 92.

This early milestone in his cricketing career was the catapult that launched him into international test cricket one year later. It was the 5th. and final test at Sabina Park, Jamaica against the English touring side. The call came as Sobers was playing a game of road cricket, a common practice in Barbados at the time. *"We got....a cable from Jamaica, from the West Indies selectors asking me to make myself available to go to Jamaica for the last test. Well then you knew how I felt. Playing with the three W's* (Barbadians, Frank Worrell, Clyde Walcott and Everton Weekes) *was some-thing that I never dreamed of at that age. Within about two and half hours to three hours I was in the field. I was out....padded up to bat. The West Indies team had collapsed...But when I walked down the steps onto the playing area...the ovation I got being a youngster – it was something overwhelming; it was something that one can never forget. You look around and you see all of those people and you think, well I am here; I've...made it; I've arrived."*

England won the match, but, once more, Sobers made a good bowling impression, taking four for 75 in England's first innings, including a wicket in his opening over.

As his cricketing career unfolded, Sobers was emerging as an outstanding left-arm batsman and bowler. In the bowling department, he could deliver from spin to medium fast, but was more effective with fast bowling. *"As a boy I'd bowl fast because....we used to play a game called 'Ferms', and Ferms was: who would have gotten the ball bowled. And spin in those days wasn't very good; you had to bowl quickly and try and get the fellow out because...whoever caught the ball batted. So it meant that the bowler had to bowl the fellow out or catch the ball himself, or run him out or do something....so you had to learn to bowl all different styles. But it didn't end here. When I went to the League* (Barbados Cricket League) *as a youngster then I realized that I had to do practically everything. Had to open the bowling – which I loved anyhow – and then when you were tired bowling fast you came on and you spin...."*

His fielding position was usually close to the wicket, where he was one of the most brilliant. In this position he took several extra-ordinary catches at short leg and slips, finishing his first class career with a record 407 catches in 93 tests. But it was his batting prowess that would forever etch *'King Cricket'* in the minds of fans all over the world. He was rated as one of the finest stroke players, with an ability to read both spin and swing quickly.

By the time of his retirement, his test aggregate had reached 8032, a record then, but one which was subsequently surpassed. In first class cricket he made 28 thousand 315 runs, including 86 centuries, averaging 54.6 per innings, figures which survived as West Indies records for nearly two decades. Another Sobers batting record was his perfect score of 36 from six sixes in an English county match. That record was subsequently equalled by the Indian batsman, Ravi Shastri. And who else would break the record for the highest score in a test innings? Set at Sabina Park, Kingston in 1958 against Pakistan, this record would stand for 36 years before being eclipsed by the Trinidadian West Indies batsman, Brian Lara. Lara's own record was subsequently taken down by Australian Matthew Hayden and himself.

Sobers recalls the story this way: *"It was not until I got 300 runs and Clyde Walcott who was batting with me at the other end – he came down and said to me… 'it's only 60-odd runs to get and you've got all the time. The wicket is playing so well and you might not even get to 300 again. Here's a great opportunity.' And that was when I started to think. So I decided then to cancel out the 300 completely and to just think – well I've just gone in to bat and all I need was 64 runs. And I put my head down and I started all over again."*

The Sabina Park run feast was significant for Sobers in more than one way. Not only did it set a cricketing record, it was also a personal record for him: it was the first time he had scored a test century, after being put under pressure from observers. *"I was never really conscious of not getting a hundred. I think that people were more conscious of that, and I think that after a while being reminded by people that I'd played so much test cricket and hadn't scored a hundred I think I started thinking about it myself."*

After his first tour of England with West Indies in 1957 Sobers lent his talents to the English county team, Radcliffe. He spent five seasons with Radcliffe, from 1958. And following the 1962 England tour with West Indies in 1962 he switched to Norton club, helping them to win the league title in 1964. Just before his foray into English club cricket, he played the first of three seasons with South Australia in the Sheffield Shield. Such a hit he was *"down under"* that attendances rose by nearly 90% leading to a two-and-a-half-times increase in gate receipts. He topped both the batting and bowling averages at South Australia that year.

But it was the iconic Tied Test between West Indies and Australia in 1960 that left Sobers with his best memories of cricket down under. Hailed by cricketing enthusiasts as the greatest game of all time, the tied test set a cricketing first for tied games. Sobers remembers it as a particularly exciting match.

"It looked as though Australia had had it all sown up…and then we had that breakthough when Wes (Hall) bowled the bouncer that Sir Frank told him not to bowl – but Wes decided he's going to bowl it anyhow…That was a tremendous match and I don't think there will ever be

another one, because it was the last ball, the last second,
the last run and the last wicket – the last everything."

It was a moment of cricketing magic that would take its
rightful place in the annals of the game. As Wes Hall remembers
it: *"one of the best cricket matches ever played"*. Sobers captures
the aftermath of the occasion in his auto-biography thus:

> *"It was chaos. Everyone in the ground was going ber-*
> *serk... We all realized the magnitude of the moment when*
> *the Australians came out to meet us on the way in to the*
> *pavilion to congratulate us on the first tie in 498 tests....*
> *We danced into the dressing room, jumping for joy... The*
> *Australians were as confused as we were and they came*
> *into our room to join the celebrations... Some of us did not*
> *leave the dressing room until after ten o'clock that night.*
> *We just sat there and let it digest. This was history."*

It was inevitable that the prince of West Indies cricket would
one day ascend to the cricketing throne, and in 1965 when Sir
Frank Worrell retired, he logically fell into the position of captain. Sobers enjoyed immediate success as captain when his team
defeated Australia in the first test at Sabina Park, Jamaica. West
Indies went on to win the series and claim the Frank Worrell
trophy. It was the first time West Indies had beaten Australia in
a test series. In 1966 he enjoyed spectacular success in England
and in the euphoria was christened with the sobriquet *"King
Cricket"*, and celebrated as the greatest cricketer in the world by
the calypsonian, Sparrow, in the song, *"Sir Garfield Sobers"*:

> *"Who's the greatest cricketer on Earth or Mars?*
> *Anyone can tell you, it's the great Sir Garfield Sobers!*
> *This handsome Barbadian lad really knows his work.*
> *Batting or bowling, he's the cricket King – no joke!*
> *Three cheers for Captain Sobers!"*

But his overall record as a captain is a shadow of the brilliance he displayed as an individual player. Out of 39 tests in which he captained the West Indies, his side lost ten, drew 20 and won only nine. Unlike his performance as a batsman and bowler, his captaincy has been known to put him on the wrong side of fans; but Sobers has no regrets.

"I've been criticized as probably one of the worst captains in the world, but I have always seen leadership different from other people, and I feel that a captain has got to do what he thinks is best at the time he's leading the team. He's got to see the game the way that he thinks it should go and not the way he thinks other people would have looked at it."

Dark clouds are wont to cast a pall over the most brilliant sunset, and an otherwise illustrious career was tarnished by what many saw as two unfortunate errors in judgment by Sobers. West Indies versus England at Port of Spain, 1968. West Indies are on top of the game and declare in the first innings. Then in the 2nd. Innings, with a lead of just 122, Sobers declares again leaving England a mere 215 runs to chase with nearly three hours on hand. The English side rose to the occasion, winning the match with seven wickets in hand and three minutes to go. The loss caused an uproar among West Indies fans, some of whom vented their anger by burning an effigy of the West Indies captain. But Sobers remains unapologetic:

"I feel that games should be played that way and interest should be created at all times in a cricket match. Otherwise what we should have done is batted right through the evening. It's no sense making a declaration and giving a team half an hour to bat for eleven men to go out there and just stand up, give away a lot of silly runs.....because there is nothing left in the game – the people who've come to watch are bored because there is no interest.....No. I never felt that way. I felt that if you're playing a cricket match,

*at all times there should be interest up to the end; and that
is how I captained my team...and if I had to do it again I
would do it all over the same way that I did it when I was
captain."*

But if Port of Spain 1968 was an awakening for Sobers, his
moment of truth was yet to come. Two years later he accepted
an invitation and played in what was then Rhodesia (now Zimbabwe), at the time under United Nations sanctions for deny-
ing the vote to black people, and the object of protest by many
Caribbean people. In Rhodesia he received a standing ovation all
the way to the middle, endorsed with a rendition of "*For He's a
Jolly Good Fellow*". That night he had dinner with the minority
Rhodesian leader, Ian Smith. The story broke on September 7th.
1970 when a London newspaper reported the proposed visit, and
the outcry was immediate.

All hell erupted on his return to the Caribbean. The "*jolly good
fellow*" for Rhodesian whites was about to be thrown under the
bus by his own people. Antigua's Workers' Voice, a trade union
paper, labelled him "*a white black man*", while others, including
the Jamaica Labour Party, demanded he resign or be stripped of
the captaincy. The outrage was not confined to the Caribbean;
the then Indian Prime Minister, Indira Gandhi, indicated that
the Indian tour of the Caribbean in 1970 might have been called
off if the West Indian side included Sobers.

Things came to a head when the then Prime Minister of
Guyana, Forbes Burnham served notice that Sobers would not
be welcome in Georgetown unless he apologized. A settlement
of the issue was finally brokered by the then Prime Minister of
Trinidad & Tobago, Eric Williams, who drafted a letter of apology for the West Indies Cricket Board, which Sobers would later
sign. The emissary was West Indies player and friend of Sobers,
Wes Hall, who was coaching in Trinidad at the time.

It read:

*"When I was invited to play cricket in Rhodesia,
I thought of only two things: my love of cricket and my*

hope that I would be able to contribute to greater West Indian dignity. I had not realized the deep feelings of the West Indian People in this issue of Rhodesia. I have since learned of the wider international issues involved on the question of Rhodesia. If I had known or thought of these matters before going, I would never have gone to Rhodesia. If another opportunity came my way to go to Rhodesia, I would not now accept it." Sobers signed the letter and the flames of a raging inferno were quietly extinguished.

Sir Donald Bradman

Opinions may vary as to his greatest performance but that of another luminary of the game, the late Australian cricketer, Sir Donald Bradman, is worthy of note. Sir Donald – himself regarded as the greatest test batsman of all time – points to the Third International between Australia and the World Eleven at the Melbourne Cricket Ground, January 1972, when Sobers scored 254.

In Bradman's words, *"it was an incredible innings, full of the most savage power, the most brilliant shots, the most delicate placements – some of his foot work was absolutely perfect; at other times even when his feet were not absolutely in the right place, the ball still sped off the bat to the boundary with such speed that it left the field man standing like stumps...I count myself privileged to have been there and to have had the opportunity of commenting on this innings which will live in the minds of all who saw it for as long as life should last."*

The Sobers statue at Kensington Oval

We erect monuments as lasting memorials to the events and people who take us beyond the boundary of the mundane into new avenues of glorious possibilities. One such, bearing the likeness of Sir Garfield, adorns the entrance to Kensington Oval, a place where he would have executed some of the strokes of his cricketing genius. It's but one in a long list of accolades bestowed on the Barbadian hero.

The list includes: Wisden Cricketer of the Year; the Karl Nunes Award; the Walter Lawrence Trophy; Hall of Fame Inductee in Hartford, Connecticut and in Antigua; a players' pavilion named in after him at Kensington Oval; the Garfield Sobers Sporting Complex in Barbados; inductee in the I.C.C Hall of Fame; an international schools tournament named in his honour; the Order of Australia; a Knighthood from the Queen and national hero status in Barbados with the title, '*The Right Excellent*' before his name.

It was a journey of epic proportions, fuelled by sheer talent. From the humble Barbadian village called Bay Land, he soared on a wave of national and international acclaim to the pinnacle of honour and glory, securing his memory in Barbadian and world cricketing history for all time. Of him, it can truly be said:

Memories will fade, of ordinary folk whose earthly
journeys cease,
But the stroke of a genius will forever be
Etched in the sands of eternity.

New Frontiers

So what is the prognosis for Barbados as we advance into the uncharted waters of the 21st. century? Sadly, from my vantage point, the picture is not a rosy one. Clouds without silver linings are billowing on the horizon, waiting to usher us into new frontiers of uncertainty if not doom. We are sailing towards them with all of the luke-warm, visionless leadership that has retarded our development over the years. And we all know what happens to the people when there is no vision.

The so-called Willie Lynch formula for making a slave may not be rooted in fact, but it is certainly based on a factual principle: that if you indoctrinate the mind for a sufficiently long period, the effect will often last for centuries. Much of the under-development afflicting our country is attributable to this lingering legacy of colonial indoctrination. It's as simple as: the mind that lack confidence in itself – that harbours feelings of inferiority; that takes its values and cultural norms from elsewhere; that looks for leadership from outside is unlikely to think big ideas that will advance a country.

It is exactly this mentality that our foremost Pan Africanist and thinker, Elombe Mottley, is up against when he constantly implores us to brand our products – tangible and intangible – and take on the world. How can you take on the world when you lack confidence in who you are and what you have to offer. Had we that confidence, perhaps by now textiles produced from West Indian Sea Island cotton, regarded as the best in the world, would have been earning us premium prices internationally. Perhaps the much touted black belly lamb would have been a gourmet meat in hotels and restaurants – of course with a much more palatable name. We've been playing pussyfoot with these two potentially lucrative product brands for the past forty years, and today have nothing to show for it. It is the same inertia that has kept us from moving beyond primary producers of sugar after nearly four centuries of a sugar industry. Cricket is sometimes described as a religion in the Caribbean. We've produced one of the greatest – if not the greatest cricketer in the world, yet we don't make a single stump, bat nor ball in this region.

The fortunes of a people hinge very much on the kind of leaders they choose. Wise and visionary leadership can be their salvation; weak and visionless leadership, their downfall. The examples of Singapore and Cuba are there for all to see.

The remarkable story of the Cuban literacy programme of 1961 is one of the best demonstrations of visionary leadership at work. When Fidel Castro and his revolutionaries took over the country in the late fifties, about one quarter of the Cuban people were illiterate – mostly peasants in the rural areas. The Revolution immediately set itself the goal of eliminating illiteracy and organized a campaign to achieve this.

Groups of young people or *"Literacy Brigades"*, as they were called, were trained and sent into the country to teach the peasants to read and write. One hundred and five thousand of them volunteered for the campaign, which began on the 1st. of January and ended on December 22, 1961. At its completion more than 700 thousand Cuban peasants joined the category of the literate, pushing the national literacy rate to 96%.

Education has continued to be a principal plank of the Cuban government's policy. It's free up to university level; and today Cuban students will score higher in standardized tests than their counterparts in the rest of Latin America.

We leave the Caribbean and head for south-east Asia, stopping at a group of islands at the southern tip of the Malay Peninsula. The territory is made up of a main island less than twice the size of Barbados and about sixty associated islets. This is Singapore of *"the Singapore model"* fame. The transformation of this archipelago from an impoverished nation with high levels of illiteracy and unemployment into one of the world's most developed states is one of the best testimonies to the power of visionary leadership.

Lee Kuan Yew

The first thing the government headed by Prime Minister , Lee Kuan Yew, did was to establish an infra-structure for industrial activity by creating a series of industrial estates. It then established the Singapore Economic Development Board to promote the country among foreign investors as a place they would want to put their money. In time, branches of the Board would be set up in Europe, Asia and the United States. At the same time the government invested heavily in the training of Singaporeans, both at home and abroad, in high tech industrial skills. Foreign direct investment flowed into Singapore over time, by the year 2001 accounting for 85% of manufactured exports.

Singapore

Today, Singapore, with no mineral resources, is one of Asia's and the world's most prosperous nations. Its port is the second busiest in the world; its unemployment rate among the lowest and its quality of life among the best in Asia.

Barbados has had its own experience with foreign industrial development. In the 1960's and 70's during the tenure of national hero, Errol Barrow, we did manage to attract some industrial investment from North America. Very few, if any, of those businesses are with us today, and we certainly never achieved anything approximating the success of Singapore. I am not aware of any major effort at industrial development since the Barrow initiative. Indeed, it is my firm belief that the economic morass into which we've fallen in recent years is partially attributable to our failure to expand our industrial base. Successive governments since universal adult suffrage in 1950 have rested on the laurels of sugar and tourism and failed to expand the island's industrial base, except for the modest efforts mentioned earlier. Unlike Singapore, they almost completely ignored the revolution in computer technology.

India has also made a huge industry out of information technology and is now said to be one of the largest I.T capitals of the world. The industry, launched in the early 1970's, earns billions of dollars in foreign exchange and employs hundreds of thousands. Exports of soft-wear products and services are made to nearly a hundred countries, with North America accounting for more than 60% of that. The foreign investment in soft ware industry in the Asian state has had a positive impact on the domestic I.T sector. There are now more than 500 local soft ware companies in India.

Barbados is much closer to North America with a highly literate and educated English-speaking people. So, with these advantages, what have we done to capitalize on the I.T goldmine? Nothing. A thriving soft-ware sector at a time like this would have been the salvation of the hundreds of young people leaving school each year and looking for meaningful employment. The dim prospects as relayed to them by a junior Minister of government are that they can't look to local sources anymore and might have to consider migration as an option. Those of us with children about to enter into adulthood have good reason to bite our nails as we contemplate their graduation to this new phase of their lives. Will they really have to leave this country in order to make a living? That is what our fore-parents did in the hard times following Emancipation. Have we regressed to that point in our history?

I know we have regressed, but never for one moment did I think we had gone that far back – to the pre-1960's when our people were forced to depart these shores in search of work in Panama, Guyana, Trinidad, England and North America. The spirit of our visionary Father of Independence, the late E.W. Barrow is surely weeping in the ultra-marine waters of the Caribbean Sea.

This dim prognosis certainly makes no allowance for the much touted goal of us graduating to developed world status in the near future, a prospect being held out by some of our political leaders. For while we may score highly on the United Nations Human Development Index, we will certainly not cross the threshold into "*developed*" status in the present mental culture.

Singapore has no natural resources, yet today she is one of the most prosperous and well ordered island nations in the world. The same can be said for Bermuda, much smaller than Barbados, but with little to no poverty and an obvious attention to aesthetics that makes it one of the most beautiful and well kept tourist islands in the Americas. Everyone who's been there remarks on how clean and trim the place is. Tourism is their main industry and they know it. For the past 11 years the island has been voted the "*Best Island in the Caribbean & Atlantic*" in the annual Readers' Choice Awards of the traveller's magazine, Condé Nast.

Barbados, too, is a tourist island. But what do visitors encounter when they come here? Well, if they are taking a trip into the city it's very likely they will travel on some roads in various stages of disrepair, and pass piles of uncollected garbage beside the road and litter on the streets. In the city itself they may be confronted by vendors' shanty-towns in Fairchild Street and

Cheapside – clusters of wooden shacks and make-shift sheds at which food, vegetables and drink are sold.

Should they decide to mingle with the *natives* and take a public bus back to their hotel they might end up sitting in the bus terminal for nearly two hours waiting on the Transport Board service (In Bermuda the buses run every 15 to 20 minutes). A trip to the beautiful St. John's Church will be worth the panoramic view of the island's east coast, but they'll miss much of the equally beautiful sight of the verdant Claybury valley on the border between St. John and St. George. Over-grown shrubs have now all but blocked this landscape from view, and apparently it has never occurred to anyone that with a bit of de-bushing the beauty of this landscape could add to a positive visitor experience. Sometimes the difference between development and under-development is in the size of the mind.

The lack of vigour in the management of our economic and social affairs contrasts with the vibrancy in our artistic culture. Of one thing we can be sure going into an uncertain future: there will be no lack of song and dance. For if there's anything we've learnt over the past two decades or so, it is how to fete. There is no shortage of musical entertainment options in Barbados these days – at least not in the realm of pop music. From the Crop Over fetes to the reggae festival to the dancehall fetes to Gospelfest, to Jazz On De Hill, to the Back to School fete, to the Wet Fete, to the St. Philip and Christ Church and St. John carnivals – Barbadians are well served with opportunities to jump up and move *"we"* waist – or *wuk-up*, as we say. Is it a case of misplaced energy? I leave you to decide.

There was a time in our modern history when we placed great emphasis on personal development – when people would seek to equip themselves educationally, whether academically or by way of skills, to be able to live meaningful lives. The less academically minded would learn what was called a trade – tailoring or carpentry or dressmaking. Others would pursue training in short-hand and typewriting and other fields. Some of this self-development is still happening today, but there appears to be a much larger number of mostly young – but older people also, who see the fete as the raison d'être of their existence; who live for the fete; whose incantation might well be:

Let the party swing!
Let the people dance!
Dance!
Dance!
Raise your hand and juck!
Free up your body!
Free up your mind!
Pooch back and shake your behind!

Don't stress with decimals and fractions,
Similes and metaphors.
The only metaphor is the fete itself –
A metaphor for the 'now generation',
Human capsules of energy and enthusiasm
Free! – liberated from the fetters of primordial values:
education, ambition, morality.
There is now one new value:
The value of the fete.
To this, all other values must bow.
So let's fete.
Fete on the hill,
Fete in the yard,

Wet fete,
Beach fete,
Bikini fete,
Uniform fete,
Fete in the morning,
Fete in the night,
Fete from morning 'til twilight.
While others sleep we fete.
While others work we fete.
Cash registers ringing on Broad Street
But we fêting.
Dollars rustling on Swan Street
But we fêting.
The rich getting richer
But we fêting.
We let them deal with stocks and shares;
We take their loans and buy their wares.
We hew their wood and draw their water
But when we get paid
It's fêting thereafter.
Fete like it's going out of fashion.
Fete without rhyme,
Fete without reason.
When I awake in the morning I looking to fete.
When I come home on evenings I dressing to fete.
When I go to sleep at night I just done fete.
When I dreaming at night I dreaming 'bout fete.
No metaphor can supersede the fete;
No decimal can take its place.
No stocks and shares with it can compare.
The fete is the most important of all human activities.
Without it planet Earth as we know it would cease to be.
We were destined to fete –
And we will fete.
No matter who,
No matter what
WE WILL FETE.

But as we jump and wind our waist into the 21st Century, the evidence mounts of a society crying out for prudence and accountability in the management of its financial affairs, if the recent reports of the Auditor General are anything to go by. The 2014 report is typical of those for the years immediately preceding and the one that followed. It reports a litany of irregularities in financial transactions and procedures during the year reviewed, including dubious charges, millions of dollars in over-payments to taxpayers, pensioners and suppliers; misuse of funds and under-reporting by several leading state agencies. Inappropriate charges were identified in the books of the Psychiatric Hospital, which the Audit Department said were not directly related to cost of assets under construction.

At the Ministry of Transport and Works, there were over-payments to suppliers, involving substantial sums. In one case, a financial institution was overpaid by 1.2 million when the actual amount owed was 6.5 thousand. The ministry also overpaid another supplier to the tune of 29 thousand while yet another company was paid twice for a photocopier valued at just under 19 thousand dollars.

In another revelation, a contractor employed at the department's vehicle equipment and workshop section was paid $60,000 over a six month period at a rate of $10,000 a month, despite failing to satisfy the contract. The Auditor General also highlighted discrepancies at the Land Tax Department where there was a $12 million difference in the revenue figure reported for that department and the amount recorded for it in the Treasury.

In the case of the National Assistance Board, it was also revealed that the agency had been paying full pensions for 75 employees even though only two should have received such benefits, resulting in overpayments in the amount of 714 thousand dollars. The Auditor General also reported overpayments to suppliers and staff, as well as numerous instances of *"misuse of funds"* at the Barbados Licensing Authority, for which *"no evidence of further investigation or action taken was seen by the Audit Office"*.

The discrepancies included just under eight thousand dollars collected by cashiers but not accounted for, and seven thousand for services which the department did not receive. The Auditor General also pointed out that the process for appointments in the Public Service needs to be reformed, and raised a red flag over agencies which were blatantly ignoring Cabinet decisions pertaining to increases in staff. Missing contracts also hampered the work of the Audit Department. In one instance a firm in the United States was paid 1.3 million dollars by the Registration Department but there is no contract information available. The same obtained at the Solid Waste Unit of the Ministry of the Environment, where in excess of one million dollars was paid out to various contractors for digging wells and providing other maintenance services, in many instances without the support of valid contracts. A further 1.3 million dollars was also paid to a United States-based company for facilities management at the Judicial Centre without any formal contract in place.

Quite damning a report, you might think. So how does the government respond? Silence – stony silence. No reproach of anyone, no announcement of investigation – nothing. That is the Barbados with which we are heading into the 21st. century. Since he did not report it, I must assume that the Auditor General was not aware of the lower level government functionaries who book first class tickets, then fly economy class and pocket the significant refunds. Barbados, we are told, is among the least corrupt countries in the world, and least corrupt in the Caribbean. How thankful we are for that.

The response – or lack thereof – to the infelicities reported by the Auditor General is a reflection of the national malaise I spoke of earlier. I suspect it will be with us going forward.

The 21st. century is also unlikely to change the often contemptuous and dictatorial attitude of public officials to ordinary folk. It is an endemic personality trait among the "*negrocrats*" who populate our public service. They are to be found in every facet of the service, as heads of departments, supervisors, Policemen, Principals of schools – anywhere where black people have been given the proverbial bunch of keys and a big stick. The notion of service to the people is as far removed from their beings as the north pole is from the south, and their treatment of the ordinary citizen reflects this.

A request for public information, for instance, might be met with questions about what use is to be made of the information and it would not be unusual for that information to be withheld. Letters might go unanswered, and efforts to reach people by telephone often turn out to be unsuccessful – they are always at meetings or out of office. Their most contemptuous behaviour is reserved for persons at the lower end of the economic scale: street Vendors and Fisherfolk. In one alarming, recent incident Fisherfolk who sell from the Bridgetown Fish Market turned up for work one morning to find a hand-written note posted by the management of the market, informing them that the market was closed for cleaning. Not a word of notice. The Market officials didn't think they needed to give these working men and women any prior notice of their intended actions. Angry fish Vendors called in the Press who sought clarification from the management. Well, you can guess what their response was: *'no comment'*.

Journalists, too, are often victims of this official arrogance. They'd be millionaires if they could match with dollars the number of times they've heard the words *"no comment"* when seeking information or confirmation of some matter involving a government department.

When I worked as a Producer with CBC I once phoned up an official of the department responsible for electoral constituency boundaries to update information we already had on the boundaries. On this occasion the official was offering the information, but with such trepidation. Indeed they confessed to me that the reason for this was that *'You have to cover your ass'*. I had to remind the official that the information was, indeed, public and not state secrets. How much more public can you get than the boundaries of a constituency?

In one high profile case Journalists trying to cover a mass casualty event at the country's main hospital were evicted from the premises by Policemen acting on instructions from the hospital's management. Two newspaper Journalists were man-handled by the Police in the incident and one video Journalist arrested.

Three cheers for press freedom in this parliamentary de-mocracy called Barbados. The Journalists were not hindering the emergency operation in any way; they simply wanted to take some pictures of a very public event. It was naked exercise of power for no rhyme nor reason – except that Sarg, the negrocrat, is large and in charge here and he wants you to know it:

My name is Sarg
And I large and in charge.
I got my keys and a big stick to boot
And I got the power to make *wunna poop,
Cause my name is Sarg
And I large and in charge.
I descend from the lineage of the blue, black and gold.
From Westminster's palace I took over control.
I reigning supreme over these fields and hills,
Commanding respect from every John, Jack and Jill.
Cause my name is Sarg
And I large and in charge.
I've conquered the chains of the triangular trade
And turned the trident into a broken spade,
So don't deny me my due, if I may beg;
I deserve the honour of strutting on my hind legs
Cause my name is Sarg
And I large and in charge.
I feel important; I feel like a man.
It is a feeling I don't think you can understand.
You got to walk in these shoes to know what I feel –
To experience the clout and power that I wield.
Cause my name is Sarg
And I large and in charge.
I got the power to change up the rules;
I en got to consult with man, child nor mule.
I can get up one morning and issue a decree:

Forty years of vending on this spot must cease.
Cause my name is Sarg
And I large and in charge.
I run my own system of democracy
Although you might call it autocracy.
You got all the rights and freedoms you need
But only if I approve of your deeds.
Cause my name is Sarg
And I large and in charge.
I can toll the bell of freedom for all to see;
But freedom carries certain responsibilities.
That's why I institute the Public Order Act.
Not a man can meet nor speak without reference to that.
Cause my name is Sarg
And I large and in charge.
All roads lead to me and I control all things.
Every town hall meeting must have my blessing.
No fisherman can march unless I say so
And every vendor must have a licence to show.
Cause my name is Sarg
And I large and in charge
I feathering my nest and taking care of my kin.
Only two terms in office and a fat pension I getting.
The rest o' wunna can wait 'til 65
But I making sure my clan and I survive.
Cause my name is Sarg
And I large and in charge
So always remember – as I wish you adieu –
My big stick and my keys give me power over you.
I make the decision as to what you can do
And if you don't like that you can complain 'til you blue
Cause my name is Sarg
And I large – and in charge.
* *You:* 2nd. person plural

The national Initiative for Service Excellence, which is working to raise the quality of service throughout the public and private sectors has been focussing its efforts on the customer relations experience. But much more of its attention needs to be devoted to the quality of management and supervision, with special focus on the interaction between management and the public. Someone has to disabuse our public sector managers and supervisors of the notion that they are lords in ivory towers. Sarge may indeed be large and in charge, but he's there as a servant of the people and it is going to be very difficult to serve those people while he is still perched high up in his lofty towers.

The absence of hope must never stop us from dreaming, and as I wind up this essay I am daring to hope for a few things. My first hope is for better relations between black and white Barbadians. Inter racial relations in Barbados have never been a model to be emulated. The naked racism of the pre and immediately post-Emancipation periods gave way to a state of cool, racial apartness: white Barbadians in their little corner and black Barbadians in theirs. For reasons best known to themselves, the whites have tended to avoid events involving large gatherings of blacks. They will socialise as members of organizations or at national events, but when it's time for recreation or ceremonies such as weddings and funerals, it's an all-white affair. They need to mix more freely among the general populace.

Barbadians are quite familiar with the notorious Yacht Club, that infamous symbol of white separatism in Barbados where black people were persona non grata. There was also the Aquatic Club, of which the (white) wife of the island's first Premier, Grantley Adams, was a member. The story goes that Grantley would drop her off to club meetings and return to collect her. He was not a member. Across the board we had these white institutions and associations set up by and for white people: Wanderers Cricket Club, Barbados Rally Club, the Polo Club, St. Winifred School. In the field of business, there were companies, some of them public, with all white directors – and in some cases all white top Managers. It took the Barbados Light and Power Company

– established in 1911 – one hundred years before it appointed its first black General Manager in a country with 95% black people!

But we must resist the temptation to draw the lines exclusively in black and white. A class factor was most definitely a part of the equation. For example, Barbadian *"Poor Whites"* – descendants of indentured servants from the United Kingdom, were just as barred from the Yacht Club as blacks. Karl Watson, a white Historian, tells us he and other poor whites were chased from the Yacht Club beach. The parameters for membership at the time were limited to foreign whites and local upper and middle class whites.

I am not aware of any deliberate avoidance by black Barbadians of white company. Because they are such an overwhelming majority, black Barbadians tend to be predominant in any gathering. The presence of all-black gatherings must therefore be viewed somewhat differently from the converse.

So my dream, as we face the uncertainty of the future, is that African and British descended Barbadians will finally tear down the Berlin Wall of racial division and see themselves as equal citizens of one country. That white Barbadians will reverse the indoctrination which tells them they have to avoid mixing with black Barbadians at all costs. Already some white Barbadians have demonstrated that it is possible to transcend racial boundaries and be integrated members of the society – Julian Hunte, Karl Watson, Henry Fraser, Frances Chandler, Bizzy Williams, the late Olga Lopes-Seale are some that come to mind.

For their part, blacks need to be less awed by the presence of whites, seeing beyond the tone of skin to find the person within. Let us discard the view of whites as special beings with an unfair economic advantage. There also needs to be greater recognition of the progress made in inter-racial relations – e.g: that the Yacht Club of today and other previously all-white institutions are no longer exclusive. Let us recognise that the injustices of the old plantation order are no more. I think I may have something on the late Frank Sinatra, because everything I see tells me my dream is quite possible.

If it appears I have ignored the East Indian presence in Barbados, it's simply because relations between Indians and the rest of the black population have always been cordial. Indian immigration is traced back to 1913 when a Bengali man arrived in the island. The Indians who came here were mostly itinerant traders who would go from house to house selling household items and other merchandise, mostly on credit. Barbadians, in their innocence, would refer to them as *"the coolie man"*, a derogatory term in India. On a Sunday afternoon a child might shout to his parent *"the coolie man out here!"* This was a signal that the itinerant trader had come to collect his instalment for that week – usually about 50 cents to one dollar. The Indians were no more integrated than the whites – probably for religious reasons (They are mostly Hindus and Muslims); but somehow there was never that tension between them and the African Barbadian.

Economic inequities apart, then, black and white Barbadians must rise above the pettiness of race and embrace one another as citizens of the common space called Barbados. It would be the most glorious transformation of the ugly duckling of plantation slavery and oppression into the swan of racial harmony and love.

So let's break these walls down. And what greater example could we look for than that of Jesus in his encounter with the Samaritan and Canaanite women. Jewish tradition forbade men talking to women in public or having contact with gentile races, like the Canaanites, but Jesus – as he was wont to do – defied these rules. He saw beyond the gender and ethnicity of the Samaritan woman at the well and asked her for a drink of water. He saw beyond the gender and ethnicity of the Canaanite woman and healed her daughter.

We, too, must look beyond the skin
Beyond the surface, to the man within.
For when you go beyond the face
You realize we're all members of the human race.

But my optimism about a thaw in race relations is counterbalanced by the foreboding I sense in the general arena of social relations. It has become apparent that traditional values governing public conduct, morals and inter-personal relations are making a quantum shift. This movement is manifesting itself in the incidence and nature of violent crime, the lewd conduct at musical entertainment shows – very often by the artistes themselves – and the decadent manner of dress of both men and women. There used to be a time when we could attend public events and feel quite safe. These days you have to consider what type of event it is and the kind of people it would attract. I have to confess that for the first time in my life I now consider social class when making decisions about what I or my children will attend.

You are driven to this point when, at what should be a fun-filled football game, a *"Wild West"*-type melee erupts, with bullets echoing in the air; when your personal safety at public gatherings can be threatened by violent confrontations involving the use of dangerous weapons and missiles; when householders are forced to dive for cover to avoid the bullets of feuding gangs of young men. Passengers on a private transport vehicle are forced to flee for safety when one man pulls out a gun and shoots another in the vehicle; a little boy is hit in the head by a stray bullet while on a trip to town with his mother.

In 21st. century Barbados young men walk around with their pants waist half-way down their buttocks exposing their underwear, and women force themselves into the tightest and most provocative garments, very often offering us more than a modest view of their breasts and other sensual areas. Standards of dress and public conduct have plummeted to appalling levels, manifestations of a society very much heading in a downward direction.

We have definitely crossed the frontier into a new social sphere with all of the ominous portents that has for life in 21st. century Barbados. In more ways than one:

The sun has set on Westminster's jewel;
Its golden glow has waned.
Its seven years of plenteous yield
Will never be seen again.

And now she is like any other stone
Sitting in lustreless gloom,
A shadow of her former self
Never again to bloom.
Her night is long, her darkness deep
In blissful ignorance she sleeps,
Unable to rise and shake off the dust
From three centuries of colonial mush.
And claim her own identity
As a proud, national entity,

Free from the fetters of mental slavery.
And so she sleeps and takes her rest
As the golden sun sinks into the west.

THE END

N.B: All poetry written by the Author, except otherwise indicated.